ANTHROPOLOGICAL PAPERS
MUSEUM OF ANTHROPOLOGY, UNIVERSITY OF MICHIGAN
NO. 17

LAKE SUPERIOR COPPER AND THE INDIANS: MISCELLANEOUS STUDIES OF GREAT LAKES PREHISTORY

edited by
JAMES B. GRIFFIN

ANN ARBOR
THE UNIVERSITY OF MICHIGAN, 1961

ISBN (print): 978-1-949098-28-0
ISBN (ebook): 978-1-951519-50-6

Browse all of our books at
sites.lsa.umich.edu/archaeology-books.

Order our books from the University of Michigan
Press at www.press.umich.edu.

For permissions, questions, or manuscript queries,
contact Museum publications by email at umma-
pubs@umich.edu or visit the Museum website at
lsa.umich.edu/ummaa.

FOREWORD

This publication was conceived in 1953 as the result of my participation in the first excavation on Isle Royale by Professor Roy W. Drier, which he describes in the first section of the volume. Professor Drier was to write up the results of the field work and prepare a section on the metallurgy of the prehistoric Indians. My task was to describe the archaeological finds from the excavation and to prepare a statement on the cultural relationships of the material. As a part of this program I collaborated with George I. Quimby, Curator of North American Archaeology and Ethnology at the Chicago Natural History Museum, in two summer surveys of archaeological sites and collections around the Lake Superior basin in 1956 and 1957. In the summer of 1959 another field survey with Mark Papworth was again made along the southeastern and eastern side of Lake Superior.

For a variety of reasons I was unable to seriously begin the writing and compiling of the data presented in this volume until the fall of 1960. Unless otherwise identified, the responsibility for the material in this volume is mine. I am indebted to Professor Drier for his patience at my delay and for his valuable contributions. George I. Quimby has not only prepared valuable sections of the volume but has also shared with me his extensive knowledge of Great Lakes prehistory. The drawings of many of the copper artifacts were done by Barbara Gagnon of the Exhibits Museum of the University of Michigan.

The transformation of this manuscript into its publishable form has been ably accomplished by Mrs. Clara D. Johnston of the University of Michigan Publications Office.

James B. Griffin

CONTENTS

ILLUSTRATIONS

Plates
(Plates I - XXIII following page 189)

Maps

Figures

TABLES

THE MICHIGAN COLLEGE OF MINING AND TECHNOLOGY ISLE ROYALE EXCAVATIONS, 1953-1954

Roy W. Drier

PREFACE

Many accomplishments in the fields of scientific endeavor would not have been possible if it were not for interested financial sponsorship and other assistance of various kinds. This was certainly true of the 1953 and 1954 Michigan College of Mining and Technology Prehistoric Copper Mining Investigations.

Sincere appreciation is hereby expressed to Joseph C. Gannon of Marquette for initiating the investigation and for his financial and personal support. The 1954 field party was largely supported by the Wenner-Gren Foundation for Anthropological Research. The Michigan College of Mining and Technology supplied most of the personnel, supplies, and equipment. The National Park Service, through Robert Gibbs, then Superintendent of Isle Royale National Park, gave permission for the excavations, made the Belle Isle Resort Lodge available to the field parties, provided transportation from Houghton, Michigan, to the Island and return, and the use of a National Park Service boat for traveling around Isle Royale.

The personnel of the 1953 expedition included the leader, Professor Roy W. Drier of the Department of Metallurgical Engineering, and the following members of the staff of Michigan College of Mining and Technology: Albert Archambeau, Clyde Bice, Grover Lanctot, James Lauren, Wayne Maki, J. Harry Stalf, and Matt Usimaki. The remainder of the crew was as follows: Paul L. Beaubien, archaeologist of Region 2 of the National Park Service; Dr. Walter S. White and Dr. Henry Cornwall of the United States Geological Survey; Joseph C. Gannon; Professor James B. Griffin, Director of the Museum of Anthropology at the University of Michigan, and his two sons.

The 1954 field party consisted of Drier, Archambeau, Lauren, Wayne Maki, Stalf, and Gannon of the first seasons party and of Professor U. J. Noblet of the Forestry Department, Professor T. R. Maki of the Chemistry Department, and Al Manniko and Ned Watson. Professor Drier assumed the administrative and organizational responsibilities of the two expeditions, contributed personal funds to the support of the field parties and devoted a great deal of his energies to the furtherance of the studies of Lake Superior copper mining and metallurgy.

The field success was due to the interest, efforts, and skill of the personnel in providing comfortable living quarters, and to their labor in excavating in the ancient copper pit and in the Chippewa Harbor village site.

The account of the 1953 and 1954 field parties was prepared by Drier and has been revised by Griffin to incorporate notes and photographs taken by Griffin and Beaubien in 1953.

Two of the radiocarbon dates on wood and charcoal from the pit excavated by Drier and his associates were determined by the University of Michigan, Phoenix Project Radiocarbon Laboratory under the direction of Professor H. R. Crane. The third date was obtained from the United States Geological Survey Laboratory through the courtesy of Dr. Meyer Rubin.

THE 1953 SEASON

In the late spring of 1953, Professor Drier visited Isle Royale and chose the Belle Isle Resort Lodge on the north side of the island as the field party headquarters because of its relative accessibility to an old copper pit in the Minong area which he selected for excavation (Fig. 1). The field party left Houghton on the morning of June 12 and landed at the Lodge late that afternoon. The ancient copper pit excavated by the party is located about one mile west of the south end of McCargoe Cove, and about 190 feet above the level of Lake Superior. This pit was near the crest of Minong ridge in the W 1/4 corner of Section 26, T66N, R34W.

Figures 1 and 2, from an unpublished report by White and Cornwall, locate the pit and its relationship to the historically and prehistorically mined area and something of the topography of the region. According to their report the strike of the pre-Cambrian basaltic and andesitic flows, which predominate in the region, is about N65E, the dip is 20° SE. A single finegrained andesitic flow topped by an amygdaloid, makes up the massive central core of the rocks of the region. A rare occurrence of felsite porphyry is found in the upper part of the andesitic flow. Figure 2 shows the manner in which the continuity of the bed rock is broken by fissures, which occasionally contain masses of native copper. These fissures, which were mined prehistorically, seem to follow a general trend which is parallel to the Minong ridge. The Minong deposit has, associated with its native copper, such accessory minerals as quartz, epidote, calcite, chlorite and adularia. Native copper is found in the upper part of these late pre-Cambrian felsites, the richest portions usually being the regions of physical penetration of these flows by fissures. The fissures follow a zone southeast of, and parallel to, the Minong ridge. A minor zone of fissures cuts the ridge at about N25E. These are not as rich in copper as the fissures more nearly parallel to the Minong ridge.

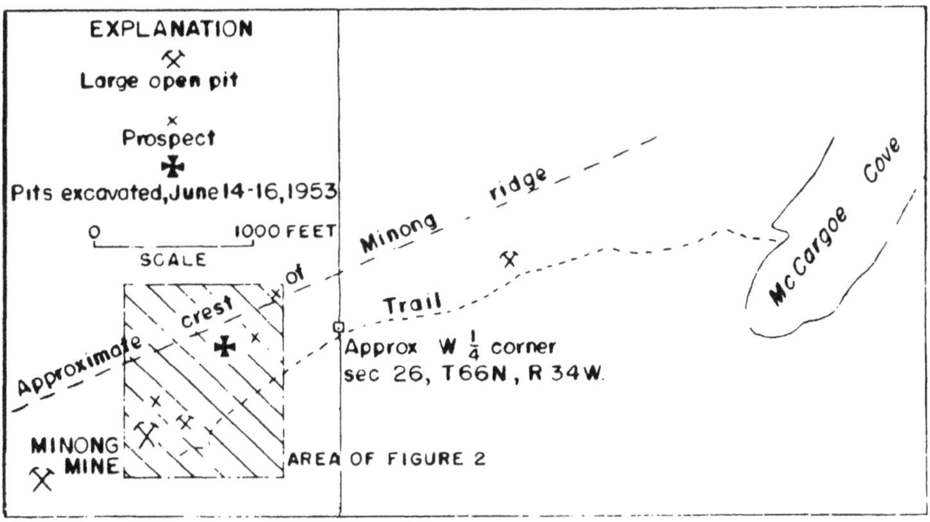

Fig 1. Index map showing location of Minong mine and pits excavated June 14-16, 1953.

The pit chosen for excavation is now known at Pit 25. The aboriginal work had been done along a fissure and there was a northern and southern section of the excavation. Both were filled with water and the southern, or lower section, was bailed before digging was started (Pl. I, Fig. 1). In the upper foot a number of hammerstones and hammerstone fragments were found, as well as small charcoal fragments, earth, and tailings from the prehistoric mining (Pl. I, Fig. 2). The excavation was slow and there was considerable difficulty in maintaining levels because of the necessity of bailing and of the mucklike consistency of the vegetation, charcoal, and soil. Charcoal and wood samples were taken at 1-foot levels, placed in aluminum foil and then in paper bags.

As the excavation proceeded downward it was clear that there had been no recent (historic) excavation in this pit as the vegetational debris was thick and matted, also fire-cracked and

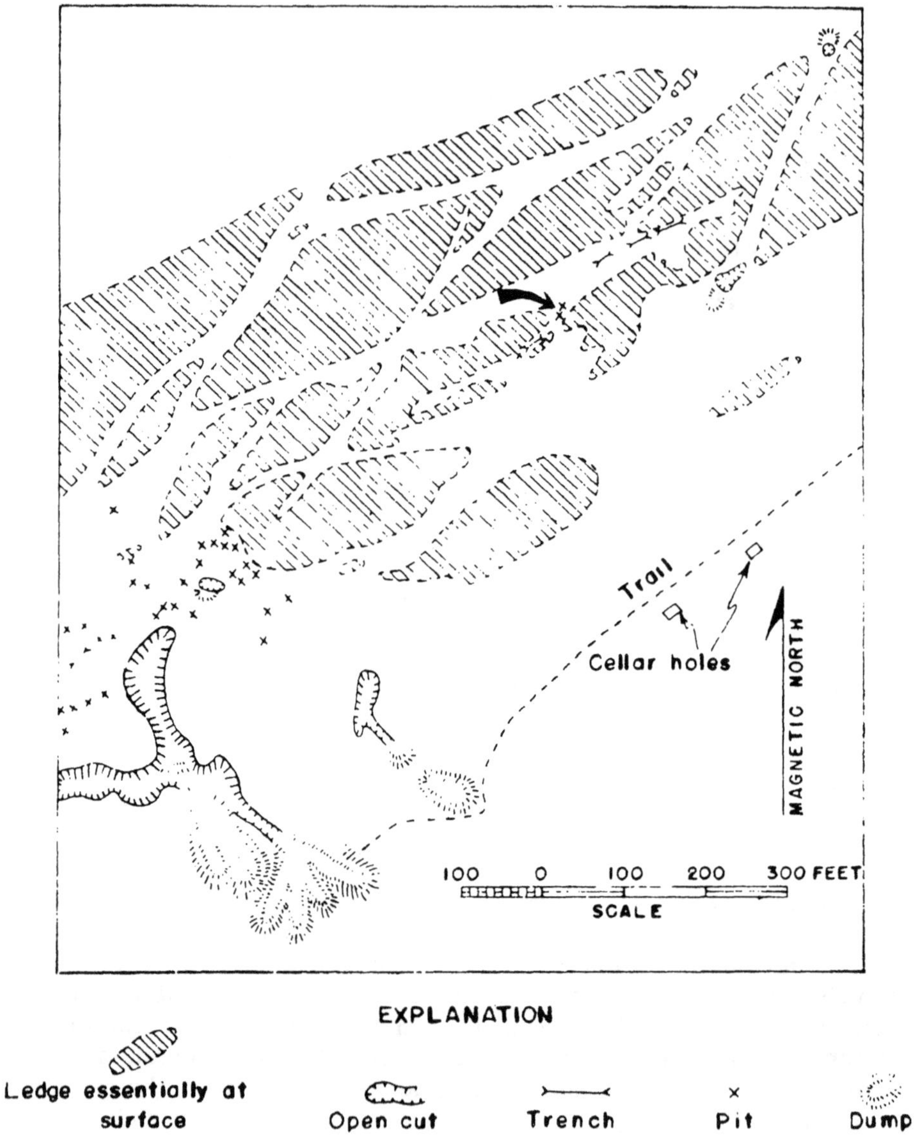

Fig. 2. Openings on south flank of Minong ridge. Arrow indicates pits excavated June 14-16, 1953. Open cuts with dumps dug by white men, many pits and trenches probably dug by Indians. For location of this sketch map, see Fig. 1.

hammered rock fragments, charcoal, sand, soil, and an occasional hammerstone were present.

At a depth of 72 inches a charred piece of black or white spruce was recovered and has been given a date of 3000± 350 B. P. (M-320), or 1047 B.C.± 350. This was the first sound date for one of the ancient copper pits in the Lake Superior area. Other types of wood from the pit were birch, Norway pine needles, and conifer cones. Because of the difficulty of the excavation in the pit during the spring season (Pl. II, Fig. 1) it was decided to forego further excavation for the first season and to investigate some of the other known sites on the Island.

The Chippewa Harbor Site

One day was devoted to a trip to the Chippewa Harbor village site on the south side of the Island. The area we investigated is on a projecting spur on the north side of the Harbor (Pl. II, Fig. 2). The soil is sandy loam and the present surface is some 4 to 5 feet above Lake Superior. Our excavations consisted of a trench 15 feet long and 5 feet wide. There was aboriginal material in the upper 6 to 8 inches. There was also considerable evidence, in the top few inches, of recent American occupation.

The humus zone was about 5 to 6 inches deep and there were numerous pits dug into the subsoil, including a number of fire pits, with fire-cracked stones. The excavation was extended to a depth of 12 to 15 inches and a cross section was made of the north wall in order to photograph a fire pit which extended from near the surface to almost 2 feet into the brownish sandy loam subsoil.

As the area was being excavated it was clear that we were obtaining the same Late Woodland pottery, copper, and other artifacts which had been obtained by earlier excavators (Pl. III). The materials recovered are described by Griffin in the following section (pp. 8-11).

McCargoe Cove Village Sites

One day was spent in investigating a number of locations on Indian Point where Paul Beaubien had picked up some pottery while the main party was excavating in Pit 25. Sherds were found in the soil adhering to the root area of a number of felled trees. Some of the Blackduck-style pottery was recovered in this area (Pl. IV). A search was made on Birch Island but no surface specimens were seen.

THE 1954 SEASON

This field trip was made by the personnel listed in the Preface and took place after the park season rather than before it. The trip to the Island was made on August 30. A gasoline motor-driven pump was obtained from the Michigan Department of Conservation and a similar pump from the Houghton County Road Commission.

The first day's excavation in Pit 25 reached a depth of 9 feet from the surface and during the second day a depth of 10 feet was reached. At the 10-foot depth, according to Professor Noblet, there was a concentration of cones, matted needles, and bark of the Norway pine. The pieces of birchbark were in an excellent state of preservation. At the 9- to 10-foot depth a burned log about 12 inches in diameter and 3 to 4 feet long required splitting in order to remove it from the pit. Hammerstone and chips were near the log. Cones and matted needles of the Norway pine were very common as were pieces of birchbark as large as 5 by 8 inches. Birch and maple leaves were found and were in very good condition. One cone was found that Noblet believed to be white pine. No signs of soot or smoke were noticed on the hanging or foot walls.

After the water in the pit had been bailed and pumped out the excavation was carried down to the 11-foot level during which charred wood, knots, and hammerstones were recovered. The last level excavated was from the 11- to 12-foot depth. In this zone there was charred wood, charcoal, birchbark, and birch branches. The bottom level seemed to have less dirt and organic material and more small rock. Much of this rock differed from the rock higher up, in that the lowest fragments seemed shattered and had sharp edges. Higher up in the pit they seemed to be the result of ice fracturing of the rock along cleavage planes, the angles approaching right angles. At the northwest end of the pit were areas or layers of what seemed to be yellow- or orange-colored ashes.

A section of a 4 inch thick, charred log from the 11- to 12-foot level was dated at 3800 ± 500 years old (M-371e) or 1645 B.C. ± 500. Another section from the same log was dated by the United States Geological Survey laboratory (W-291) as 3310 ± 200 B.P. The age of the log is, then, about 1500 B.C.

The final excavation reached a depth of 14 feet. Hammerstone chips, charred wood, and small rock fragments with sharp edges suggesting they had been fractured, formed the evidence for prehistoric activity at this depth. Occasionally, the rock pieces were blackened as though they had been exposed to fire. The exposed pit was covered with poles and the ladder used to reach the 14-foot depth.

About 20 feet northwest of Pit 25 there is an area of broken rock, and investigation indicated that this location was an area where the prehistoric miners crushed the rock which they had removed from pits. Numerous small pieces of free copper were found in the crushed rock. One of these, 1/3 by 1 inch was flattened on both sides, and one edge had breaks in it as though it had been hammered. Numerous hammerstones and many spalls were noticed in the debris. The hammerstones were smaller than those found in the pit. This was apparently a prehistoric stamp mill.

The field party examined the area of the historic Minong mining activity, particularly the area north of the mine (Pl. VII). It was estimated that there were more than two hundred "pits." Numerous hammerstones were found, some even on top of the hill or cliff to the east. On the surface of the Minong rock dumps a hundred or more hammers were visible. The 1870 estimate of three thousand pits and one thousand tons of hammers does not seem to be out of line considering that hammers have been removed from the area for some eighty years.

CONTRIBUTIONS ON ISLE ROYALE PREHISTORY

NOTES ON THE POTTERY FROM THE MICHIGAN COLLEGE OF MINING AND TECHNOLOGY EXCAVATIONS

The Chippewa Harbor Site

The largest amount of pottery was collected from this best-known of the Island's prehistoric villages. The pottery was badly fragmented. None of the rim fragments recovered belonged to the same vessel and most of the body sherds were in very small pieces.

There are forty-three small fragments which do not have sufficient identification characteristics to do much with except to indicate that they are from vessels similar to the larger body and rim fragments. There are twenty-six smooth-surfaced body fragments and forty-three cord-marked body sherds. Most of the body fragments are 4 to 7 mm thick. One cord-marked fragment is 1.4 cm thick and is probably a basal section from near the base of a large jar.

The first four rims are all cord-marked up to the lip on the outer rim (Pl. III, Fig. 1). Two of the four lips have broad indentations in the lip surface, one perhaps caused by the finger tip of the potter and the other by oblique indentations across the lip surface made by the edge of the paddle. The other two lip surfaces are flattened and have been cord-marked in the same way as was the outer surface of the rim.

Two rims and three lower rim fragments were smoothed on the outer surface. The lip surface on the two rims is shallowly indented but the type of impression cannot be determined. On the outer surface of the two rims there are short (1 cm) oblique impressions about 3 and 5 mm apart forming a horizontal decorative band (Pl. III, Fig. 1). The three lower rim fragments also have punctate impressions forming a band of decoration.

One lower rim and shoulder area sherd has a smoothed rim and a cord-marked body. The latter is set off from the smoothed upper area by a horizontal row of closely spaced (3 mm) punctates which were punched from above (Pl. III, Fig. 1).

Two of the rim sections are castellated and thus follow a common Late Woodland rim treatment. The first of these has only a low, raised area and the lip has closely spaced oblique incisions across it. These incisions are 2 mm wide and spaced

2 mm apart. On the outer rim surface there are three horizontal rows of small punctates placed 8 mm below the lip and forming a band 1.3 cm wide.

The second has a marked rim castellation and in the available section has a group of right to left parallel oblique lines from upper right to lower left made by a linear-punctate or stab-and-drag technique (Pl. III, Fig. 1). The lip surface is transversely incised by 2 mm wide, closely spaced lines. The inner rim is also decorated by short (5 mm) oblique incisions made just below the lip surface. This is bordered on the lower side by an incised line placed 1.2 cm below the lip surface.

Perhaps the most unusual sherd is a lower rim fragment of thin (5 mm), lightly tempered, fine paste. It has a well-smoothed and lightly scraped interior surface. The exterior surface had also been well smoothed before being decorated. The design is formed by groups of left to right oblique shallow lines made by a linear punctate technique. The lines are 5 mm wide with their transverse impressions made about 1 to 2 mm apart. The zone of oblique lines is terminated by a series of at least three horizontal lines of the same linear punctate technique (Pl. III, Fig. 1).

Another unusual fragment is from a temperless bowl which has smoothed outer and inner surfaces (Pl. III, Fig. 3). The lower rim wall is 1 cm thick, but near the slightly incurved lip it is narrowed markedly. There are three other rim sections, but they are too small to warrant description. They are not parts of any of the other rims.

The Chippewa Harbor excavation uncovered a section of a clay pipe bowl. This section had been broken off just above the juncture with the stem and is the bowl half, which would have faced the smoker (Pl. III, Fig. 2). The height of the pipe to the stem hold is 3.8 cm and the bowl depth is 2.1 cm. The greatest diameter of the pipe is 3.6 cm, but the capacity of the bowl is much less because of the thickness of the upper bowl and the incurved upper rim which becomes horizontal before the orifice is formed. The lower bowl diameter is 1.8 cm. There are three rows of small (1 mm) punctates placed about 1 mm apart on the outer bowl rim. The row adjacent to the lip is separated from the next row by a narrow incised line. The next two rows of punctates are also set apart by an incised line. Below the thickened bowl section with the horizontal punctates there is a meander pattern of the same small punctates. The pipe clay is apparently temperless.

Indian Point

Paul Beaubien found eight fragments of pottery at the extreme northeast point of the entrance to McCargoe Cove. These were taken from the matted roots of trees that had blown down or in the soil which had fallen from the roots. The location was just above the present water level. Seven of the sherds are thin (5 mm) cord-marked fragments (Pl. IV, Fig. 3). Of these, five have rather sparse, small, crushed-rock tempering, and may belong to one vessel. The other cord-marked body sherd is badly eroded on the outer surface and has large- to small-temper fragments. It is also thicker (8 mm). The eighth sherd is also badly eroded and probably had a plain surface.

At a second timber fall near the first one, a larger group of sherds was found, including three rim sections. Nine of the fragments are so small or broken that they can only be identified as pottery and that they are similar in tempering, firing, and other characteristics to the rest of the collection. Eight of the body sherds have a plain exterior surface. They are 4 to 6 mm thick and have the same kinds of grit tempering as the cord-marked body sherds. There are thirty-eight cord-marked body sherds. Most of these are thin (4 to 5 mm) and some of them may be parts of the two larger rim sherds from this location.

The largest rim sherd has been repaired from eleven fragments and there are six additional body sherds which probably belong to this vessel (Pl. IV, Fig. 2). This rim belongs to a ceramic group called "Blackduck" in Minnesota (Wilford, 1941, 1945, 1955). The body and shoulder area is cord-marked. It has a constricted shoulder area and a slightly flaring rim with a flattened, slightly extruded lip. The lip is 7 mm wide and is decorated with a criss-cross pattern of oblique lines spaced 4 mm apart. Immediately below the lip on the outer rim there is a row of right-to-left oblique, cord-wrapped stick impressions which are 1 cm long. Below them are three horizontal lines made by a fine-toothed implement which was dragged lightly against the surface from one line to the next, and for 1.6 cm below the lowest line. The horizontal lines are 4 mm apart, and there are about 8 of the dragged or brushed vertical lines per centimeter. Between the two upper horizontal lines there are cylindrical holes punched from the outer surface and which formed a low boss on the inner surface. These punches are 2.2 cm apart and are 3 mm in diameter. The rim thickness is 6 mm, and the shoulder is 4 mm. The estimated diameter at the lip is 11 cm.

The second rim fragment also has a flat lip and a similar decoration of criss-cross, cord-wrapped stick impressions (Pl. IV,

Fig. 2). It is 6 mm wide. On the outer rim just below the lip there is a single row of a herringbone design with apex toward the left. It was made by two oblique, short impressions of a cord-wrapped stick element. This vessel has a low, almost vertical rim and has very little flare to the body. The rim area is smoothed 1.8 cm below the lip and the design occupies the upper 1.2 cm of this area. The body is cord-marked. It had an estimated lip diameter of 9 cm.

The third rim fragment is very small and thin (3 mm) and is of the size which is often called a "children's pot" (Pl. IV, Fig. 2). It has a plain outer surface and two horizontal rows of small vertically elongated punctates placed just below a flattened lip. The lip is decorated by two groups of two incised lines spaced 1 cm apart which slant in opposite directions toward the vessel interior. There is little or no tempering material in this small vessel.

Interpretations

Quimby (1939*a*) has described earlier collections of pottery from Isle Royale which were made by the Milwaukee Public Museum expedition (West, 1929) and by field parties from the University of Michigan Museum of Anthropology. This paper, written while Quimby was a graduate student at the University of Michigan, identifies most of the pottery as Woodland and a few specimens as Iroquois. The Iroquoian sherds appear to belong to western Iroquoian complexes which developed around the southern end of Georgian Bay and which reached as far north as the mouth of the Michipicoten River in northeastern Lake Superior (Ridley, 1957). The estimated age of the Iroquoian sherds on Isle Royale would be somewhere about A.D. 1500-1600. I am indebted to Mr. Ridley for his help in assessing the age of the Iroquoian sherds on the island.

All of the Woodland pottery illustrated by Quimby and all of the pottery collected by the Drier party in 1953 belongs to a broad grouping of prehistoric pottery which is called "Late Woodland" (Table I). Pottery belonging to this group is in existence from about A.D. 400 to 1700 in the Upper Great Lakes. Almost all of this pottery from Isle Royale probably dates in the latter half of this time span. Most of it is more closely related to pottery in northern Wisconsin and Michigan than it is to the pottery from northeastern Minnesota and the north shore of Lake Superior. The pottery type referred to as Blackduck (Pl. IV, Fig. 2) is located in the latter area, and in Minnesota has been

TABLE I

CORRELATION OF CULTURAL GROUPS, FLORA, FAUNA, AND LAKE STAGE IN THE LAKE SUPERIOR BASIN

Time Period	Indian Groups and Prehistoric Cultures	Flora	Fauna	Lake Stage
A.D. 1600-1700	Various bands of Ottawa, Chippewa, Cree, Sioux, and Huron.	Lake forest formation of hemlock-deciduous forest on south side of Superior. North side is spruce-fir or boreal forest.	Essentially boreal on north shore and Isle Royale. Southern shore is boreal deciduous, and some prairie.	Contemporary
A.D. 1200	Development of Late Woodland cultures such as Effigy Mound, Blackduck, Iroquoian.	Essentially contemporary flora.	Essentially boreal on north shore and Isle Royale. Southern shore is boreal deciduous, and some prairie.	Post-Algoma
A.D. 500	Middle Woodland cultures such as Laurel and Point Peninsula II along north shore of Lake Superior.	Essentially contemporary flora. Possibly with a higher deciduous component than at present.	Essentially boreal on north shore and Isle Royale. Southern shore is boreal deciduous, and some prairie.	Post-Algoma
200 B.C.	Early Woodland			
1000 B.C.	Late Archaic complexes including Old Copper, and beginning of Early Woodland ceramic-using groups.	Essentially contemporary flora. Maple and birch known to be present on Isle Royale.	Essentially boreal on north shore and Isle Royale. Southern shore is boreal deciduous, and some prairie.	Algoma stage of Huron Michigan Basin.
2000 B.C.		Presumed initial period of essentially contemporaneous forest composition.	Essentially boreal on north shore and Isle Royale. Southern shore is boreal deciduous, and some prairie.	Nipissing stage
3000 B.C.	Beginning of Old Copper culture as a variant of northern Late Archaic culture.	Essentially contemporary but with less representatives of deciduous trees.	Gradual introduction of fauna associated with deciduous forest.	
		Initial introduction of deciduous trees.		Houghton low-water stage in Superior
5000 B.C.		Gradual forestation of spruce-fir on southern shore of Lake Superior.		
	Early hunting cultures of Lake Superior Basin during Early Archaic.	First forest composition of spruce-fir on southern shore of Lake Superior.	Moose, elk, giant beaver, deer, lynx, caribou.	
8000 B.C.	Lake Superior Basin covered by retreating glacial ice.			Correlative of Algonquin stage

attributed to Siouan tribes (Wilford, 1955, p. 136). Dr. Elden Johnson of the University of Minnesota and James V. Wright of the National Museum of Canada have both suggested that the distribution of Blackduck pottery is more compatible with a Chip pewa authorship than it is with Siouan. It is reasonably certain, however, that this pottery type comes fairly close to the historic period.

The broken pipe bowl (Pl. III, Fig. 2) has a form and decoration which is similar to one illustrated by Ridley in an unpublished manuscript from the Michipicoten site mentioned above. It is clearly connected to the pipe styles associated with Iroquoian groups.

The University of Michigan is continuing its work on Isle Royale and is collaborating with the National Park Service. Within a few years a more adequate sample of the late prehistoric material from the Island will be available. There will also be available a considerable amount of Late Woodland pottery from northern Michigan which will be of great value in interpreting the late Isle Royale occupations.

The small copper knives from Isle Royale, illustrated by Quimby, fit the styles known from other Late Woodland sites so there is little doubt that one of the attractions of the island to the late prehistoric Indians was the copper deposits. In our survey and excavation program we should find the camp sites of the earlier visitors who were responsible for much of the mining on the Island.

NOTES ON THE PLANT AND ANIMAL LIFE ASSOCIATED WITH PREHISTORIC ACTIVITIES ON ISLE ROYALE

The arboreal specimens obtained from Pit 25 by Professor Drier and his party have been identified as black or white spruce, birch, Norway pine, maple, and possibly white pine. All of these are now found on the Island, although the present tree stands are different from the prehistoric growth because of the extensive fires (Pl. VII) which were deliberately set in order to make prospecting for minerals less difficult (Brown, 1933, p. 22-25 and Potzger, 1954, p. 200). Brown points out that white pine [*Pinus strobus*] was formerly much more common on the Island but suffered severely from fire damage. The term Norway pine [*Pinus resinosa*] should be referred to as "red pine" since the term "Norway" pine carries the implication that it is native to Norway and was introduced to North America during the historic period. There are three species of maple now common on the Island.

Potzger's studies of pollen from nine bogs on Isle Royale from 900- to 600-foot elevations are of interest from the standpoint of the reforestation of the Island following the glacial retreat and during its gradual emergence as the waters of Lake Superior were lowered during the post-Pleistocene. The higher elevation bogs from 700 to 900 feet record in their lower levels the closing period of the initial spruce-fir association of this general region (Table I). The date for this would fall between 6000 and 5000 B.C. Maple is present in the middle zones of Siskiwit bog at 900 feet and at the lower third of the Farbes Lake bog at an elevation of 700 to 750 feet. In the two bogs at 650 feet, maple as well as oak are in the lowest to upper levels and a similar placement is found in the two bogs at 625 feet and the two bogs at 600 feet. By the time, therefore, of the lowering of the lake level below 700 feet we find that oak, maple, hemlock, and tamarack are significant members of the tree assemblage. Their introduction seems to correspond with the dominance and decline of pine which Potzger places around Nipissing time or about 2200 B.C.

It is clear however, from studies of the beach level by Stanley (1932) and Farrand (1960, Pls. II and V), that the location of Potzger's bogs at elevations of 650 feet and below, were under the Nipissing lake of about 2200 B.C., and did not become available for bog deposition until between the Nipissing and Algoma stages. It is also probable that the Houghton Point and Rock Harbor bogs at 625 feet did not begin to record the forest succession until after the Algoma stand of about 1200 to 1100 B.C.

The significance of this for the present study is that the date of the mining activity on Isle Royale, in Pit 25, took place during the period between the Nipissing and Algoma stage of the lakes. This period is commonly regarded as one of a gradual shift to a cooler moist period after the period of maximum warmth in the western Great Lakes which had produced the farthest northward move of the hardwood forest. The Nipissing-Algoma interval of about 2200 to 1100 B. C. is also the period during which the Old Copper culture seems to have had its greatest development. It may be regarded as reasonably certain that the Pit 25 mining operations obtained copper which was made into implements of the Old Copper culture.

The faunal affinities of Isle Royale are with the adjacent north shore of Lake Superior as might be expected from its geographical location (Adams, 1906, p. 128). The faunal remains from the village sites have been identified by Charles Cleland as follows. Most of the remains are of beaver and other mammals.

There are surprisingly few fish bones. It should be remembered that some part of the skeletal remains could have come from recent occupations, particularly at the Chippewa Harbor site where the upper level contained a considerable amount of living debris from the activities of commercial fishermen and other modern residents.

Identification of Bone Refuse from Several Sites on Isle Royale

The following animal species were identified:

Castor canadensis . . . . (Beaver)
Lynx canadensis . . . . (Lynx)
Alces americana . . . . (Moose)
Ursus americanus . . . .(Black Bear)
Rangifer caribou . . . . (Woodland Caribou)
Canis familiaris . . . . (Dog)
Bos? . . . .(Cow)
Acipenser fulvescens . . . .(Lake Sturgeon)

Beaver bones made up 61 per cent of the 126 identifiable bones. There seemed to be three characteristic fracture patterns in the beaver bone:

1. Fracture of the verticle ramus of the mandible just below the condyloid process. This would most likely occur in removal of the mandible.
2. Fracture of the scapula directly posterior to the glenoid fossa. This fracture would occur in removal of the fore limbs.
3. Fracture of the innominates at the level of the acetabulum which seems likely in the removal of the hind limbs and tail.

Evidence of the presence of the black bear on Isle Royale are the tarsals and metatarsals of one paw. This is not believed to be substantial evidence that bear inhabited the Island. The bones could have been introduced. All species present, with the exception of the black bear, have previously been reported on the Island. Three bones showed evidence of knife marks and twelve bone fragments were charred.

Species represented in the collections of the Museum of Anthropology from the three sites and from the Island are as follows:

TABLE II
IDENTIFICATION OF BONE REFUSE FROM VILLAGE SITES ON ISLE ROYALE

Site	Species	Minimum Number of Individuals Represented	Number of Bones of Species Represented
Indian Point	*Castor*	1	2
	Alcer?	1	3
Duncans Bay	*Castor*	1	1
	Lynx	1	1
	Alcer	1	2
Chippewa Harbor	*Castor*	8	68
	Alcer	1	5
	Ursus	1	4
	Bos?	2	11
	Cervis	1	1
	Dog	1	1
	Bird	2	6
	Frog	1	8
Isle Royale	*Castor*	1	6
	Rangifer	1	2

PREHISTORIC FINDS MADE BY EARLY AMERICAN MINING ACTIVITIES ON ISLE ROYALE, 1870-1880

Henry Gillman, of Detroit, who made a number of notable contributions to Michigan archaeology, made a visit to Isle Royale in May, 1873. As a result of his observations and from conversations with "a gentleman well known in mining interests, who is at present engaged in developing the mineral resources of the place" Gillman (1873) compiled a statement in which it is difficult to separate what he saw from what he was told. This "gentleman" was almost certainly A. C. Davis, who was an eye-witness to mining activities as he reports below (pp. 19-20).

> The works, generally pits of from ten to thirty feet in diameter, and from twenty to sixty feet in depth, are found scattered throughout the island, wherever examined, being sunk through the few feet of superincumbent drift, where it exists, into the amygdaloid copper-bearing rock. They invariably are on the richest veins; and the intelligence displayed in the tracing and following of the veins when interrupted, etc., has elicited the astonishment of all who have witnessed it—no mistakes having apparently been made in this respect. These excavations are connected underground, drains being cut in the rock to carry off the water. Stopes

one hundred feet in length are found. A drain sixty feet long presented some interesting features—having been cut through the surface-drift into the rock, it had evidently been covered for its entire length by timbers felled and laid across. When opened, the timbers had mostly decayed, and the centre portions had sunk into the cavity, filling it for nearly its entire length with the rotted wood.

At a deep inlet known as McCargoe's Cove, on the north side of the island, excavations such as are described extend in almost a continuous line for more than two miles, in most instances the pits being so close together as barely to permit their convenient working. Even the rocky islets off the coast have not escaped the observation of those ancient miners, and where bearing veins of copper are generally worked. The stone hammers, weighing from ten to even thirty pounds, the chief tool with which the labor was performed, have been found by cart-loads. They are either perfect, or are broken from use; and the fragments of large numbers of them are found intermingled with the debris on the edge of the pits, or at their bottom. These hammers are occasionally found grooved for the affixture of the handle, but are oftener without this adaptation. Tools made of copper, and consisting principally of chisels and knives, have also been taken from such of the pits as have been explored. Arrowheads of copper have also been picked up, both in the vicinity of the pits and scattered over the island, at the surface, as if lost in the chase. The tools, though injured from oxidation, appear to have been of fair workmanship, and were evidently hardened, apparently through the action of fire. With the exception of the stone hammers, no other tools formed of stone have been observed. A large portion of a wooden utensil, shaped like a bowl, was taken from among the débris, charcoal, etc., at the bottom of a pit. This vessel had possibly been used in bailing water from the excavation. It must originally have been about three feet in diameter, and something of the rude character of the tool employed in shaping it could be gathered from its appearance. It was not of uniform thickness throughout, the wood having been more easily removed when working in certain directions; e.g., when cutting with the grain, the vessel was thinner in those portions.

The pits which have been examined, by being cleaned out, invariably had at top a large deposit, mostly of vegetable remains, the accumulations of many a fall-of-the-leaf, beneath which lay a thick bed of charcoal and mud mingled with fragments of copper-bearing rock. Besides this, they were partly filled with water. The removal of the contents was consequently very dirty work. The method of mining pursued by those people was evidently, on turning back the overlying drift, to heat the rock through the aid of fire; then, when by the application of water the rock was sufficiently disintegrated, to attack and separate it with their great hammers.

At Isle Royale the present forest covers equally the excavations and the adjoining land; no difference can be observed in the growth. Trees, from two to four feet in diameter, are now growing in the pits, on their sides, and on the tumuli formed of the excavated debris which surround them. In one case, the partially-decayed stump of a red-oak probably *Quercus coccinea*, Linn, was found on the tumulus at the edge of a pit. This tree had not been blown down, but had grown and decayed where the stump stood. A large proportion of the rotted wood surrounded it; only the red, interior portion of the stump remaining sound. A careful enumeration of the annual rings composing this red, undecayed centre of the tree, gave as the result the number of three hundred and eighty-four. If to this be added two hundred rings, as representing the decayed, outer portion of the stump, and not considered an over-estimate, we have five hundred and eighty-four years as the period of its growth. To this will have to be added the number of years which a tree with the durability of the wood of this species takes to reach the stage of decay here exhibited; and possibly some years may also be allowed for the time which may have elapsed before it commenced growing on its peculiar site. So that the placing this period at from seven hundred to eight hundred years, as already given, may not be far from the truth. On removing this stump, the debris underlying it was found to consist of the usual fragments of copper-bearing rock, thrown out from the adjoining pit, with which were intermingled a large number of stone-hammers, some perfect, others fractured from use, and, more interesting still, a knife made of copper. Pine-trees of the present forest, in which three hundred and eighty annual rings have been counted, have frequently been cut on the tumuli.

From another pit, beneath a thick deposit of vegetable matter, the remains of the skeleton of a deer were taken out. The bones were so decayed, however, that they crumbled to pieces; and it was only through the undecayed portion of an antler that the animal was recognized. It had evidently fallen into the pit long after it had been deserted, and, unable to escape, had perished. Another interesting relic consists of a sheet-like piece of copper, which had apparently been exposed to the action of fire, and then partially hammered into a shape approximating to a bowl-like utensil. This, too, exhibits the character of the copper generally sought by those men. It is manifest, from the working of the veins, that they followed the deposits of sheet-like copper, which varied from a quarter of an inch to an inch in thickness, rejecting as unmanageable the fragments of rock which contained even large-sized nuggets of the metal. The latter are found in large quantitites in the débris forming the tumuli at the mouths of the pits, as well as in the excavations themselves, where, mingled with considerable amounts of charcoal, they seemingly had been pushed behind those miners as they advanced in the exploration of the vein, the walls of which were generally left unbroken.

At an indentation of the coast on the south side of the island, where a stream about forty feet in width had cut a passage through the rocks, and formed quite a fall of water, was discovered what is taken to be the site of the town, or the habitations of these people. It occupies an elevated slope, giving an extensive view of Lake Superior, and over-looking the intervening point of land which makes the little bay an excellent harbor. The remains consist of a series of shallow excavations, generally about four feet in depth and occupying the successive terraces of the slope. Some of these pits are circular, others are quadrangular, and they vary from ten to thirty feet in diameter. Indications suggest that timber or bark was used in their construction, the soil being thrown up around them to a sufficient height. But time did not permit a satisfactory examination of this interesting locality, which, with other points on the island, it is hoped will afford, on a thorough exploration, many valuable facts connected with the life of this remarkable people. They, doubtless, shipped the copper, the object of their toil, to the south shore of Lake Superior, the wonderful metal finding its way thence to other parts of the country, as is testified by the articles of copper found in the burial-places of the mound-builders. This point, therefore, was well selected as a town-site. The good landing, the admirable harbor, the abundant stream and fall of water, the sheltered and yet commanding hill-side, which enabled them to watch the departure and return of their copper-laden flotillas, were all strong recommendations even to these semi-savage inhabitants. (Gilman, 1873, pp. 173-74.)

Gillman returned to Isle Royale in August of 1873 and faithfully reported new data which dealt, in the main, with Triangle Island on the extreme west end of Isle Royale. He mentions that the island was sandstone, that there were circular pits, 2 to 5 feet in diameter, of the "ancient miners" but he could find no implements, or apparently no indications of copper. Subsequent investigations have not indicated that prehistoric mines were located on this Island.

A. C. Davis was the agent and superintendent of the Minong Company for two years beginning in 1875. His report (Davis, 1875, pp. 369-70) is on the first of the large copper masses to come from the Minong area. In writing to the Smithsonian Institution Davis said:

I send you three photographic views of a mass of copper found in clearing some ancient mine-pits on Isle Royale, Lake Superior. The mass was found in the bottom of a pit sixteen and a half feet deep, and was completely detached from the surrounding rocks. All the wings have been beaten off by the ancient miner with his stone hammers-evidences of which can be seen all over its upper surface. The section it was taken from is 27, 66 north, range 35 west. The belt of rock in which it was found is of a sedimentary character, highly metamorphosed, from twenty to forty feet wide, and for a distance of two and.a half miles has been completely worked over by the ancient miner. I have been mining for the last twenty-five years on Lake Superior, but I have never seen anything to compare with this locality for ancient work.

I am confident that, when this district is thoroughly mined, discoveries will be made throwing more light than we now have on the character of the people who did this work.

In the depression in the outlying trap was found clean lake sand, and the rock thrown out of the pit first was thrown on the sand. There was no sign of vegetable mold between the rock and sand, but over all there was three and a half feet of made soil or decomposed vegetable matter.

In the pit there are tons of stone and stone-hammers, and a large quantity of ashes and charcoal.

In one I opened on a transverse vein on the same property, I found the scales of white-fish. At this pit the ancient miner had used large granite boulders to hold up the hanging ground. These boulders would weigh from 300 to 400 pounds, and were put in where the modern miner would place timber, to secure the ground. Nearly all the brands and timber we found in the pits were roots and stumps. This with the fact of their using these large stones for timber, leads me to think that the ancient miners had used up all the timber in their reach, and consequently could not prosecute mining further.

There is another peculiarity in the hammers found in these mines—I only found one that was grooved, while on the south shore of the lake I never saw a stone-hammer that was not grooved.

Gillman's description of the first large copper mass from Minong was prepared after the "nugget" had been brought to Detroit for exhibition (Gillman, 1876, pp. 330-31):

> Late last autumn, there was brought to our city a mass of copper which, in the latter part of the summer, was taken from an ancient pit on the property of the Minong Mining Company, at McCargoe's Cove, Isle Royale. On cleaning out the pit of the accumulated debris, this mass was found at the bottom, at the depth of sixteen and one-half feet. It is of a crescent-like shape, and weighs nearly three tons, or exactly 5,720 pounds. Such a huge mass it was evidently beyond the ability of those ancient men to remove. They could only deal with it as best they knew how. And as to their mode of procedure, the surroundings in the pit and the corrugated surface of the mass itself bear ample testimony. The large quantities of ashes and charcoal lying around it, show that the action of fire had been brought to bear on it. A great number of the stone hammers or mauls were also found near by, many of them fractured from use. With these the surface of the mass had evidently been beaten up into projecting ridges, and then broken off. The entire upper face and sides of the relic present repeated instances of this; the depressions, several inches deep, and the intervening elevations with their fractured summits, covering every foot of the exposed superficies.
>
> How much of the original mass was removed in the manner described, it is, of course, impossible to say. But from appearances, in all probability, it had, at least, been one-third larger. Innumerable fragments of copper chips lay strewn on all sides; and even the scales of fish, evidently the remnants of the meals of the miners, were recovered from the pit.

This copper "nugget" as Winchell mentions (p. 22) was sent to Philadelphia. Hinsdale (1931) illustrates a drawing of this mass and stated that it was made from a photograph. Fortunately, for this contribution, the Burton Collection of the Detroit Public Library has two glass negatives of the boulder which were taken in 1874, in Detroit, by J. J. Bardwell, a famous photographer of that period. Many of his photographs are valuable historical documents and those in this publication are in the same category.

The photographs (Pls. V and VI) clearly show the depressions and ridges on the boulder which resulted from Indian efforts to obtain sections from it that could be worked into implements or ornaments. The photographs sent to the Smithsonian Institution by Davis were probably similar, if not identical to, the ones we illustrate.

The field-work program of N. H. Winchell carried him, in 1879, to Isle Royale where he studied the formations and collected specimens as State Geologist of Minnesota. Item 584 of his listed collections was "battered copper, found about the large masses worked by the ancients." Item 585 was "stone hammers used by the ancient miners at the Minong mine, Isle Royale. These are generally rounded or oval pebbles of fine basalt, evidently transported from the north shore of the lake, where they got their form by the action of the waves on the beach. They are not withed. They are found in the debris about the old pits." Item 586 was "wood, found in the ancient dumping pits." Winchell (1882, p. 54). These pieces of wood were called "charred" in the catalogue of archaeological specimens of the previous year. The statements in this field report were limited to a record of the collection of his specimens, but Winchell also published a short popular article in *Popular Science Monthly* with illustrations (Winchell, 1881) of his observations of mound building on Isle Royale, along with extensive material on the use of copper by the Indians. He concludes with the observation that:

> Every known trait of the mound-builder was possessed by the Indian at the time of the discovery of America. It hence becomes unnecessary to appeal to any other agency than the Indian. It is poor philosophy and poor science that resorts to hypothetical causes when those already known are sufficient to produce the known effects. The Indian is a known adequate cause. The assignment of the mounds to any other dynasty was born of that common reverence for the past, and for the unexplainable, which not only unconsciously augments the actual, but revolts at the reduction of these works to the level of the existing red-man. (Winchell, 1881, pp. 619-20.)

Winchell's comments on Isle Royale are both his own observations and those reported to him. They are as follows:

> These mines are rude, irregularly disposed, shallow pits in the general surface, which, on being cleared of rubbish, are found rarely to exceed the depth of ten feet but in some instances reach the depth of twenty. They seem to have been located by the accidental outcropping of native copper, over large areas the rock being entirely bare. In other cases, the mining seems to have been systematically prosecuted along the strike of a known copper-bearing belt of rock. In this case it is a rock of marked lithological characters, being of a red color, and, when once its trend was established by a series of pits, it was followed under the drift-materials, that were thrown off into heaps, in which are found, mingled with charred wood and other relics, a great many stone hammers. In one instance, a cross-drift ran under a rude archway from one red belt to another, through a thin partition of darker rock; but, in general, no planning for easy excavation or skillful and prolonged effort in the operations of the miners can be discovered. So far as can be ascertained, they

resorted to the very simplest and most laborious methods of excavation in the rock, using their stone hammers, wielded in the hands alone, sometimes aided perhaps by the application of heat, and by repeated blows battered and broke away the rock surrounding the copper masses. When once a mass was detached or sufficiently uncovered, it was parted into smaller pieces by the same means. Some of the masses found, being too large for removal from the pits, show the marks of long-continued pounding and about them in the pits are a great many small, thin chips of metallic copper, of irregular shapes, with concavo-convex surfaces, exactly such as would be produced by battering a small nugget of copper to a thin layer by pounding it continuously on the same side. The finding of these thin chips of copper is the first indication to the present miners of the proximity of a large mass. In the summer of 1874 the first of these large masses was discovered. It was sixteen and one half feet below the surface, and under it were poles, as if it had been entirely detached, but it had not been much displaced. This mass was exhibited publicly in the yard of the court-house at Detroit, and was also on exhibition at the Centennial Exposition [Philadelphia] in 1876. It was subsequently fused and sold as commercial copper. It weighed 5,720 pounds, and has been described by Mr. Henry Gillman, in the annual volume of the American Association for the Advancement of Science for 1876. In the summer of 1879 two other large masses that had been wrought by the ancients were found at the Minong Mine, which is at the head of McCargoe's Cove. One had a weight of 3,317 pounds, and the other 4,175 pounds, the latter being about nine feet long. The largest mass yet found at that place was taken out the previous summer, weighing six tons, but the ancients had not discovered it, though one of their drifts ran within two feet of it. The large masses discovered by the ancients show the labor that has been spent on them in their hammer-marked and pitted surfaces. They seem to have been beaten up into ridges and points, by hammering alone, for the easier removal of parts. One of those found in 1879 was not detached from the inclosing rock, though it was wholly uncovered and undermined. . . .

Various articles have been found in these old pits or in their neighborhood. Several copper implements, such as a gad, a chisel, knives, and arrow-heads, have been discovered, both on Isle Royale and in the vicinity of similar old mines on the south shore of Lake Superior. Mr. Gillman reports that a large part of a "wooden bowl," originally about three feet in diameter, which had probably been used for boiling water, was taken from one of these pits. The timber found in some of these excavations bore the marks of an axe, the bit of which must have been about two inches in width. Fragments of charcoal and partially consumed sticks abound. The bark of the white birch is still preserved, though the interior woody portion is wholly rotted. At McCargoe's Cove, Captain William Jacka discovered a wooden shovel or paddle, which showed by its worn and battered side that it had been used in moving dirt. The blade was four and three quarters inches wide, and about twelve inches long. The handle had been broken, but still showed the length of about a foot. It was all perfectly wrought and smooth, and very true in form. A rounded ridge on the upper and lower sides of the blade extended along its middle, tapering off along the same sides of the shaft or handle upward. It was wet and swollen when found, but, on drying, it shrank to a width of three fourths of an inch, and curled out of shape.

A restoration of this ancient paddle or shovel is seen in Fig. 2[1], as drawn under the direction of Captain William Jacka, and a cross-section of the blade in Fig. 3[1]: a represents the upper side of the blade, and the ridge, evidently designed to strengthen the instrument, extends to within an inch or two of the end, and gradually and smoothly sinks to the level of the surface. This shovel was found within a few feet of one of the large masses of copper, in the summer of 1879.

Dr. G. K. Bailey also discovered a piece of string, about a foot long, made of some raw-hide, supposed to be of the caribou, tied in the middle by "a square knot and a half-hitch." This lay under one corner of the copper mass found in May last (1879), and seemed to break on being pulled out, but the remainder could not be secured. When examined, this string seemed to possess the fiber and much of the strength of dried raw-hide, a circumstance that will not allow the assignment of a very great antiquity to the date of the last mining. Caribou were on the island till a few years ago, and are now common on the shore directly north of the island.

In regard to the main implements of the mines, the stone hammers, they seem not to have been made for the purpose for which they were used. Great numbers of them are found in moving the dirt which the miners handled. They are of various sizes and forms, but generally about five inches in diameter, though some are eight and even ten inches, and of a rounded oval outline. They were certainly gathered as pebbles along the shore of the lake, north from the island, where there are still others of the same shapes and sizes, and of the same varieties of rock, formed on the beach by the action of the waves. The great profusion in which they are scattered among the debris of the pits would itself indicate the ease with which they were obtained. They are not grooved for the reception of a withe, like those found on the south shore, near Ontonagon, but they were apparently used for the most part by simply swinging them in the hand, or probably in both hands clasped, thus by repeated blows breaking away the surrounding rock or hammering the desired metal into such shapes as to facilitate its separation in smaller pieces. The rock of which they are composed does not occur as pebbles on Isle Royale, and indeed it is doubtful if it exists at all on the island. It forms the coast of the mainland for several miles opposite the island. It is an igneous rock, usually a diabase, as shown in thin sections under the microscope, consisting essentially of a triclinic feldspar and augite, with magnetite. Sometimes the grains are coarser, and the rock would more properly be styled a dolerite or a gabbro. They belong to the formation designated by Sir William Logan *The Lower Volcanic Group*, but since styled *Animiki Group*, by Professor T.S. Hunt.[2] Occasionally, however, the workmen seem to have gathered rounded stones of other varieties of rock, though nothing equaling the firmness of the above, and so fit for the purpose of a ride hammer in simple mining, can be selected among all the rocks of the region. One or two, of a granite containing red orthoclase, were seen at the mine, and a few of other granites are reported to have been found. These other varieties are also seen mingled sparsely with the diabase stones along the Canadian shore, and are referable to the drift forces which transported them from farther north and east in Canadian territory.

1. These figures have not been reproduced in this publication.
2. Vide, "Trap Dikes and Azoic Rocks of Southeastern Pennsylvania," *Second Geological Survey of Pennsylvania*, pp. 68, 240.

Although these hammers, as a rule, are not withed, it is still true that occasionally one is found that is withed—i.e., grooved for the reception of a withe handle. One seen at the time of this visit was owned by Dr. Bailey, and was not well wrought. The groove was evidently made by an unskilled hand, and was unfinished. This allies these miners with those of the south shore of the lake. The absence of these hard, rounded stones on the shores of the south side of Lake Superior,[3] owing to the strike of the formation producing them across the interior of the States of Michigan and Wisconsin, made it necessary for the miners on that side to manufacture their hammers, which they did with greater perfection and symmetry than are seen in the beach-wrought hammers of the Isle Royale miners; and they almost invariably grooved them for a withe. Those found on Isle Royale are generally broken with use on one end or on both, a fact which probably caused their abandonment. Fig. 5[4] shows the imperfectly grooved hammer belonging to Dr. Bailey. Fig. 6[5] shows the outline and irregularity of three others, also found at the Minong mine. These are a fair average for form, of the most of those found. They are also evidently such as would result from the constant attrition of angular fragments on the beach, and show no evidence of designed shaping. Their battered and even fractured extremities are the only sign of the agency of man in giving them shape.

If we inquire now who were the men, and when did they live, who did this work, we enter on a very interesting question, but one on which we are not in total darkness. A single observation at the pits at once places them *later than the last glacial epoch.* The dirt that they moved lies on the drift-clay. This is shown by the subjoined diagrammatic sketch taken on the spot (Fig. 7).[6] It is also shown by the fact that some of the pits are but a few feet above the present lake-level (about thirty feet); since during the period of the drift, and particularly toward its close, the interior lakes and rivers of the North American Continent were much higher than they are now. (Winchell, 1881, pp. 601-6.)

ARCHAEOLOGICAL INVESTIGATIONS ON ISLE ROYALE, 1892-1930

Among the individuals who have pursued archaeological studies on Isle Royale are W. H. Holmes, George R. Fox, Samuel A. Barrett, George A. West, Fred Dustin, and Carl E. Guthe. There are also the excavations of William P. F. Ferguson (1923, 1924), who misinterpreted the evidence from prehistoric pits mentioned by Gillman as "the remains of a Stone Age town or "city," and as "fortified pits." The Milwaukee Public Museum also investigated this site (West, 1929, pp. 27-30). Of these men, the best published accounts of pit excavations are furnished by Holmes and Barrett.

3. Shiploads of these stones are transported from the north shore of Lake Superior for paving streets in Chicago and other cities.
4. This figure has not been reproduced in this publication.
5. *Ibid.*
6. *Ibid.*

Holmes was an accomplished archaeologist and his discussion of the *Aboriginal Copper Mines of Isle Royale, Lake Superior* (Holmes, 1901) is a model of accuracy and careful interpretation. He made his excavation in 1892 while collecting material for the Worlds' Columbian Exposition in Chicago to prepare an exhibit on ancient mining and quarrying. He dug in the area of the abandoned Minong Mine (Pls. VII-X):

> Wishing to examine the ancient pittings more in detail, I searched the walls of the modern mines for a favorable exposure in which to begin excavation, and finally selected a spot where the complete section of an ancient mine, some ten feet in depth and probably twenty feet in diameter, was exposed in a steep slope. The ancient pit was filled nearly to the top with well-compacted material, mainly crushed trap-rock and earth, the notable feature of these excavations was the ever-recurring sledge-hammers. Plate XXIII [Pl. IX, this publication] shows these implements projecting from the excavation face and clearly defined because of their light-colored smooth surface and entire unlikeness to the other material in the pit. The work of excavation continued until a large part of the contents of the mine was removed and complete vertical sections were exposed to view and photographed. In the plate upward of a dozen of the sledges are seen in place in the evenly-dressed front wall, and others already removed appear at the right and left in the bottom of the excavation. A silver dollar placed near the base of the front wall serves as a scale, as does also a pick resting on the bed-rock. It is seen that the rocky walls rise from the floor of the pit at an angle of about forty-five degrees, extending almost to the surface. How much of the excavated space was originally solid rock, removed by ancient workmen, no one can say; but judging from the very large percentage of shattered trap found in the filling, and the multitude of sledges broken in the work, it is fair to assume that a considerable body of the rock in place was crushed and removed.
>
> The discovery of considerable quantities of charcoal scattered through the mass indicates pretty clearly that fire was used to aid the sledge in breaking up the rock. I was not so fortunate as to encounter any copper nuggets or masses in this excavation. If such were found by the miners they were not too large to be disposed of, but there were many fragments of rock impregnated with the green oxide indicating the copper-bearing nature of the formation.
>
> The question of the disposal of the larger masses of copper encountered was no doubt a very serious one with the native miners, and when they were too large to be carried away to the shops or to distant settlements, efforts were made to break them up. All protruding parts were belabored with hammers and if possible removed, as shown by the appearance of several masses deserted by the old miners because they were too large to be in any way utilized. They bore evidence of long-continued battering with sledges. (Holmes, 1901, pp. 690-91.)

Perhaps the most constantly present and remarkable feature of these sites is the stone quarrying sledges, varying from three to twelve inches in length and from an inch to eight inches in diameter, a few specimens reaching a weight of perhaps sixty pounds. They occur in countless numbers upon the surface and in and about the pits, proclaiming the aboriginal character of the work. The bruised and shattered remnants of these sledges literally fill the ancient mining debris, as already shown, and in sections of the deposits made by recent mining operations they are seen protruding at all points, being rendered distinctly visible by their smooth surfaces and general bluish or light-gray colors contrasting with the dark earth. In places cascades of sledge-charged refuse descend into the recent mines, as shown in some of the views taken. Upward of twenty specimens had fallen into a little heap of gravel from an ancient pit at the top of the wall in front of the entrance to one of the modern mines.

The presence of multitudes of stone sledges in and about the mines tells a clear story of the character of the aboriginal work. Wooden implements would have served to loosen and remove the superficial materials, laying bare the rock surfaces and exposing protruding masses of copper, but the globular boulder-sledge could have served no purpose in the work save that of breaking up the enclosing rock and freeing the lumps of metal. Although these sledges are natural boulders rarely modified by art, they are by no means rude affairs, or mean makeshifts. They are as perfectly adapted to the rock-crushing work as if shaped for the purpose. Doubtless they were carefully selected, and it is believed that they were brought from the beach several miles away, or, more likely, from deposits of water-polished boulders along the northern shore of the lake.

Holmes was impressed by the amount of work evidenced by the pits in the Minong Mine area, and he had had extensive experience in studying Indian mining operations for flint and other raw material.

The operations of our modern miners, although extensive, have by no means obliterated the ancient work. All over the slopes, above and between the recent excavations, are traces of the ancient diggings, and the extent of this work was a matter of great surprise to me. As in the flint quarries previously examined, I found myself wandering over the wilderness of pits and their accompanying mounds of excavated material, marveling at the enterprise and perseverance of the aborigines. For a people with only primitive tools, the work seems colossal. A long, narrow area amounting to at least half a mile square of the surface has been worked over, pit connecting with pit, the impression given being that hardly a square rod of ground within the particular area has been left unexplored. The pits are neither so deep nor so wide as those of the flint quarries, but they do not afford a good index of the work accomplished. The earlier pits were often filled up as the work advanced, and the crumbling debris has gradually been leveled by gravitation and the growth of forests.

From the surface indications it is difficult to say how far the ancient excavators penetrated the rock in place. It is apparent, however, that there was little tunneling. The rock was too massive and refractory, save where somewhat decomposed near the surface to permit of successful manipulation by men having only stone tools. The work of the miner consisted in uncovering the rock surface with a view of discovering protruding masses of the metal, and these, when found, were removed by crushing the enclosing rock with sledges. The deeper and larger pits probably often mark the spots where important masses of the metal were found and removed, while the smaller openings are those resulting from general and, probably in many cases, bootless exploitation. It is said that in some of the old excavations bodies of copper were found by our own miners only partially liberated from the enclosing rock, while in other cases the masses encountered were so large that native devices were not equal to their removal. Indeed, some of the masses uncovered by the white miners defied for a long time the most advanced breaking-up and transporting contrivances of a civilized age.

The pit depressions are rounded or irregular in outline and seldom are more than three or four feet in depth. Numerous examples of the battered stone sledges are in sight. The plenitude of these sledges is everywhere apparent, and it was not unusual to see them turned up among the roots of the fallen forest trees. The battered, truncated ends of the originally symmetrical water-worn forms clearly tell the story of their use by ancient men. (Holmes, 1901, pp. 688-89.)

Dr. Barrett made his excavations in 1924 in order to prepare an exhibit for the Milwaukee Public Museum, of which he was the director. He excavated in the Minong Mine area and the results of his careful explorations are given below. The text has been altered slightly to conform to the illustrations in this volume:

This pit [Pl. XI, Fig. 1] was selected more or less at random, simply because it looked as though it might yield interesting results and it is safe to assume that it is typical of a large number of such pits among the thousands along this slope.

It was located near the top of the ridge and was directly in the bare rock, though farther down the slope the rock is covered with a thin dressing of soil and, of course, quantities of fire-cracked stone, for here the old Indian mines are so numerous that the edge of one pit touches the next and the debris from one pit half fills an older one near by.

Above and to the sides of this particular pit, are others of various sizes and just west of this one, are several fire-cracked spots in the rock where mining operations were started, but apparently not carried beyond an initial fire or two.

The general appearance of this rock surface, after the pit was finally excavated, is shown in [Pl. XI, Fig. 2]. The ground plan of this pit was a double one. . . .

When the excavation was begun the exposed vertical rock face at the rear of the pit measured about three feet, but the pit at its deepest point measured about seven and a half feet, the other four and a half feet being filled chiefly with fire-cracked stone and debris from the pits higher up the slope. This, combined with a tangle of roots of trees and bushes, made extremely difficult digging.

In the upper portion of the pit, we found no evidence that the Indians' quest for copper had been successful, but in the lower portion we found a malachite stained spot a foot in diameter, and all evidence that a good sized lump of copper had repaid the Indian miners for many days of arduous labor. Certainly, to excavate in this solid, hard rock by these crude means, a pit ten feet long, five feet wide and ranging from three to seven and a half feet in depth, must have required many toilsome days. And this is one of the smaller pits. . . .

Immediately above this pit is another one, much larger. In fact, it averages eight feet wide by twenty-two feet long. Much of the debris from this pit was thrown down, or later washed down, into the one we excavated, which probably accounts for its being so well filled. Still others lie farther up the slope and have contributed their share to the filling process.

Much has been said about the hammerstones or mauls used in this mining, and the claim has been made that there are none to be found at this old site. They are, as a matter of fact, very numerous on the surface about the pits and during the excavation of this one pit alone we removed fifty-two mauls and fragments [Pl. XII].

It has been stated that many of these mauls were grooved for hafting. No evidence of such grooving was found anywhere about these old sites. Further, it has been stated that these mauls are very uniform in size, weighing about fifteen pounds each and that they were brought by the aboriginal miners from the Canadian mainland. Neither of these statements appears correct. We found mauls varying from the size of a fist to that of a large human head. In fact, some were so small that they could and probably were used in one hand. Others were so large as to be very unwieldy, even when used with both hands. Some idea of these mauls may be obtained from a few shown in Plate XII.

As for the source of these implements, attention need only be called to the fact that the glacial drift of the island has cobblestones of sizes, shapes and materials identical to those of the hammerstones found in the pits. The use to which these hammers were put caused them to break and wear out quickly. Hence, it is only reasonable that the Indians should use materials at hand and should put into the making of such an implement no more time and labor than was absolutely necessary. This is exactly the case. They took suitable cobblestones from the glacial drift immediately at hand and used these without any working whatsoever, either grooving or otherwise.

Our next task was to determine the extent of these ancient workings. To this end, Mr. West and the writer, made a rather careful walking survey of the region covered by the pits and found it to be about a quarter of a mile wide by about five miles in length. Conservatively estimated, we can say that it covers a square mile in total area. Over this entire area are pits of all sizes, ranging from some thirty feet across and at present six feet deep . . . to others perhaps a quarter that size. All are more or less filled in and some have been very much filled by the accumulation of debris from one or more of the surrounding workings. In some places these pits are rather widely scattered, but over most of this large area, they are so closely spaced, that their edges touch. In fact, they might be said to, in many places, actually overlap. Conservatively estimated there are from ten to fifteen of these pits per acre or upwards of ten thousand pits at this site.

Assuming very conservatively that each pit required on the average ten mauls for its working, we find that at least 100,000 of these crude implements were required at this site. It is, therefore, not strange that they are still present in great numbers.

Assuming that only one thousand of these pits yielded copper, we have here the source of a very large supply of this metal. However, the infinite labor entailed in the aboriginal mining methods, means that the product of these mines was very costly and the extent of the workings leaves little doubt that these mines were operated by the Indians over a very long period of time, probably hundreds of years.

It is, therefore, not surprising that with such a source of supply the trade in copper would take on a very important aspect, not only locally, but among the more distant tribes. (Barrett, 1925, pp. 25-31.)

George R. Fox made a survey of the island in 1911 and published a report (Fox, 1911). He made no excavations but summarized some of the earlier work. Fox also accompanied the McDonald-Massey Isle Royale Expedition of 1928 but the report on this project was published by the late George A. West, an amateur archaeologist, who was the Chairman of the Board of the Milwaukee Public Museum (West, 1929). This expedition recovered skeletal material from a rock ossuary. This collection is in the Milwaukee Public Museum. They visited the sites of Ferguson's diggings and were unable to find any evidence which differed significantly from that obtained by Holmes, Barrett, and others of normal Indian excavations. Their main excavations were at Chippewa Harbor where they obtained the pottery summarized by Quimby in 1939.

During 1929 and 1930 the Museum of Anthropology at the University of Michigan supported, with funds from the legislature (Dustin, 1957 and Bigelow, 1957), an archaeological survey by the late Fred Dustin of Saginaw, and some limited excavation by Dr. Carl E. Guthe, then Director of the Museum. Dustin's survey covered much of the ground of previous workers on the island but he also located additional sites and prepared a map of the location of sites and of his travels (Map 1). Dustin was an amateur archaeologist, a student of Western United States History, and a competent individual in identifying stone and rock by inspection. Dustin did not believe it was necessary to leave the island in order to find the raw material for the Isle Royale hammerstones:

The statement has been made that all these artifacts came from the Canadian mainland; this was based upon insufficient observation, as it is possible to duplicate any hammerstone with a pebble from either the present or ancient lake beaches which rise in a succession of terraces around the isle. The rocks are relics of the Ice Age, brought from the northern mainland and dropped on the isle, to be rolled and smoothed later by the waves of the inland sea. (Dustin, 1957, pp. 29 30.)

Many of his other observations are sound and reasonable. He concluded that:

1. The probable route by the miners was from the Keweenaw Peninsula to the Island and back, rather than from the north shore.

2. The ancient miners were probably the ancestors of the Algonquian and perhaps Iroquois of the Upper Great Lakes.

3. Isle Royale did not offer much inducement for permanent settlement.

4. The major mining area was McCargoe Cove.

THE ACQUISITION OF ISLE ROYALE BY THE UNITED STATES

One of the more romantic stories connected with Isle Royale is that it was included as United States territory after the Treaty of Paris, in 1783, because "some report of its mineral wealth is said to have reached Franklin, perhaps through the *Jesuit Relations* and through his French friends, and to have led him in making the treaty with Great Britain which defined the limits of the United States, to curve the boundary line slightly so as to take Isle Royale and separate it from the Canadian shore, nearest to which it lies." (Lane, 1898, pp. 2-3.) After carelessly repeating this story a number of times I talked with Professor Verner W. Crane, of the University of Michigan Department of History, who is a well-known student of Benjamin Franklin and his times. Professor Crane told me that he had never seen any data which would support the thesis that Isle Royale was included in United States territory because of Franklin's knowledge of the copper deposits on the island. The quotation from Lane is the earliest reference to the story that I have located.

The American-Canadian boundary set by the Treaty of Paris became involved in serious discussion primarily over the line in northern New England. The boundary line was to run through the middle of Lakes Ontario, Erie, and Huron and their connecting rivers into Lake Superior. From "thence through lake Superior northward of the isles, Royal and Philipeaux to the long lake, thence through the long lake and the water communication between it and the lake of the woods, to the said lake of the woods; thence through the said lake to the most northwestern point thereof, and from thence on a due west course to the river Missisippi; thence by a line to be drawn along the middle of the said Missisippi, until it shall intersect the northernmost part of the thirty-first degree of north latitude." This quotation is from

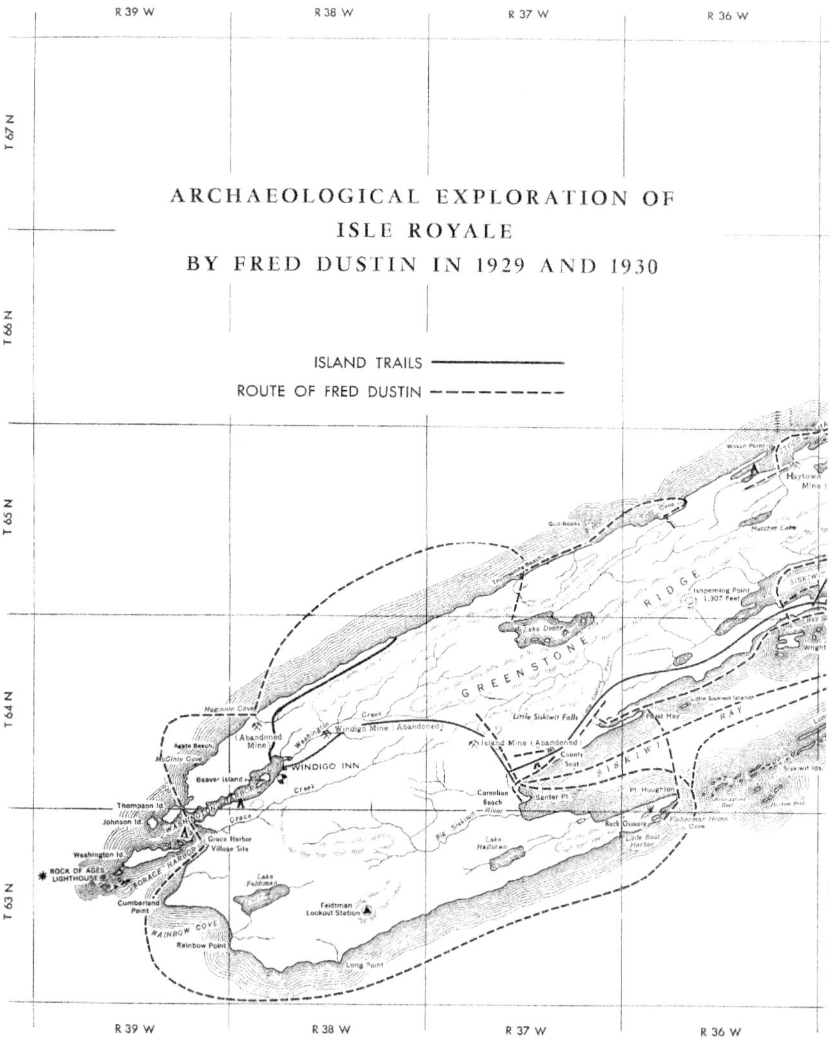

Map. 1. Isle Royale archaeological sites based on information comp

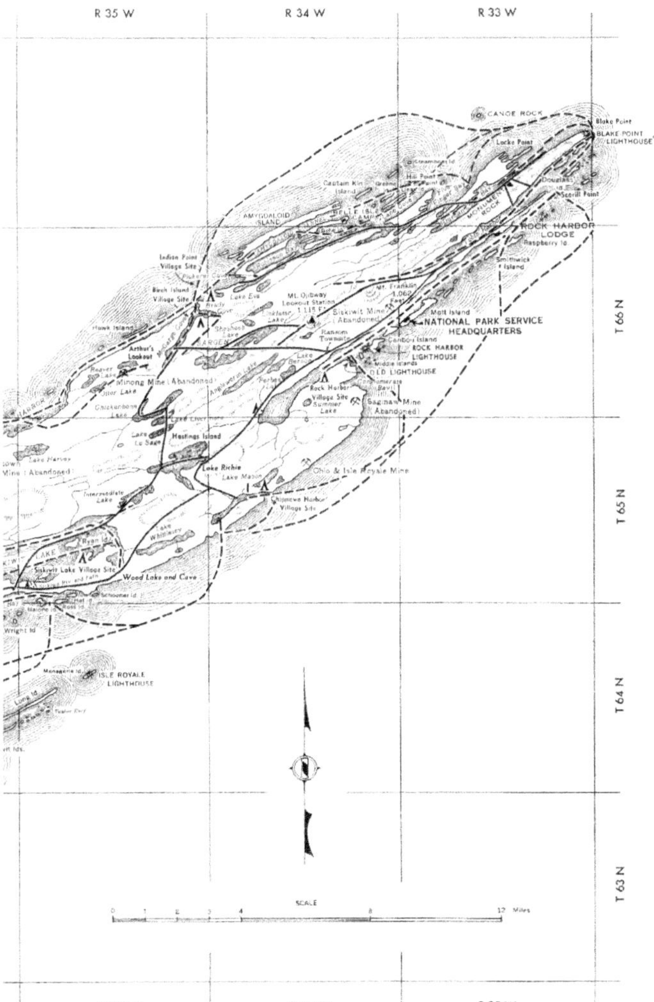

compiled by Fred Dustin

Winsor (1888, p. 167) who reproduced a broadside entitled "By the United States in Congress Assembled, A Proclamation."

Actually it was John Jay who insisted that the western boundary of the United States should be from the Mississippi River down to the 31st parallel. (Bemis, 1935, p. 216.) On the Mitchell map of 1755 which was used during the treaty negotiations, the Mississippi, although its upper course was covered by an inset of the Hudson Bay area, seemed to rise quite a distance north of Isle Royale and of the nonexistent Philipeaux island to the south of it. "The negotiators assumed that a line due west from the northwestern corner of the Lake of the Woods—the final language of the treaty--would strike the Mississippi; but actually the source of that river lies south of such a latitude" (Bemis, p. 234.)

EARLY HISTORICAL ACCOUNTS OF THE LAKE SUPERIOR COPPER DISTRICT

One of our major sources of Indian knowledge and use of Lake Superior copper is from the historical accounts of the French, English, and Americans. Pertinent passages are quoted in this section in order to present the opinions of various writers on the subject. It is difficult to correctly assess these sources because of the handicap of imperfect understanding by the French of what the Indians actually meant and vice versa. In the accounts of the seventeenth century there is a further hindrance in the fact that some part of the reporting of the discoveries in Lake Superior was done by individuals who were summarizing the activities of others and were not themselves participants in the voyages. The general intent of this chapter is to indicate that the Indians of the upper Great Lakes area (Map 2) were aware of the major copper deposits in Lake Superior, were obtaining copper from the deposits, and were distributing it to other groups to the east and south. Archaeological records indicate that during the period from A.D. 1000 to A.D. 1700, a moderate amount of copper was shaped into small knives, awls, and beads in the upper Great Lakes area. Active exploitation of the copper by the Indians seems to have been at a relatively low level during the A.D. 1500 to 1700 period.

The earliest sound reference to the Lake Superior area copper deposits (Map 3) is provided by Cartier's second voyage of 1535-36 when he reports the results of his information obtained from Laurentian Iroquoian-speaking Indians who were then located in the area between Montreal and Quebec (Fenton, 1940, pp. 167-76). The first reference merely identifies the direction from which the copper had come. "Our Indians told us that this was the beginning of the Saguenay and of the inhabited region; and that thence came the copper they call *caignetdaze*." (Biggar, 1924, pp. 105-6.) The word "caignetdaze" is close to a Mohawk word for metal.

The second reference to copper was obtained from some of the Iroquois who had taken Cartier to the top of Mount Royal to explain to him what they knew of the surrounding country. In the quotation below, which identifies the Ottawa River as the route to the copper country, it is not clear just which tribe or tribes are referred to as the "bad people" or *Agojuda*. It might have been

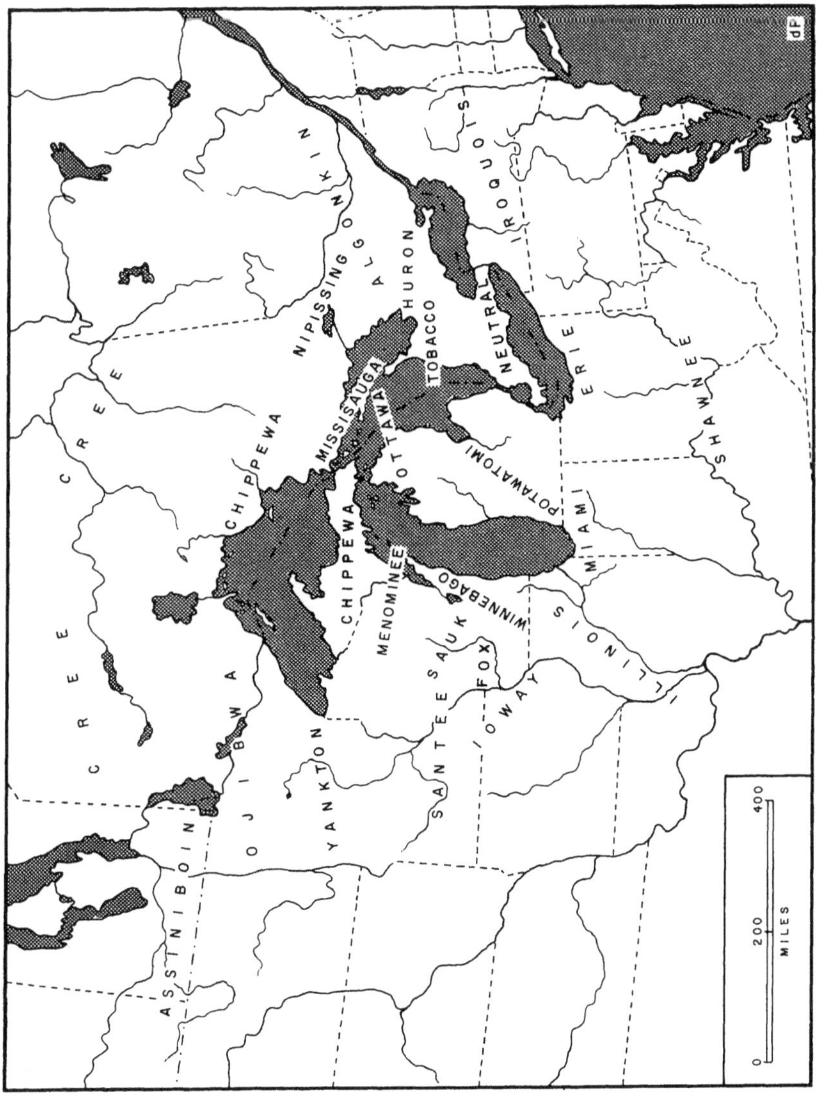

Map 2. Distribution of some of the Indian groups of the early historic period about 1600-1700. This map is a compromise between strict historical reality, the research design of this paper, and available space on a single map. It has been compiled from several sources. The Assiniboin, Yankton, and Santee represent the forest and prairie Sioux of Minnesota-Manitoba; the Winnebago, another Siouan-speaking group, located in Wisconsin; while the Erie, Neutral, Tobacco, Huron, and Iroquois were Iroquoian-speaking groups. The rest of the named groups were Algonkin-speaking.

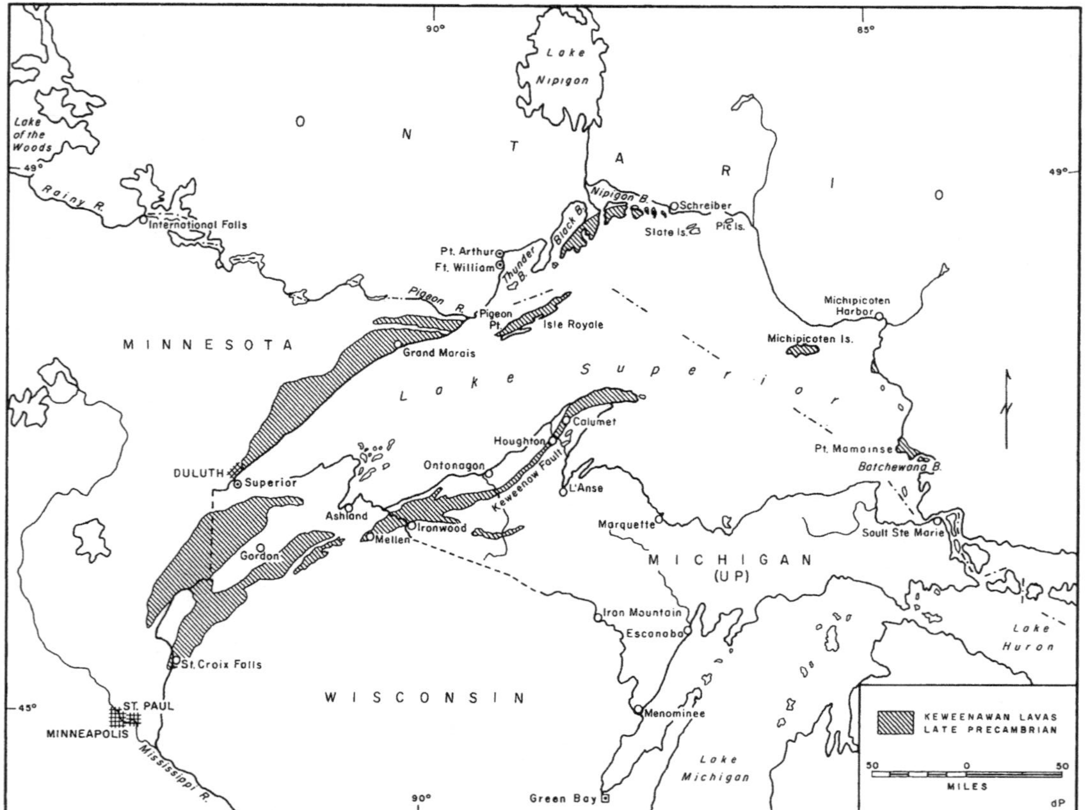

Map 3. This map of the location of the copper-bearing formations of the Lake Superior Basin was sketched by Professor F. S. Turneaure of the Department of Geology of the University of Michigan. We annotated the map and the data was then placed on it by A. L. Petrucci, graduate assistant in the Geography Department, who also prepared maps 2 and 5.

the Huron, but could be a reference to the Ottawa or another Algonkin group. It is necessary to distinguish between the Saguenay River of Quebec flowing into the lower St. Lawrence and the land of the Saguenay which is apparently on the east side of Lake Huron.

> We thought this river [Ottawa] must be the one that flows past the kingdom and province of the Saguenay; and without our asking any questions or making any sign, they seized the chain of the Captain's whistle, which was made of silver, and a dagger-handle of yellow copper-gilt like gold, that hung at the side of one of the sailors, and gave us to understand that these came from up that river [Ottawa], where lived *Agojuda*, which means bad people, who were armed to the teeth, showing us the style of their armour, which is made with cords and wood, laced and plaited together. They also seemed to say that these *Agojuda* waged war continually, one tribe against the other, but through not understanding their language, we could not make out what the distance was to that country. The Captain showed them some copper, which they call caignetdaze, and pointing towards the said region, asked by signs if it came thence? They shook their heads to say no, showing us that it came from the Saguenay, which lies in the opposite direction. (Biggar, 1924, pp. 170-71.)

The third reference to the copper source was obtained after Cartier returned to Quebec, from the Laurentian Iroquois of that area. They also identified the Ottawa River as a route to the land of the "Saguenay." The accuracy of this passage, in detail, may be inferred from the reference to "gold" which was almost certainly only in the minds of the French when the Iroquois word for metal was spoken, and does not imply that the Indians were referring specifically to gold. Even the connotation "honest folk" is one that seems to be a poor understanding by the French of what the Iroquois actually said. The references to people "clothed and dressed in woolens" is again a failure on the part of the French to understand what was being said to them. Donnacona, the chief of the Indian group at Quebec claimed to have been to the Lake Huron area.

> On our return from Hochelaga [Montreal] with the bark and the long-boats, we held intercourse and came and went among the tribes nearest to our ships in peace and friendship, except for a few quarrels now and then with some bad boys, at which the others were very angry and much annoyed. And we learned from Chief Donnacona, from Taignoagny, Dom Agaya and the others that the above-mentioned river, named the "river of the Saguenay," reaches to the [kingdom of the] Saguenay, which lies more than a moon's journey from its mouth, towards the west-north-west; but that after eight or nine days' journey, this river is only navigable for small boats; that the regular and direct route to the [kingdom of the] Saguenay and the safer one, is by the river [St. Lawrence]

to a point above Hochelaga where there is a tributary, which flows down from the [kingdom of the] Saguenay, and enters this river [St. Lawrence], as we ourselves saw, from which point the journey takes one moon. And they gave us to understand, that in that country the natives go clothed and dressed in woolens like ourselves; that there are many towns and tribes composed of honest folk who possess great store of gold and copper. Furthermore they told us that (pp. 200-201) the whole region from the first-mentioned river up as far as Hochelaga and [the kingdom of the] Saguenay is an island, which is encircled and surrounded by rivers and by the said river [St. Lawrence]; and that beyond the [kingdom of the] Saguenay, this tributary flows through two or three large, very broad lakes, until one reaches a fresh-water sea [Lake Huron], of which there is no mention of anyone having seen the bounds, as the people of the [kingdom of the] Saguenay had informed them; for they themselves, they told us, had never been there. (Biggar, 1924, pp. 200-203.)

The significance of these early references is cleared up to some degree by the data obtained from Champlain. While Champlain was sailing up the St. Lawrence in 1610, he met two Indians, one of whom gave him a bar of copper. Apparently, by this time, the Indians had learned that copper not only had value to them, but also to the Europeans, for from Cartier's trip to those of Champlain, an increasing amount of French trading activity was going on, and not all of the European participants left journals such as Champlain did.

I DEPARTED from Quebec on June 14, to go and meet the Montagnais, Algonquins, and Ochateguins who were to be at the mouth of the river of the Iroquois. When I was eight leagues from Quebec, I met a canoe in which were two Indians, one an Algonquin and the other a Montagnais, who were coming to ask me to push on as fast as possible. They said that in two days Algonquins and Ochatequins [Ottawa], to the number of 200 would be at the rendez-vous, and that 200 more would come a little later with Iroquet, one of their chiefs. They asked me if I was pleased with the arrival of these Indians, and I said that I could not be displeased with it, since they had kept their promise. They got into my pinnace, where I entertained them well. After conversing with them a short time about a number of things touching their wars, the Algonquin Indian, who was one of their chiefs, drew out of a sack a piece of copper a foot long, which he presented to me. It was very fine and pure. He gave me to understand that the metal was abundant where he had obtained it, which was on the bank of a river near a large lake. He said that it was taken out in pieces, and when melted was made into sheets and smoothed out with stones. I was much pleased with this gift although it was of small value. (Biggar, 1925, pp. 122-23.)

The records of the period from 1603 to about 1630 definitely set the major trade and transportation routes from the St. Lawrence to the Lake Superior copper area and suggest that it is primarily the eastern side of the Superior area with which the French were familar. It may be regarded as settled that the inhabitants of Lake Superior were primarily the Chippewa-Ojibwa with some incursions of other groups, including the Iroquois.

Gabriel Sagard is often referred to in his 1632 account for his reference to copper which we can accept as being adequate for the time, but also contains statements which reflect the general level of knowledge of the mineral resources. Sagard provides the records for the Recollect missions to the east of Lake Huron. From Brule (?), who was in Champlain's service, and another Frenchman named Grenoble, Sagard, in the 1620's, learned of a "place where the Indians were taking copper from a mine" (Kellogg, 1925, p. 59), on Lake Superior and of its size and of the rapids discharging from it to Lake Huron. The first individuals into Lake Superior, and who had some first-hand knowledge of the copper deposits, were those primarily engaged in trade and in extending the French domain. There is no indication in the historical accounts as to where, in Lake Superior, the copper sources were located.

> Here then, you who are without religion, here are the treasures and riches to which alone you look with so much concern. They consist chiefly in quantities of furs, from various species of terrestrial and amphibious animals. There are in addition copper mines not to be despised, from which profit might be derived if there were a population and workmen who were willing to work them conscientiously. This might happen if colonies had been established, for about eighty or a hundred leagues from the Hurons there is a mine of copper, an ingot from which was shown me by the interpreter [Brule, an associate of Champlain] on his return from a journey made in the district. It is believed that there is some also in the direction of the Saguenay, and even that gold, rubies, and other wealth are found there. Moreover, some persons are certain that in the Souriquois country there are not only copper mines, but also steel contained in the rocks, which when melted out might make excellent knives. Then there is a kind of transparent blue stone, not less valuable than turquoise. In the rocks containing copper are also found sometimes small pieces of rock covered with diamonds adhering to them; and I may say that I myself picked up some near our convent in Canada and kept them, and that they seemed as if they had come from the hands of a lapidary, they were so beautiful, glittering, and well cut. I will not assert that they are pure, but they are pretty and they write on glass. (Wrong, 1939, pp. 242-43.)

The account of Father Bressani, an Italian Jesuit in the *Jesuit Relations* of 1653, is still apparently based on the stories and accounts of copper from Champlain's and Brule's (?) information and from stories of the Indians: "There is a Copper ore, which is very pure, and which has no need of passing through the fire; but it is in places far distant and hard to reach, which render its transportation almost impossible. We have seen it in the hands of the Barbarians, but no one has visited the place." (Thwaites, 1899, Vol. XXXVIII, p. 243.)

It is not until after the voyages of Médard Chouart, Sieur des Groseilliers and Pierre Esprit Radisson and their Jesuit associates that from 1660 on, the data about Lake Superior copper deposits becomes more explicit, and that sound knowledge of the size and main features of Lake Superior begin to appear on European maps (Kellogg, 1925, pp. 104-16; Nute, 1943). Radisson gives a description of their passage from Keweenaw Bay to the lake in 1659 and mentions the activities of the beaver near the portage. It was primarily Ojibway Indians who were making the trip across the lake from Keweenaw Point to Isle Royale and to the north shore.

> Having passed that place, we made a carriage through the land for 2 leagues. The way was well beaten because of the commers and goers, who by making that passage shortens their passage by 8 dayes by tourning about the point that goes very farr in that great lake, that is to say, 5 to come to the point, and 3 for to come to the landing of that place of carriage. In the end of that point, that goeth very farre, there is an isle, as I was told, all of copper. This I have not seene. They say that from the isle of copper, which is a league in the lake, when they are minded to thwart it in a faire and calme wether, beginning from sun rising to sun sett, they come to a great island (Isle Royale), from whence they come the next morning to firme lande att the other side; so by reason of 20 leagues a day that lake should be broad of 6 score and 10 leagues. The wildmen doe not much lesse when the weather is faire.

In describing Siouoan dress at a celebration near Knife Lake, Minnesota, a reference is made to copper: "Their ears are pierced in 5 places; the holes are so big that your little finger might pass through. They have yellow waire that they make with copper, made like a starr or a half moon and there hang it". (Upham, 1905, p. 497.)

The often quoted account, by Father Allouez, of the copper along the south shore of Lake Superior is given below. It is suggested that Allouez's concept of the attitude of the Indians toward the copper is not completely factual. Prize it, they certainly did, perhaps had a "superstitious" attitude, but they also were clearly using it.

> On the second of September, then after clearing this Sault (de Sainte-Marie),—which is not a waterfall, but merely a very swift current impeded by numerous rocks,—we entered Lake Superior, which will henceforth bear Monsieur de Tracy's name, in recognition of indebtedness to him on the part of the people of those regions.

The form of this Lake is nearly that of a bow, the Southern shore being much curved, and the Northern nearly straight. Fish are abundant there, and of excellent quality; while the water is so clear and pure that objects at the bottom can be seen to the depth of six brasses.

The Savages revere this Lake as a Divinity, and offer it Sacrifices, whether on account of its size,—for its length is two hundred leagues, and its greatest width eighty,—or because of its goodness in furnishing fish for the sustenance of all these tribes, in default of game, which is scarce in the neighborhood.

One often finds at the bottom of the water pieces of pure copper, of ten and twenty pounds' weight. I have several times seen such pieces in the Savages' hands; and, since they are superstitious, they keep them as so many divinities, or as presents which the gods dwelling beneath the water have given them, and on which their welfare is to depend. For this reason they preserve these pieces of copper, wrapped up, among their most precious possessions. Some have kept them for more than fifty years; others have had them in their families from time immemorial, and cherish them as household gods.

For some time, there had been seen a sort of great rock, all of copper, the point of which projected from the water; this gave passers-by the opportunity to go and cut off pieces from it. When, however, I passed that spot, nothing more was seen of it; and I think that the storms —which here are very frequent, and like those at Sea—have covered the rock with sand. Our Savages tried to persuade me that it was a divinity, who had disappeared for some reason which they do not state.

This Lake is, furthermore, the resort of twelve or fifteen distinct nations—coming, some from the North, others from the South, and still others from the West; and they all betake themselves either to the best parts of the shore for fishing, or to the Islands, which are scattered in great numbers all over the Lake. These peoples' motive in repairing hither is partly to obtain food by fishing, and partly to transact their petty trading with one another, when they meet. But God's purpose was to facilitate the proclaiming of the Gospel to wandering and vagrant tribes—as will appear in the course of this Journal. (Thwaites, 1902, pp. 31-32.)

The following account attributed to Father Dablon of the Lake Superior deposits is a considerable improvement over that of Allouez, since it was put together where a considerable amount of information had been gathered from many people:

Hitherto it had been thought that these Mines were found only in one or two Islands; but, since we have made more exact inquiries on the subject, we have learned from the Savages some secrets which they did not wish to reveal. It has been necessary to use artifice to elicit this information, and to distinguish the true from the false.

Still we do not vouch for the truth of all that we are about to relate, upon their simple deposition, until we are able to speak with more assurance after having gone in person to the places referred to; and this we hope to do this Summer, at the same time when we go in search of lost and wandering sheep all through the region of that great Lake.

Upon entering it by its mouth, where it empties into the Sault the first place met where Copper is found in abundance, is an Island, distant forty or fifty leagues and situated toward the North, opposite a spot called Missipicouatong [Michipicoten].

The Savages say that it is a floating Island, which is sometimes far off, sometimes near, according to the winds that push it and drive it in all directions. They add, that a long time ago four Savages came thither by chance, having lost their way in the fog by which that Island is almost always surrounded.

It was in the times before they had yet had any commerce with the French, and when they did not use kettles or hatchets. These men, then, wishing to prepare themselves something to eat, adopted their usual method; taking some stones that they found at the water's edge, they heated them red-hot, and threw them into a bark dish filled with water, to make it boil, and by this device to cook their meat. While selecting these stones, they found that they were almost all pieces of Copper; accordingly they made use of some of them, and, after taking their repast, resolved to embark as soon as possible, fearing the Lynxes and the Hares, which are as large as Dogs in that region, and were coming to eat up their provisions and even their Canoe.

Before setting out, they loaded themselves with a good many of these stones, large and small, and even with some slabs of Copper; but they had not gone far from the shore when a powerful voice made itself heard to their ears, calling in great wrath: "Who are those robbers carrying off from me my children's cradles and playthings?" The Copper slabs are the cradles, because among the Savages these are made of only one or two boards joined together, on which they put their children to bed; and those little pieces of Copper that they were carrying off are the toys and playthings of the Savage children, who play together with little stones.

That voice astonished them greatly, as they knew not whose it was. Some say that it was Thunder, because there are many storms there; and others that it was a certain Spirit whom they call Missibizi, who passes among these peoples for the God of the waters, as Neptune did among the Pagans. Others say it came from Memogovissiouis: these are, they say, marine People somewhat like the fabulous Tritons or the Sirens, who always live in the water and have long hair reaching to the waist. One of our Savages told us he had seen one of them in the water, according to what he imagined.

However this may be, that astounding voice inspired such terror in our Travelers' souls that one of the four died before reaching land. A short time afterward a second was taken off, and then the third; so that only one was left, who, after returning to his Country and relating all that had happened, died very soon afterward.

The Savages, timid and superstitious as they all are, have never dared to go there since that time, for fear of dying there, believing that there are certain Spirits who kill those who approach them. And, in fact, in the memory of man, no one has been known to set foot there, or even to be willing to sail in that direction—although the Island seems to be open enough, and its trees may even be distinguished from another Island, named Achemikouan.

There is truth and there is untruth in this whole narrative, and the following is what is most probable: namely, that those four persons were poisoned by the water that they boiled with the pieces of copper, which communicated their poison to it, owing to their very great heat; for we know by experience that this copper, when it is put into the fire for the first time, exhales very malignant vapors, which are thick and infectious and whiten the fireplace. It is not, however, a poison so immediate as not to operate more promptly in some cases than in others, as happened with those of whom we are speaking; who, being already affected by the poison, may have easily imagined that they heard those voices, if they heard, however slightly, some echo, such as is commonly found among the Rocks bordering that Island.

Perhaps this fable has been invented since the event, from not knowing to what to attribute the death of those Savages; and when they say that it is a floating Island, it is not incredible that the mists with which it is often laden, by becoming thin or dense under the Sun's rays, make the Island appear to the observer sometimes very near, and at other times farther away.

What is certain is that, in the common opinion of the Savages, there is a great abundance of Copper in that Island; but they dare not go there. It is there that we hope to begin the discoveries which we purpose making this Summer.

Advancing as far as the part called "the great inlet," one comes to an Island three leagues from the land, renowned for the metal that is found there, and for the name *[Thunder]*, which it bears because it is said to thunder there all the time.

But farther toward the West, on the same North side, is found the Island which is most famous for Copper, and is called Minong [Isle Royale]; this is the one in which, as the Savages have told many people, the metal exists in abundance, and in many places. It is large, and is fully twenty-five leagues long; it is distant seven leagues from the mainland, and more than sixty from the end of the Lake. Pieces of Copper, mingled with the stones, are found at the water's edge almost all around the Island, especially on the South side; but principally in a certain inlet that is near the end facing the Northeast, toward the offing, there are some very steep clay hills where are seen several strata or beds of red Copper, one over another, separated or divided by other strata of earth or of Rocks. In the water even is seen Copper sand as it were; and from it may be dipped up with ladles grains as large as a nut, and other smaller ones reduced to sand. This large Island is almost all surrounded with Islets that are said to be formed of Copper; they are encountered in various places, as far as the mainland on the North. One, among others, is only two gunshots distant from Minong; it is between the middle of the Island and the end that faces the Northeast. Again, on this Northeast side, far out in the lake, there is another Island which, because of the copper in which it abounds, is called Manitouminis [i.e., "Island of the Spirit"]; of this it is related that those who came here formerly, upon throwing stones at the ground, made it ring, just as brass is wont to ring.

Going on to the end of the Lake, and coming back a day's journey along the South side, one sees at the water's edge a Rock of Copper weighing fully seven or eight hundred livres, so hard that steel can scarely cut it; yet, when it is heated, it may be cut like lead.

Twenty or thirty leagues this side of that spot is situated Chagaouamigong [Chequamegon] point, where we have established the Mission of saint Esprit, of which we shall speak hereafter. Near that place are some

Islands, on the shores of which are often found Rocks of Copper, and even slabs of the same material.

Last Spring, we bought from the Savages a slab of pure Copper, two feet square, and weighing more than a hundred livres. It is not thought, however, that the mines are found in the Islands, but that all these Copper pebbles probably come from Minong or from the other Islands which are the sources of it, borne upon floating ice or rolled along in the depths of the water by the very impetuous winds—particularly by the Northeast wind, which is extremely violent.

It is true that on the Mainland, at the place where the Outaouaks raise Indian corn, half a league from the water's edge, the women have sometimes found pieces of Copper scattered here and there, of the weight of ten, twenty, or thirty livres. It is in digging up the sand to plant their corn that they make these chance discoveries.

Still returning toward the mouth of the Lake and following the South side, at twenty leagues' distance from the spot we have just mentioned one enters the river called Nantounagan [Ontonagon], in which is seen a height from which stones of red Copper fall into the water or on the ground, and are very easily found. Three years ago we were given a massive piece of it, a hundred livres in weight, which was taken in this same spot; from it we have cut off some fragments, and sent them to Quebec to Monsieur Talon.

All do not agree as to the precise spot where it is found, some maintaining that it is where the river begins to narrow, and others saying that it is encountered very near the Lake, by digging in the clay. Some have said that at the place where the River forks, and in the channel farthest to the East, on this side of a point of land, one must dig in the rich earth to find this Copper; and that pieces of this metal are even found scattered in the channel which is in the middle.

Still continuing in this direction, the long point [Keweenaw] of land presents itself which we have called the arrow of the bow; at its end there is only an Islet, which appears to be six feet square, and is said to be all of copper.

Finally, not to leave any part of this great Lake that we have not explored, we are assured that in the interior, toward the South, mines of this metal are found in different places.

All this information and other besides, which it is not necessary to give more in detail, make it worth while to undertake an exact investigation in these matters; and that is what we shall try to do—as also to examine a certain verdigris which is said to run down through the crevices of certain Rocks at the waterside, where one even finds among the pebbles some rather soft pieces, of a pleasant green hue. If God guide us in our enterprise, we shall speak about it next year with more certainty and knowledge. (Thwaites, 1902, pp. 72-76.)

The importance of the following quotation from the Jesuit records, which deals with the French outpost at Chequamegon on the south shore of Lake Superior, is that it provides an excellent example of the type of Indian settlement which developed around trading posts and mission centers:

More than fifty Villages can be counted, which comprise divers peoples, either nomadic or stationary, who depend in some sort on this Mission; and to whom the Gospel can be proclaimed, either by going into their Country, or waiting for them to come to this to do their trading.

The three Nations comprised under the name of Outaouaks, of which one has embraced Christianity, and that of Etionnontatehronnon Hurons [Tobacco Nation]—among whom there are more than five hundred baptized persons—inhabit this point; they live there on fish and corn, and rarely by hunting, and number more than fifteen hundred souls.

The Illinois, tribes extending toward the South, have five large Villages, of which one has a stretch of three leagues, the cabins being placed lengthwise. They number nearly two thousand souls, and repair to this place from time to time in great numbers, as Merchants, to carry away hatchets and kettles, guns, and other articles that they need. During the sojourn that they make here, we take the opportunity to sow in their hearts the first seeds of the Gospel. Fuller mention will be hereafter made of these peoples, and of the desire which they manifest to have one of our Fathers among them to instruct them; and also of the plan formed by Father Marquette to go thither next Autumn.

Eight days' journey from here toward the West is the first of the thirty Villages of the Nadouessi [Sioux]. The extensive warfare carried on by them with our Hurons, and with some other Nations of those Regions, keeps them more confined, and obliges them to come hither only in small numbers, and as if on an Embassy. Of them also mention will be made hereafter, and of what the said Father has done to put them in a state of peace and keep them there.

Of all the Nations toward the North, there are three, among others, who come to trade here; and very recently two hundred Canoes passed some time here. (Thwaites, 1902, Vol. XVI, pp. 77-78.)

By 1670, which is the date of this account, the main Indian tribes at Chequamegon were bands of the Ottawa, and of the Huron who had fled from the southern Georgian Bay area under pressure from the New York Iroquois. The latter group had been supplied with guns by the Dutch and English and were attempting to control the fur trade of the Great Lakes area in order to obtain the economic benefits from such control. The account is also of interest because of the emphasis on agriculture as a primary food supply; because of the variety of Indians who came from considerable distances to trade, such as the Sioux and Illinois; and because it was at least partly from such Illinois and other Indians from the south that Joliet heard of the river system leading from Green Bay into the Mississippi. Joliet was sent by the French officials in Montreal to explore the copper country of Lake Superior in 1669 (Thwaites, 1902, p. 89). His demonstrated ability caused him to be chosen to lead a party to find and explore the Mississippi in 1673. Father Marquette accompanied him.

In the latter part of the seventeenth century, both in Canada and in Paris, the French colonial administrators were aware of the commercial importance of the Lake Superior copper, and also of the stimulus such an operation could provide for French colonists to develop the copper deposits (O'Callaghan, 1855, pp. 63, 70-72, 89, 336). The interest was not sufficient, however, to overcome the difficulties of starting the project.

Between 1725 and 1740, the French made an effort to initiate commercial mining in the Lake Superior region, particularly along the south shore. Many of the documents dealing with this attempt are in Thwaites (1906, Vol. II) account of "The French Regime in Wisconsin." Much of this activity was promoted by Louis Denys, Sieur de la Ronde, who was the commandant at the French post at Chequamegon. He had the active support of French officials in Canada and was encouraged in his proposal by the King and his Minister in Paris. De La Ronde agreed to build a twenty-five-ton boat on Lake Superior in order to transport the copper from the mines to Sault Ste Marie, and another of fifty tons to operate on Lakes Huron and Erie. Ingots of copper had been sent to France and, with De La Ronde's urging, two miners were sent from Germany in 1738 to pass judgment on the suitability of extensive mining operations. These attempts continued over a ten-year period but for a variety of reasons mining activites were not started.

From these records something of value may be learned about the knowledge of the copper deposits at that time. From the Indians of the Chequamegon area De La Ronde gained his knowledge of deposits along the Ontonagan and Black Rivers. He also was told repeatedly about the tradition of copper on Isle Royale. The Ontonagon boulder, which is now in the United States National Museum, had been known to the French since the middle of the seventeenth century and no one knows how much copper was chipped away by individuals who visited it before its removal in 1843. The other enormous copper mass, reported by the many French, which was located along the south shore of Lake Superior did not survive into the nineteenth century.

In 1735, Corbin, a carpenter employed by De La Ronde visited copper deposits on the Ontonagan River to which he was guided by one of the Indians whom he took on board at L'Anse. This Indian "asserted that he had a thorough knowledge of the Mines and of the copper in the said River of Tonnagane." Corbin made a report on a number of locations but did not visit three others which were known to his guide. In August of 1736, De La Ronde brought "About 500 pounds of ore taken from two large masses of copper, one of which is at the Tonnaganne River, and the other on the Shore of Lake Superior near the Piouabic [Iron] River." It was reported to France that "All the savages assert that copper is to be found at a great many Places on Lake Superior; from time to time they have brought pieces which they have given to Frenchmen and in particular to Father St. Pé, a Jesuit Missionary at Missilimakinac." These copper pieces were sent to Paris (Thwaites, 1906, Vol. II, pp. 252-54).

In the latter half of the eighteenth century there are a number of reports by English explorers and travelers who had acquired some knowledge of the copper district and deposits from various French accounts. Some of these are quoted or mentioned in other parts of this paper. The English did make some efforts to get a commercial mining activity under way but were not any more successful than the French had been. The copper deposits were not developed until the next century when the Americans and Canadians, with improved transportation and mining techniques, less trouble with Indian groups, and a stronger market incentive, began the exploitation of the Lake Superior copper.

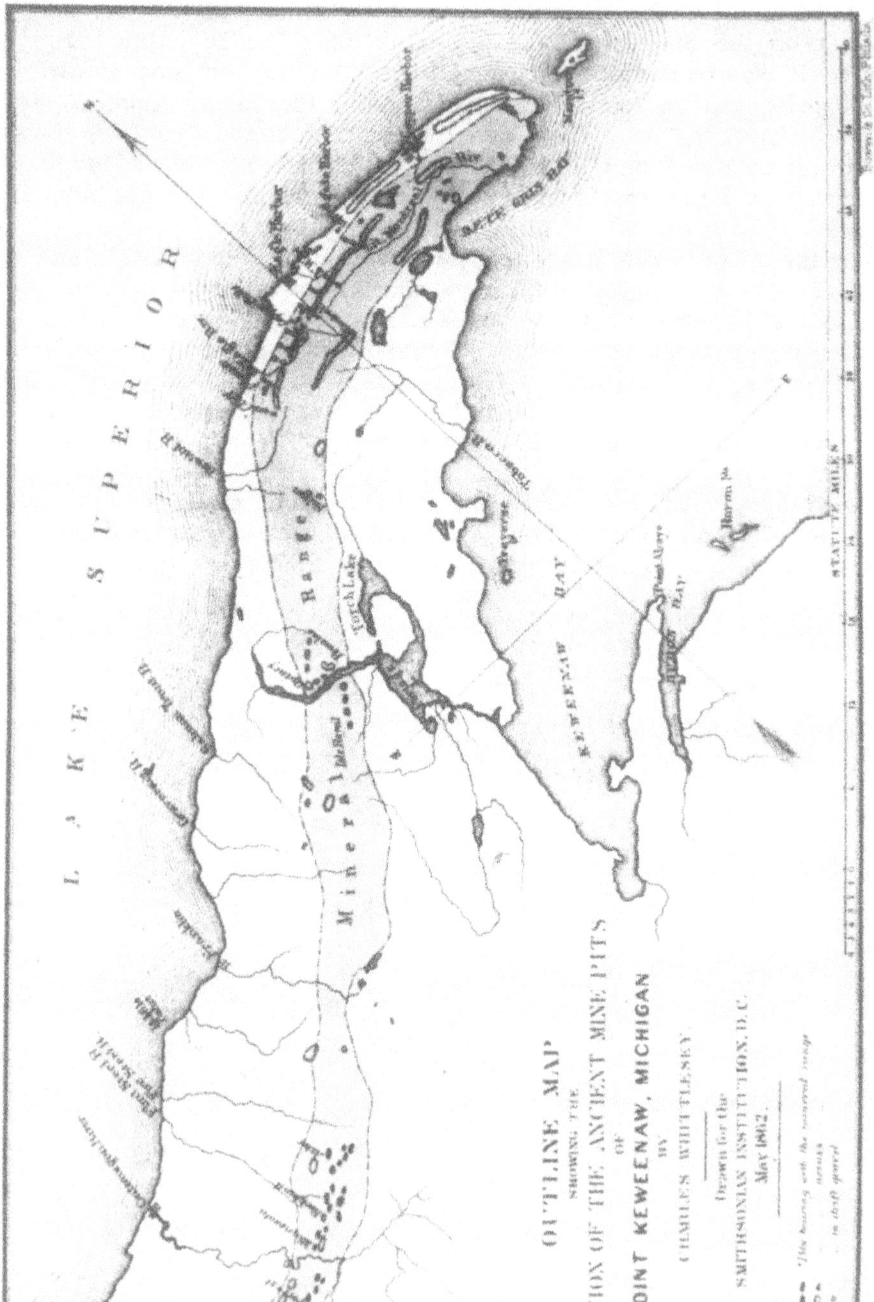
LAKE SUPERIOR
Mineral Range
Torch Lake
BETE GRIS BAY
KEWEENAW BAY
STATUTE MILES
OUTLINE MAP
SHOWING THE
POSITION OF THE ANCIENT MINE PITS
OF
POINT KEWEENAW, MICHIGAN
BY
CHARLES WHITTLESEY
Drawn for the
SMITHSONIAN INSTITUTION, D.C.
May 1862

Map 4

EARLY AMERICAN MINING IN THE UPPER PENINSULA OF MICHIGAN AND THE FIRST RECOGNITION OF PREHISTORIC MINING ACTIVITIES

The earliest and longest record on the discoveries of prehistoric mining activities in the Lake Superior copper deposits (Map 4) is that from the Keweenaw peninsula, and west from there to the Ontonagan area. Valuable as these observations are, they still leave a great deal to be desired in systematic recording. The best accounts of the early American and Canadian observers are quoted below in an effort to put these data on record under one cover. There are apparently few, if any, prehistoric mines in the Upper Peninsula that have not been examined and destroyed since 1850. Considering the large number of pits reported we have very few accounts on which to base an evaluation of the prehistoric mining activities. These published records are, therefore, the basic data on which archaeologists will have to rely both now and in the future.

At the Minnesota Mine in Ontonagan County, Foster and Whitney (1850, pp. 159-62) report some of the earliest observations regarding the ancient mining activities:

> We will now proceed to the details of the discoveries thus far made. The most extended excavations are found in the vicinity of the Ontonagon river; and to Mr. Samuel O. Knapp, the intelligent agent of the Minnesota Company, belongs the credit of having first laid before the public an account of their nature and extent.
>
> In the winter of 1847-'48, while passing over a portion of the location now occupied by the Minnesota Mining Company, he observed a continuous depression in the soil, which he rightly conjectured was caused by the disentegration of a vein. There was a bed of snow on the ground three feet in depth, but it had been so little disturbed by the wind that it conformed to the inequalities of the surface. Following up these indications along the southern escarpment of the hill, where the company's works are now erected, he came to a longitudinal cavern, into which he crept, after having dispossessed several porcupines which had selected it as a place of hybernation. He saw numerous evidences to convince him that this was an artificial excavation, and at a subsequent day, with the assistance of two or three men, proceeded to explore it. In clearing out the rubbish they found numerous stone hammers, showing plainly that they were the mining implements of a rude race. At the bottom of the excavation they found a vein with ragged projections of copper, which the ancient miners had not detached. This point is east of the present works.
>
> The following spring he explored some of the excavations to the west, where one of the shafts of the mine is now sunk. The depression

was twenty-six feet deep, filled with clay and a matted mass of mouldering vegetable matter. When he had penetrated to the depth of eighteen feet, he came to a mass of native copper ten feet long, three feet wide, and nearly two feet thick, and weighing over six tons. On digging around it the mass was found to rest on billets of oak, supported by sleepers of the same material. This wood, specimens of which we have preserved, by its long exposure to moisture, is dark-colored, and has lost all of its consistency. A knife-blade may be thrust into it as easily as into a peat bog. The earth was so packed around the copper as to give it a firm support. The ancient miners had evidently raised it about five feet and then abandoned the work as too laborious. They had taken off every projecting point which was accessible, so that the exposed surface was smooth. Below this the vein was subsequently found filled with a sheet of copper five feet thick, and of an undetermined extent vertically and longitudinally. The position of the copper block, and the extent of the exploitations along a portion of the lode, may be seen by reference to the plan of the Minnesota mine [p. 62]. The vein was wrought in the form of an open trench; and where the copper was the most abundant, there the excavations extended the deepest. The trench is generally filled to within a foot of the surface, with the wash from the surrounding surface intermingled with leaves nearly decayed. The rubbish taken from the mine is piled up in mounds, which can readily be distinguished from the former contour of the ground.

A few rods to the west is another specimen of ancient mining, where they have left a portion of the veinstone standing, in the form of a pillar, in order to support the hanging wall. The rubbish in this excavation has not been cleared away, so that its extent is unknown.

These evidences are observed on this location for a distance of two and a half miles. Upon a mound of earth we saw a pine stump, broken fifteen feet from the ground, ten feet in circumference, which must have grown, flourished, and died since the earth in which it had taken root was thrown out. Mr. Knapp counted three hundred and ninety-five annular rings on a hemlock, growing under similar circumstances, which he felled near one of his shafts. Thus it would appear that these exploitations were made before Columbus started on his voyage of discovery.

The amount of ancient hammers found in this vicinity exceeded ten cart-loads, and Mr. K., with little reverence for the past, employed a portion of them in walling up a spring. They are made of greenstone or porphyry pebbles, with a groove, single or double, cut around, by which a withe was attached. The following is a sketch of one of the larger class, the dimensions of which were 12 x 5 1/2 x 4 inches, and the weight 39 1/2 pounds. The smaller class, weighing five or six pounds, were probably wielded in one hand. The annexed sketch will convey an idea of their form.

In addition to these relics, a copper gad, with the head much battered, and a copper chisel, with a socket for the reception of a handle, were brought to light. It contained the fragment of a wooden handle, when discovered, which crumbled very soon after being exposed. The timber in the excavation before described showed the marks of an axe, the bit of which must have been about two inches in width.

Mr. Wm. H. Stevens, the agent of the Forest mine, has discovered other workings on the southwest quarter of section 30, township 50, range

39, almost of equal extent and interest. They occur on the southern slope of a hill, and consist of a series of pits, some of which, on being opened, are found to be fourteen feet deep. They are arranged in four lines, following the courses of four veins or feeders.

In cleaning out one of these pits, at the depth of ten feet the workmen came across a fragment of a wooden bowl, which, from the splintry pieces of rock and gravel imbedded in its rim, must have been employed in bailing water.

Remnants of charcoal were found, not only there, but at numerous places, lying on the surface of the rock. Some have supposed that fires were kindled for the purpose of melting the copper, but the more reasonable supposition is that heat was employed to destroy the cohesion between the copper and the rock. Before the introduction of gunpowder, fire was the great agent in excavating rock; and even now, in the Harz and at Altenberg, two of the old mining districts of Europe, this agent is employed to break down rocks of extreme hardness. It is quite as economical where fuel abounds as gunpowder in destroying silicious rocks.

We can hardly conceive it possible for them to have made such extensive excavations with such implements simply as they have left behind, without availing themselves of the aid of fire.

In one of these pits—southwest quarter of section 35, township 51, range 38—were found the bones of a deer in a pretty good state of preservation. Fragments of the cranium, humerus, and of one horn (which, to use the language of sportsmen, was in the "velvet" at the time of the destruction of the animal) were taken out. The smaller bones had mouldered away. They reposed on clay, a foot above the surface of the pit, and were covered with accumulations of clay, leaves, gravel, and sand to the depth of nineteen feet. It would appear that the animal either fell into the pit or ventured in to procure water, and, unable to extricate himself, perished.

These pits, filled as they were with water, would not become the dens of carniverous animals, and to no agency of theirs are we to attribute the position of these bones.

In the northeast quarter of section 16, township 50, range 39, near a small stream, there is a mound which has the appearance of having been the work of art. Mr. Hill, from whose notes much of the above information has been derived, states that from the want of tools he was unable to penetrate it, to determine whether it was stratified or not. It is about ten feet high, in the form of a square, the sides of which are fifteen feet in length, flat on the top, and slope regularly to the base.

There is another tumulus on the right bank of the Ontonagon river, six miles above its mouth, forty feet high, and nearly circular, which has been supposed to be artificial, but has not been explored with a view to determine the point.

From the northeast quarter of section 31, township 51, range 37, to section 5, township 49, range 40, a distance of nearly thirty miles, there is almost a continuous line of ancient pits along the middle range of trap, though they are not exclusively confined to it.

Upon Keweenaw Point they have been found extending from Eagle river eastward to range 28, a distance of twelve miles, along the base of the trap range. A great number of hammers were discovered on the present site of the Northwest Company's works, which first led the explorers to suspect the existence of a valuable lode of copper. They have also been found at the Copper Falls mine, and at the Phoenix, formerly the Lake Superior, mine. At the latter place a copper knife was discovered, in the early explorations of that tract.

Mr. C. G. Shaw pointed out to us similar evidences of mining on Isle Royale. They occur on what is known as the Middle Finger, and can be traced lengthwise for the distance of a mile. Mr. Shaw remarks that, on opening one of these pits, which had become filled up with the surrounding earth, he found the mine had been worked through the solid rock to the depth of nine feet, the walls being perfectly smooth. At the bottom he found a vein of native copper eighteen inches thick, including a sheet of pure copper lying against the foot-wall.

The workings appear to have been effected simply by stone hammers and wedges, specimens of which were found in great abundance at the bottom of the pits. He found no metallic implements of any description, and is convinced, from the appearance of the wall-rocks, the substances removed, and the multitude of hammers found, that the labor of excavating the rock must have been performed only with the instruments above named, with the aid perhaps of fire. From the appearance of the vein and the extent of the workings, he conjectures that an immense amount of labor had been expended. He endeavored to find some evidences of the antiquity of these workings, but could discover nothing very satisfactory to his own mind, except that they were made at a remote epoch. The vegetable matter had accumulated and filled up the entire opening to a level with the surrounding surface; and, in a region where it accumulates as slowly as it does on the barren and rocky parts of Isle Royale, this filling up would have been the work of centuries. Upon this vegetable accumulation he found trees growing equal in size to any in the vicinity.

One of the most detailed and perhaps the best account of the discovery and identification of prehistoric Indian mining operations was written by Charles Whittlesey (1863) at Eagle River, Keweenaw County, in 1856. He belonged to the generation of American scholars who believed that the "Indians" were at a lower cultural level than a prehistoric group called the "Moundbuilders." These latter people had vanished before the Europeans arrived and had no doubt been driven out by the Indians. Many significant historical documents describing the historic Indians' knowledge of copper sources and of working the copper had not been published and were not available in the 1850's. Whittlesey's interpretation was that the historic Indians had nothing to do with copper and that their ancestors probably did not have such competence.

After briefly describing the presence of "Indian diggings" at the mines of the Native Copper Company and the Northwest

Mine near Agate Harbor where stone mauls were abundant, the following record of mining activity is given for the following locations:

DESCRIPTION OF THE SEVERAL WORKS.

1st Group.

The Agate Harbor Company has an extensive property on the range south of Agate Harbor, on which there are reported to be *Indian diggings*, as these excavations are frequently called by the miners. They are well developed at the works of the Native Copper Company, on the northern slope of the range, and on the Northwest Company's grounds at their mines, south of the "Greenstone" cliffs. The same veins extend across both these locations, a distance of a mile and a half, indicated by the presence of old works.

At the Northwest Mine the pits are conspicuous, showing on the surface the position of *three* veins that have since been wrought. Stone mauls were abundant in them. Some of the pits had been made in a band of red conglomerate, which lies between the strata of greenstone (or crystalline) and amygdaloid trap. This conglomerate is composed of pebbles and boulders principally of red trap, cemented by argillaceous red sand, forming a very compact stratum, twelve to twenty feet thick. It here carries copper in small grains or pieces, near the veins; also crystallized calcareous spar and epidote.

The ancients did not neglect the most trifling indications of metal, but appear to have instituted a thorough investigation as to whether the copper existed in true veins, in metalliferous bands, or in detached nests. There is nothing remarkable in their operations at the "Native" Copper and the "Northwest" mines, except this closeness of pursuit, through all the veins and branches to their most minute extremities.

Waterbury Mine.—The works of this Company are situated about one mile and a half west of the Northwest Mine. A person passing to the interior from Eagle Harbor or anywhere along the northern shore of Point Keweenaw, and crossing the mineral range to the valley of the Little Montreal, witnesses everywhere the same topographical features. The mountain range rises from the lake level, in the distance of a mile, to an elevation of 500 and 600 feet; in the next mile the ascent is less precipitous, but the ground continues to rise from one to two hundred feet more. From the summit of the range there is along the whole line, from the extremity of the point to the Albion location, two miles west of the Cliff Mine, a vertical wall of naked trap rudely columnar, the upper edge, or *crest*, of which forms the summit of the range. This mineral front has the appearance of a vast upheaval from two to three hundred feet high facing the south, and about thirty miles in length. The ground from the bottom of this wall rises gradually to the south until it reaches another range of about the same elevation, thus forming a long narrow valley, through which flow, in opposite directions, the Montreal and Eagle Rivers. From the summit of the perpendicular cliff at the Waterbury Mine this valley presents a view extremely picturesque, and such as is seldom seen by the traveller in other regions. The general contour of the valley is curvilinear, so that the eye, placed at the middle of an arc in the position above mentioned, takes in the boundary ridge on each side as well as the whole inclosure. At the Waterbury Mine, which is situated near the middle of the length of the valley, there is in the face of the vertical bluff an ancient artificial recess or cavern, which is twenty-five feet in horizontal length, fifteen feet high, and twelve feet in depth. In front of it is a pile of the excavated rock, on which are now standing, in full size, the forest trees common to this region. Some of the blocks of stone which were removed from the recess would probably weigh two or three tons, and must have required the use of levers to dislodge them from their original position. Beneath the surface rubbish the remains of a gutter or trough composed of cedar bark were discovered, the object of which was clearly to conduct off the water which was baled from the mines by wooden bowls, of which mention will be made hereafter. Portions of fine or pulverized copper scales remained in the upper end of this trough. After removing the water and decayed leaves at the bottom of the excavation a piece of white cedar timber was found, one end of which exhibited the marks of a cutting instrument like those of a narrow axe.

Fig. 1.

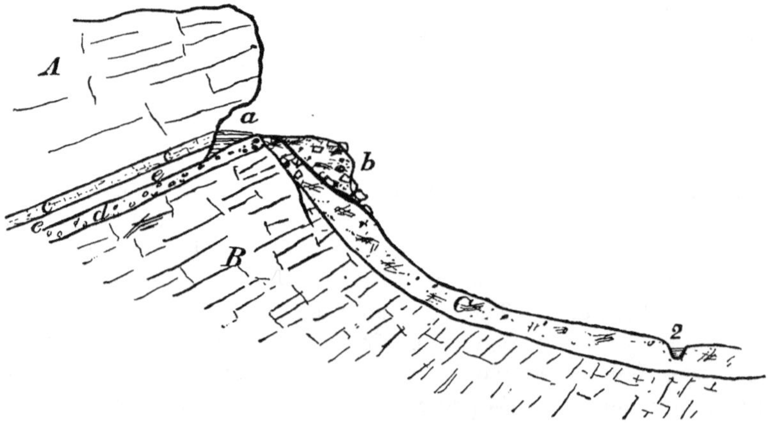

WATERBURY MINE, artificial cavern.—*A*. Crystalline or greenstone trap, dipping *N*. 28°.—*B*. Amygdaloid trap.—*C*. Talus of the bluff and drift.—*a*. Ancient rock excavation.—*b*. Rubbish thrown out of *a*.—*d*. Conglomerate bed.—*c c*. Jointed chloritic bed.—*e e*. Inclined shaft of Waterbury Company.—2. Little Montreal River or creek.

The above profile is made at right angles to the bluff, and shows the geological structure as seen from the western side. It would answer equally well for the *North*, *West*, *North Western*, *Eagle River*, *Cliff*, or any mine situated on the southern face of the coast range of Point Keweenaw.

The copper bearing amygdaloid (*B*) is separated from the crystalline or "Greenstone" trap (*A*) by a parting of conglomerate (*d*), which is however sometimes wanting, and its place supplied by a thin bed of red clay called "*flucan*" overlaid by a layer of quartz carrying specks of copper. This parting, whether it be of red conglomerate or of flucan and quartz, is known as the "slide," and sometimes (though improperly) is called a cross-course. The beds all dip northerly and at an angle of 28°. Resting immediately on the slide, and composing the inferior face of the greenstone stratum, is a bed of blackish-green chloritic rock (*c c*) very much jointed, which contains between its joints, in a leafy state and in its mass in a state more solid, scales, particles, and lumps of copper. This chloritic bed is from 12 to 15 feet thick, and in it the ancients worked forming this cavern. They did not operate on a vein at this place.

The Waterbury Company, encouraged by the labors of their predecessors, followed from the bottom of "*a*" along the surface of the conglomerate by an inclined shaft "*E E*" to a depth of 300 feet, measuring on the slide.

In removing a part of the old burrow *B*, Dr. Blake discovered several shovels, of white cedar, resembling the paddles in form now used by the Chippeway Indians in propelling their canoes. Had these been found elsewhere, they would have been regarded as ordinary paddles, but in this place they had evidently been used as shovels. This is also evident from the manner in which the blades are worn, as shown by the lines *a a*, *b b*, *c c*, in the annexed sketch.

Fig. 2.

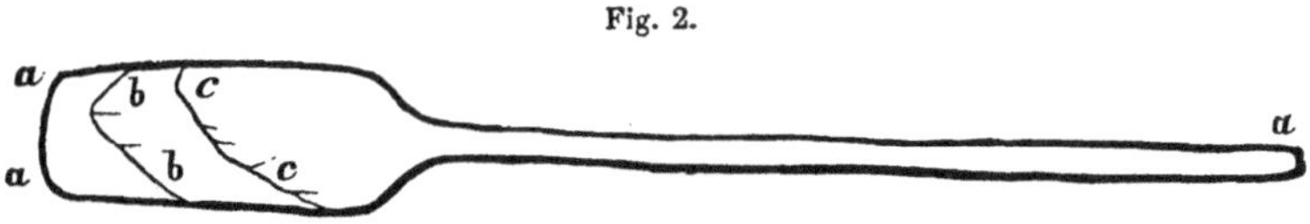

WOODEN SHOVEL, 3½ feet long—Waterbury Mine.—*a a a*. Original form.—*b b*. Partially worn.—*c c*. Worn obliquely.

The blades are more worn on the under side than the upper, as if the mineral had been scraped together and then shovelled out, as is the practice of the miners of the present day. The shovels which were found beneath the water level were sound in appearance, and the strokes of the tool by which they were formed remained perfectly distinct, but on being dried they shrunk very much, opening in long cracks, the wood retaining little of its original strength or hardness.

A birch tree, two feet in diameter, grew directly over one of these paddles.

A portion of a wooden scoop, or bowl, was found in the pit, evidently intended to dip up and to pass water. Its edge had been worn, like the shovels, by scraping over the rock; but it was so much decayed that it fell to pieces when it was taken out.

I examined the walls of this cavern minutely, hoping to find the marks of some tool of metal. The effects of blows of stone mauls were visible, and such is the hardness of the rock, that if drills or picks had been used upon it, I think the marks would be easily seen, particularly on that part which was protected from the atmosphere by water.

At one place something resembling the impression made by the point of a light sharp pick was discernible, but not very plain, and only in a single instance.

In the Porcupine Mountains I have seen works made by the English miners in the years 1769 and '70, where an adit or open cut made in the face of a cliff has been always exposed to the frost and rains. But here the marks of picks and drills appear as fresh and as perfect as if they had been recently made, although in some places the sides of the cut are covered by old lichens and mosses.

Copper Falls Location.—The ancient miners made very extensive excavations on the property of the Copper Falls Mining Company, both upon veins and metalliferous bands, which run parallel with the formations. By the profile and explanations here given the geological structure of the place will be well understood.

Fig. 3.

SECTION ON THE COPPER FALLS VEIN. *Explanations.*— Trap rock. Conglomerate beds. Sandstone.—*a a a.* Ancient pits on the vein.—*b b b.* Shafts and galleries of the mine.—*c.* Sand dunes.—*d d.* Copper bearing bed of trap.

Scale—horizontal and vertical—2 inches to the mile. 1, 6, 7, Nos. of the shafts.

This sketch illustrates the geology of the northern part of the range, or of all mines described under the head of Copper Falls Location.

From this it will also appear that when we use the term extensive, as applied to "Indian diggings," it is only in a comparative sense, and in reference to other works of the old miners. The levels and shafts constructed by the Copper Falls Mining Company, since 1851, cause the mining of the ancients to appear like mere exploratory pits.

On looking at the map, the pits will be seen to occupy a total length of several miles on this location; but none have been reopened that had a greater depth than twenty-four feet, while the modern shaft has already descended more than 250 feet, and the mine has rock galleries of greater total length than all the old trenches of the ancients. In the profile their pits are shaded, and represented at *a a a*, occupying about half a mile on the "East Vein," or as it is sometimes called, the "Copper Falls Vein." Before they were obliterated, as they are in part now, the surface appearance was that of an irregular channel or trough ascending the mountain from the edge of the sandstone beds to the band *d d*, which carries copper. Here a system of basin-shaped cavities, broad, circular, and deep, crossed those made on the vein. They are denoted by heavy black dots on the map.

The first named series were from two to five feet deep and five to ten broad, and the latter five to eighteen deep, with a diameter of twenty to 120 feet. Forest trees and underbrush stood alike within and without them.

There is a heavy vein half a mile west of the East Vein, which is styled the West or the "Hill Vein," where the old works are similar in all respects to those above noticed and sketched on the East Vein. Those on the "Owl Creek" Vein are not so extensive, because the creek occupies the "back" of the lode. Still further east other veins are seen with pits, not only on this location, but on that of the Eagle Harbor Mining Company. Broken stone mauls are common in all of them. About the point where the Owl Creek crosses the "scoriaceous" or metal bearing bed *d d*, the excavations on that bed near the creek are very marked. Here is something similar to the cave on the Waterbury Location.

A very large pit to the east of Owl Creek was partially explored by S. W. Hill, Esq., the Superintendent of the mine, in 1852. By running in an adit on a level eighteen feet below the edge of the depression, after passing some distance in the gravel, rock was met in place; cutting through this at a distance of 100 feet, the miners discovered loose fragments and rubbish that had been handled, and pieces of timber still in good preservation. The adit was not deep enough to drain the pit to its bottom, and its depth was not ascertained. I have in my possession a portion of a pine tree from the end of this adit, in complete preservation, except a part which was charred by fire. The adjacent rock contained sheet copper, and small lumps, being a part of the metalliferous band.

By examining the section, it will be seen that the order of succession in the strata is as follows:—

Beginning at the shore of the lake first, a bed of trap, that dips northerly. It rests upon a stratum of *red conglomerate* of great thickness, dipping conformably under the trap, and is succeeded by conformable and alternating beds of trap and red sandstone, known by the geologist as the "Potsdam" red.

In these beds the mineral veins are not rich enough for working; a fact which the ancients knew full well, for it was only on the regular and uniform strata of trap underlying the variable beds that they expended their labor.

On clearing out some of the old pits, Mr. Hill found wooden shovels like those at the Waterbury Mine, more or less worn and of the same size and shape. In the bottom of trenches, and among the rubbish, the workmen saw continually ashes and charcoal, with other traces of the presence of fire. They threw out frequently broken hammers or "mauls," with a groove around the middle. These mauls weigh from five to fifteen pounds, and are merely oblong water-worn boulders of hard, tough rocks. Nature has done everything in fashioning them, except the groove, which was chiselled around the middle. They were collected from the smooth boulders of the lake shore, and from banks of coarse gravel that abound in the country. Most of them are trap; but the hornblende, sienitic and granitic rocks furnish some. The ring or groove appears to have been cut for the purpose of attaching a withe, to be used as a handle, wherewith to swing the maul. In one of the trenches on the Cliff Mine, north of the upper engine, one was found with a root of cedar still twisted in the groove, but so much decayed that it fell to pieces and was not brought away. Dr. M. D. Senter, of the Cliff Mine, states that he saw it before being disturbed, and it was evidently the intention of the operators to use the twisted root or withe for a handle.

Fig. 4.

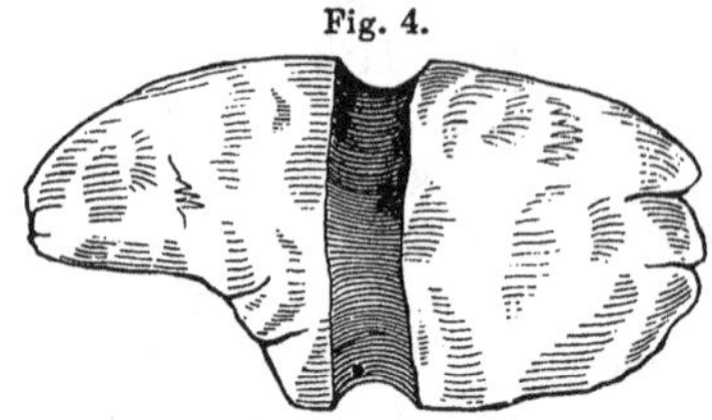

STONE HAMMER OR MAUL, with one groove, and broken by use; length 7 inches. Copper Falls Mine.

Most of these hammers are fractured at *both ends*, and the peculiar sharp cut character of the fracture in many cases indicates that the implement had been used to drive metallic wedges, such as quarrymen call a "gad." Copper gads of this kind have been found in old pits at the Minnesota Mine. It will be seen also that there are heavier mauls with *double* grooves, probably to be handled by two men.

In the description of works at the Central Mine, a class of hammers will be noticed without a groove. The one here figured was taken from a pit near Shaft No. 1 of the section above given. Not far to the south of the same shaft was found a copper spear or javelin head, in the rubbish near the bottom. Three others were found by Mr. Hill on the surface. One of them was so much corroded that the socket was nearly gone. The other I have sketched of natural size and thickness, from the original in the possession of Mr. Hill. It was evidently formed by beating the metal while cold, probably between stones, having a rough and not a polished exterior; it is not much decayed. The section of the blade *B* shows that its two faces were not symmetrical. A piece of decayed wood was found in the socket of one of them, being apparently the remnant of the shaft, by which it was hurled. As the edges of the "shank" or socket are not soldered together, but only bent around the shaft, it was probably wound with some ligament to give it strength. It is too large and heavy for an arrow-head; neither has it the shape proper for that purpose.

The description here given of the pits of the east vein will answer for almost all others.

In working the surface of the vein, or of the copper-bearing bed, the ancient operators must have wrought open to the day. They no doubt commenced as low down the slope of the range as the copper appeared to them worth being taken out, and worked upwards towards the south, in order to keep their drainage. From their rude and tedious method it was of the highest consequence to cause the water to flow away behind them, without the necessity of baling.

The "attle," or broken rock, was generally thrown back into the vacant space whence it had been taken: but little of it was cast out to right and left along the margin of the vein, which explains why the pits are so shallow at the present time.

In many places on this location, the vein is wide enough to allow men to work between its walls.

Fig. 5.

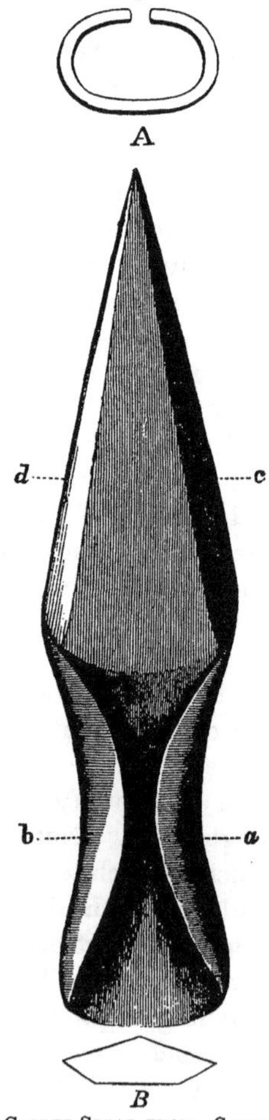

COPPER SPEAR-HEAD—Copper Falls Mine.—*B*. Section of blade at *c d*. *A*. Section of shank at *a b*. Scale, full size.

Thin sheets of copper were left standing at the bottom of the ancient excavation, which might readily have been extracted, and it seems singular that they were not.

Central Mine.—Near the road from the "North Western" to the "Winthrop" Mine, in an open grove of sugar trees, a depression was observed about five feet deep and thirty feet in length. It was generally free from water, and differed so little from cavities that are not artificial, but which are due to geological causes, that it did not attract much attention.

Mr. John Slawson, the agent of the North Western Mine, after a careful surface examination, concluded that this pit was not wholly due to nature, and the tract was on that account purchased for mining, in the fall of 1854.

Fig. 6.

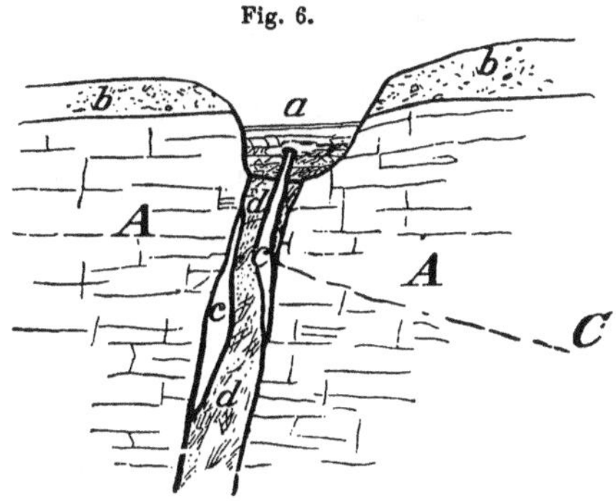

CENTRAL MINE. Section of the vein and old pit. East and west.—*A A*. Trap rock wall of the vein *d d*.—*a*. Ancient excavation partly filled.—*c c*. Masses of native copper in the vein.—*b b*. Drift gravel covering the rocks.

The Central Mining Company having been organized, a drain was constructed to take off the water, which was no sooner done than all doubts were removed; about five feet in depth of leaves and rotten sticks had accumulated at the bottom, among which a hard substance could be felt with a stick.

This proved to be a flat piece of native copper C, from five to nine inches thick, and nine feet in length, forming part of a large vein *d d*, as shown in the profile. The vein material had been worked away from one foot to eighteen inches along side of it, and it extended forward as well as downward in the vein. Its upper edge had been beaten by the stone mauls so severely, that a lip, or projecting *rim*, had been formed, which was bent downwards, over the sides. A large number of broken mauls were found in the place, and around it on the surface, all of them without grooves, of which the annexed woodcut is an illustration.

I have seen similar ones on the Humboldt Location, next west of Copper Falls. Where this class of stone hammers is found, those with grooves are wanting. The grooveless ones appear to have been used for percussion only at *one end*, as though the manner of holding them was such that a blow was not given on the other.

The Peruvians have a copper axe without an eye, or a groove, to which, however, they attach a handle in the form of a split stick, bound with thongs. The ancient miners, probably, had some such mode of tying a handle to these smooth oblong stones. Different parties of men may have preferred tools of different kinds, which would account for mauls, which are seen at one mine, being among themselves alike, but dissimilar to those at other places.

Fig. 7.

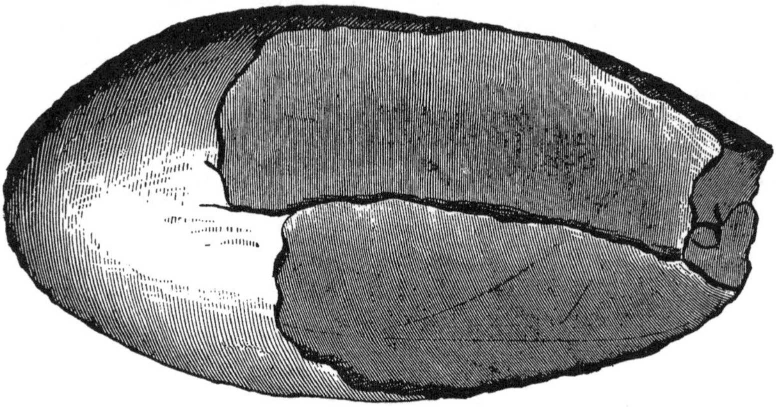

BROKEN MAUL, CENTRAL MINE.—Without groove, ½ size, weight 8½ lbs.

The usual remains were here thrown out, consisting of charcoal, ashes, and broken wall rock.

The general bearing of the vein is 10° or 12° west of north. The section is made across it, east and west, looking south, and is vertical.

As the labor of uncovering the mass of copper progressed, another one was met with, overlapping the first, and adhering to the east wall. Further on, in the adit, a third mass was found, attached to the western wall, partly overlapping the one which the ancients had left.

By stoping out a space about sixty feet in length by twenty deep, on the vein, the Company took out fifty-three tons of mass copper. Such unwieldy pieces appear to have been beyond the control of the old miners. Their object seems to have been to secure small lumps, such as could be fashioned without melting. Whatever pieces might have been detached, by diligent pounding with their stone mauls, were broken off, and the remainder was abandoned.

It was impossible for them to cut into pieces, reduce by melting, raise from the pit, or transport blocks of metal weighing many tons. There are neither marks of a cutting tool upon them, nor of the action of fire. It is quite singular that they had not discovered the art of melting copper, which can be effected so easily in an open fire made of wood, but no evidences have fallen under our notice that this was done by that ancient race.

2D GROUP.

Portage Lake Region.

Quincy and Pewabic Mines.—Portage Lake resembles in form the long, narrow, and crooked Scottish lochs. Like them its quiet surface reflects the outlines of most exquisite scenery.

It connects with Lake Superior through the channel of Sturgeon River, which has so little descent below the point of junction, that all material changes in the level of the great lake are felt throughout this inland water.

The *Quincy* landing is situated on the north side of Portage Lake, about twenty miles from Keweenaw Bay. The northern shore, which is nearly east and west at the landing, does not show rocks at the water level.

A succession of drift, knolls, points, and headlands, rising about 200 feet above the surface, overlook this shore. Above this elevation, and attaining a height of 500 to 600 feet, are seen projecting ledges and bluffs of trap rock, inclosing mineral veins. This rock is also visible at the heads of ravines where rivulets fall over low precipices forming small cataracts.

The first signs of ancient excavations occur near the lake level, and what is remarkable, are not in the rock, but in the *sand* and *boulder* "drift."

Fig. 8.

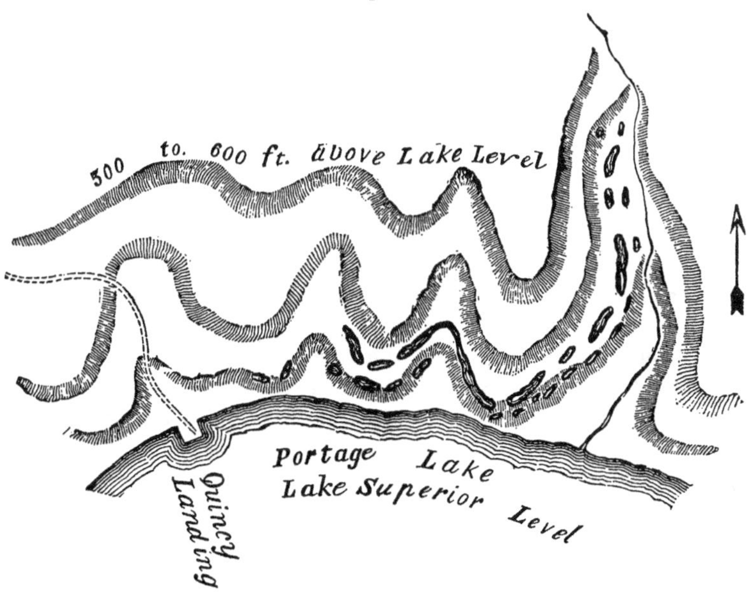

ANCIENT PITS IN THE BOULDER DRIFT OR GRAVEL, QUINCY LOCATION.

The most capacious of these gravel pits, however, occur on a line nearly level and about 100 feet above the surface of the water.

They are partly upon the land of the Quincy Mining Company and in part on the Pewabic, a short distance east of the landing, as shown in the sketch. Those constituting the upper series are even, broad, deep, and regular, having the appearance of old fortifications. They extend around the headlands of gravel, connecting adjacent ravines, as though the object was to bring water from the rivulets along the face of the bluff.

At the points of the ridges they are much broader and deeper than they are at the heads of the ravines. The resemblance to a race way, or "sluice" for running water, is such that it required much examination to convince me that they had not been used for that purpose. There are, however, no openings at the extremities, such as would have been the case in sluices, to admit and discharge water. A bench, or narrow terrace, breaking into the slope of the hill, forms a regular plateau for the uppermost group; the other groups being scattered along the slope at irregular intervals. Some of them extend down the declivity nearly to the water's edge. Pits of a peculiar shape are occasionally seen to the westward of the landing, particularly at the distance of about a mile. Here is a group of small ones covering several acres on a piece of level land, which is elevated about 200 feet above the lake, constituting one of the upper drift terraces.

There are no doubt many others, large and small, concealed by the thick brush wood with which the ground is covered. Mr. C. C. Douglass, formerly an assistant of Dr. Houghton, in the geological survey of the Upper Peninsula, and since for many years the superintendent of the Quincy and Isle Royale Mining Companies, states that lumps of water-rolled copper and small masses are frequently found on both sides of the lake in this drift gravel. In digging cellars, constructing roads, and exploring trenches, such pieces are so common, that it has been thought that they would pay for their collection by washing the earth. One mass of 1500 pounds weight was found in digging a cellar where there is no rock visible in place.

To obtain this transported mineral, Mr. Douglass conjectures to have been the object which the ancients pursued in their gravel trenches, and at the same time, that they selected from the water-worn boulders of the coarse drift such stones as had the proper size and shape for mauls, to be used in the adjacent rock excavations.

The earth from the trenches near the landing, on the slopes, was principally thrown out over the *lower* side, forming embankments with an extreme height of fifteen feet above the bottom of the ditch as it remains now after the lapse of centuries.

Some of the ditches are fifty feet wide at the present time.

The beds of trap, constituting the mineral range, at this place, have a total thickness of about a mile and a half, presenting the ends of the strata towards the lake. To reach the rock excavation of the ancients, it is necessary to follow a road from the landing up the mountain three-quarters of a mile to the north-east. Here the copper bearing rocks protrude from the soil in ledges; the intervals where no rock is seen being covered to a slight depth with earth. The veins of this part of the range have a direction different from those before described on Point Keweenaw. They have run with the formation, and not at right angles to it, like those at the Cliff, Copper Falls, Northwest, and other neighboring mines. The true lodes of the Quincy, Pewabic, Isle Royale, Portage, Huron, and other companies adjacent to Portage Lake, are called "*parallels*," while those further east belong to the system of "transverse" veins.

In the winter of 1854–5, after the land had been explored and worked ten years, a line of depressions was discovered on the summit of the range that attracted immediate attention. On this elevated ground the old operators had discovered and worked a rich deposit of copper which was nowhere visible upon the surface. The direction of the line of pits is northeast and southwest, corresponding with the range.

The mines now in operation on this lode are among the richest of Lake Superior.

At first view the excavations appeared to be irregular, like those in the gravel at the foot of the bluffs, but after clearing away the growing timber, they assumed an allignment such as I have given on the map. There are also veins in the vicinity that have a bearing different from the general course of the pits.

When the cavities came to be opened, it was evident that a deposit of great richness had been worked there in past times. Lumps of copper were found plentifully in the bottom of the old works, and with them the usual evidences of ancient mining. The pits are broad and deep, extending not far from half a mile.

Isle Royale Location.—This is on the south side of Portage Lake. Here the ground does not rise so high as on the north side, but is equally abrupt. The first escarpment on this side is rocky, its crest being reached by an ascent of 300 feet. The mining companies which have penetrated the rocky strata to a depth of at least 250 feet, are the Isle Royale, Portage, Huron, and Albion; all of them on the same vein, and situated near the south-easterly edge of the mineral range. The beds in which these companies have worked are, therefore, geologically, nearly a *mile* lower than those of the Quincy and Pewabic, which are near the westerly or north-westerly side of the range. It was, therefore, in different ground that the ancients sought for copper on the southerly side of the lake.

After having attained the summit of the lake front on this shore, we find the land nearly level for the distance of a mile, and the rocks covered with a shallow depth of earth. On this plateau the ancients discovered a rich lode that did not show itself on the surface.

In the autumn of 1851, Mr. Douglass informed me that there were indistinct signs of old works, half a mile from the lake on the northwest quarter of Section 1, T. 53, R. 34, owned by the Isle Royale Mining Company. At the request of the directors of the company, a close reconnoissance of the ground was immediately made by myself. It required some assistance of the imagination to conceive that the slight and irregular depressions, which were dimly visible among the trees, were the works of men. Applying a compass to such of them as could be seen at one view, and carrying this line forward, it passed over or near the successive pits for a distance of one-third of a mile. We then set men to work to cut down a cross trench through one of them, and in a few hours reached the bottom. The vein and its walls were distinctly visible, having been worked out to a depth of ten feet, but the space was filled with rubbish nearly to the surface. Further examination, and cross trenching, disclosed the vein along a distance of three quarters of a mile, in places very broad, with a bearing coincident to that of the formation.

It has now been worked to a depth of 250 feet, producing copper in rich masses, over a space twenty feet in thickness. In these wide places or pockets the early miners enlarged their pits to correspond, and carried their works to greater depths. Charcoal, broken mauls, and ashes are mixed with the black earth and rocky fragments of the pits.

3d Group.

Minnesota Mine.—As I have before stated, it was upon this location that the existence of mines, long since wrought, on Lake Superior was first made known to us. It is here, also, that the most extensive and interesting works of that kind are to be found.

The Minnesota lodes have a direction like those at Portage Lake, and different from those at Point Keweenaw. The veins about the forks of the Ontonagon, embracing a district of forty-five miles in length, on the mineral range, from the Douglass Houghton Mine, on the east, to the Akogebe Lake, on the west, run *with* the range, and not across it. Their bearing is, therefore, north-easterly and south-westerly, or about N. 54° East.

Fig. 9.

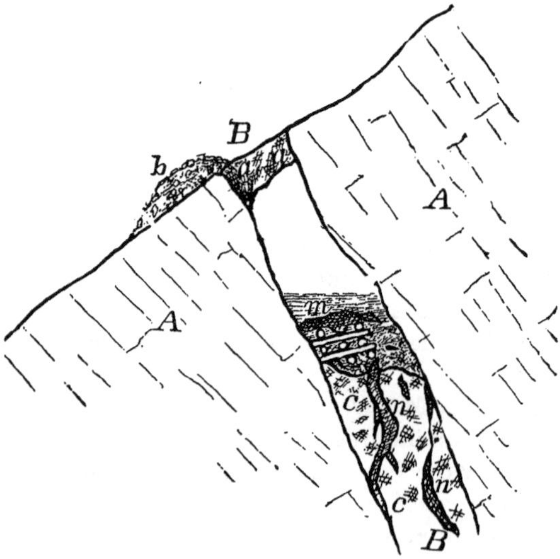

Minnesota Mine. Section across the Vein, looking from the easterly quarter. N. 30° W.—*B B*. Mineral vein dipping north.—*A A*. Wall rock of compact trap.—*a. a.* Left standing a part of the original surface support to the hanging wall.—*m*. Mass of copper sustained by timbers.—*b*. Ancient burrow or spoil bank.—*c c*. Vein matter embracing masses of copper *n n*.

On the Minnesota there is a group of veins nearly parallel among themselves, four in number, and on all these the ancients labored. The surface presents a corresponding group of rude trenches, showing the position of the veins, for more than two miles. The ground rises gradually to a height of 637 feet above the lake, but on the south drops suddenly off into a deep valley. The Ontonagon River cuts the range two and a half miles west of the mine, being navigable for batteaux to the landing.

In the above section, across the main lode, I have grouped together several remarkable objects, that were seen near each other, though not strictly in contact. The descriptions and sketches are in part due to Mr. Knapp, partly to Messrs. Foster and Whitney, and also to my personal examinations.

The vein *B B* has a variable thickness from one to nine feet, dipping northerly, at an angle of about 60° with the horizon. This is somewhat steeper than the dip of the strata, or wall rock, *A A*. On some of the veins, the excavations extend eastward, out of the Minnesota, into the grounds of the Rockland Mining Company, where they are very distinct. Being upon the southerly slope of the mountain, the ditches have become very much filled up by washing from the surface. The greatest depth of the ancient excavation is thirty feet. At the place of the above section the vein had been removed to a depth of twenty-six feet.

Not far below the apparent bottom of a trough-like cavity where shaft No. *one* is now situated, among a mass of leaves, sticks, and water, Mr. Knapp discovered a detached mass of copper weighing nearly six tons. It lay upon a cob work of round logs or skids six to eight inches in diameter, the ends of which showed plainly the strokes of a small axe or cutting tool about 2½ inches wide. These marks were perfectly distinct. A piece of this wood which I took from the mine in 1849 proved to be a species of oak, the only species known upon the range, and by some called the Spanish oak. It shrunk on drying to about two-thirds of its size, cracking open in deep gashes, and possessed little strength. Its appearance was that of water-soaked timber not rotted, preserving its original form.

The mass of copper had been raised several feet along the foot wall of the lode, on the timbers, by means of wedges. Its upper surface and edges were beaten and pounded smooth, all the irregularities taken off, and around the outside a rim or lip was formed, bending downwards. This work had apparently been done after the miners had concluded to abandon the mass. Such copper as could be separated by their tools was thus broken off. The beaten surface was smooth and polished, not rough. Near it were found, as the excavation advanced, other masses, *n n*, imbedded in the vein. After several years, this vein has been found by the modern miners uncommonly rich and valuable for the size and number of its masses of copper.

Not far to the west of this spot a portion of the vein *a a* had been left like a pillar as a support to the hanging wall, while they excavated beneath. It is cut or bruised quite smooth, but shows no marks of other tools than the mauls. This rocky support is about four feet in thickness, and is high enough above the present bottom of the trench to allow a person to pass under it. The marks of fire on the rocks of the walls are still evident. Charcoal, ashes, and stone mauls are found in all of the pits hitherto cleaned out. One of the heaviest mauls yet seen, weighing thirty-six pounds, came from this location. It has a *double* groove, as shown in the annexed figure which is not usual, and it was intended, no doubt, to be used by two men.

Fig. 10.

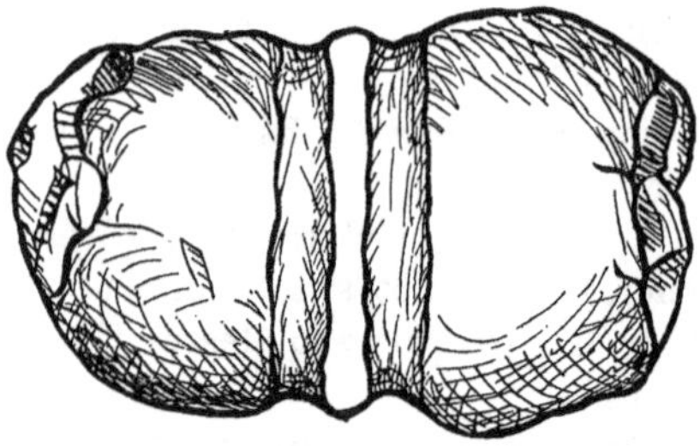

STONE MAUL, with double grooves.—Weight 36 lbs. Minnesota Mine.

Fig. 11.

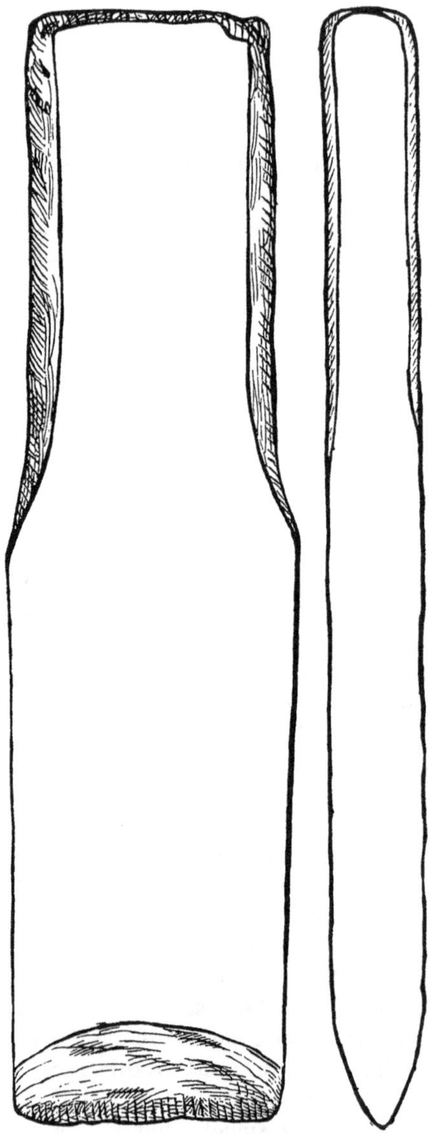

COPPER CHISEL. Full size.—Length 7¼ in.; breadth 1¾ in.; thickness ⅝ in. Minnesota Mine.

View edgewise.

In one of the pits a rude ladder was found, formed of an oak tree trimmed so as to leave the stumps of the branches projecting, on which men could readily descend or ascend to or from their work. Wooden levers are also found among the rubbish, preserved by water, which covered them continually.

On the edge of the excavation in which the mass *m* was found there stood an aged hemlock, the roots of which extended across the ditch. I counted the rings of annual growth on its stump, and found them to be two hundred and ninety. Mr. Knapp mentions another tree which had three hundred and ninety-five. The fallen and decayed trunks of trees of a previous generation were seen lying across the pits.

Near the place where the detached mass *m* was found Mr. Hill discovered a tool of which the following is a sketch, and near it a copper maul or sledge weighing from twenty to twenty-five pounds. Like all the other implements found this maul had been fashioned by pounding in a cold state. Originally the mass appeared to have had the shape of the letter T, the cross head at the top being about an inch thick and two or three inches broad, tapering towards each end. These two prongs had been folded over each other and beaten into a shape rudely resembling a man's fist, but larger. This lump of copper had evidently been battered either by pounding, to make it more compact, or by use as a maul. The handle of the maul was eight or nine inches long.

The chisel above figured was somewhat bruised at the upper end, as though it had been used. Towards the upper end the corners are taken off, apparently for the purpose of being held in one hand, while it was struck by a mallet with the other. It has a rough surface, common to these relics, but is symmetrical in form, with a bevel at the cutting edge on both sides. None of the tools show signs of having been ground to an edge on stone, but are beaten down roughly by hammers.

Artificial Caverns.—On the Aztec, Ohio, Adventure, and Ridge locations, in addition to the pits which are so common along the range, there are cavities in the mural faces of trap at various elevations, which are ancient and belong to the old copper works.

The bluffs are sometimes as high as three hundred feet above the valley. There are also breaks or gaps in the range formed by dislocations of the strata or faults, enlarged by the wearing action of the drift forces. The ends of different beds of trap are thus presented to view, rising on either side of the gorges, with precipitous fronts of different heights. One of the strata, and perhaps more than one, is metalliferous, like the scoriaceous bed worked at Copper Falls and at Phœnix Mines, on Point Keweenaw. At the Adventure the metal bearing stratum is very thick and highly charged with copper, disseminated irregularly through it. The ancients wrought upon it extensively, seeking with assiduity for the rich portions, no matter how difficult of access. Some of their excavations on the side of the bluff are scarcely large enough to shelter a bear. Others are more extensive, formed in all conceivable shapes, extending wherever indications of minerals were apparent. The agents of the Adventure Mine have followed the example of their predecessors, but on a larger scale, pursuing the strings and bunches of copper in all directions, till they disappear. When the mineral fails, like the ancients they strike off at random, and seldom proceed far without encountering other lumps or small masses.

Hitherto the true veins near the copper bearing stratum have not proved profitable. The ancients, exercising their usual skill, expended very little labor upon them. They showed in this very considerable knowledge respecting the different systems of veins, and also in regard to those anomalous deposits in which the caves are situated.

Forest Mine, Evergreen Bluffs.—On the ground known by the name of the Evergreen Bluffs ancient pits have been opened southeasterly of the Minnesota works. Some prominent ones have recently (1855) been cleared out on the "Johnson preëmption," which disclosed in a few days several tons of copper. Masses had been partly uncovered in the vein, as at the Central Mine, and thus left. On the Nebraska location and on the Rockland, the old excavations are numerous, and wherever they are reopened valuable lodes are exposed. They are not wanting on the west of the river. At the Forest Mine the present works were commenced upon the site of earlier and ancient operations. A wooden bowl was found near the bottom of one of them, that had been used for baling. Doubtless many others in the vicinity of the Ontonagon exist that are not yet discovered.

Fig. 12.

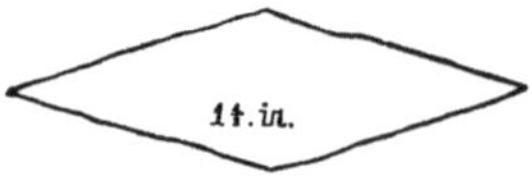

Section on *a b*, full size.

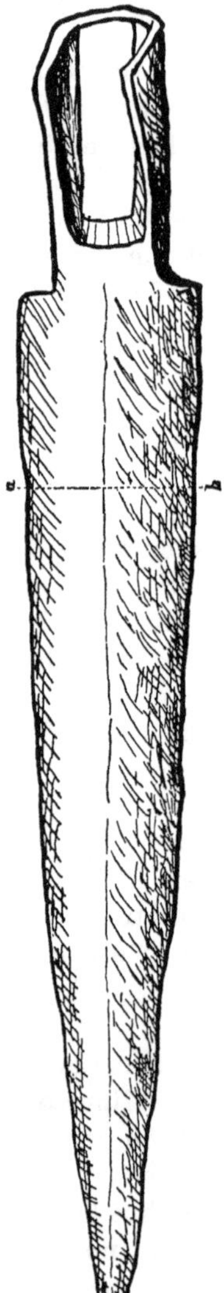

Spear Head.—Half size. 14 inches long. Ontonagon. From drawings of John F. Mullowney, Esq., Surveyor.

Fig. 13.

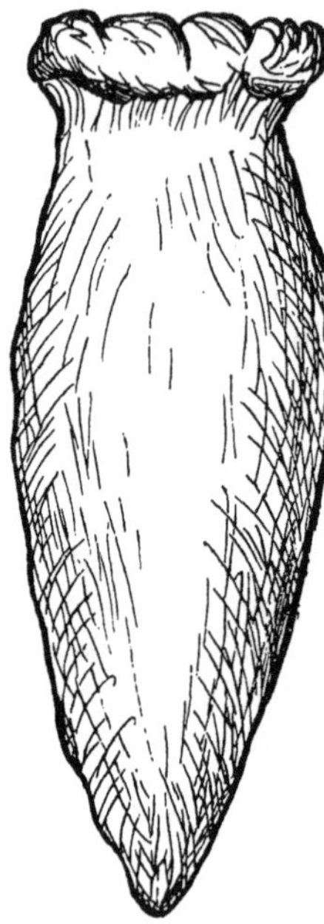

Copper Gad, full size. Minnesota Mine.

Fig. 14.

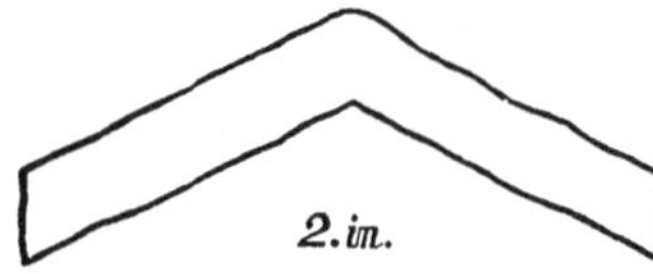

Section on *c d*, full size.

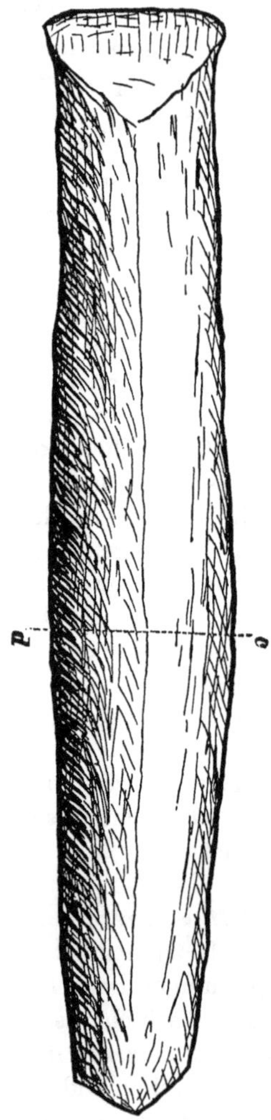

Chisel.—Half size. 13 inches long. Ontonagon.

Copper Implements, Ontonagon.—Some laborers in the employ of Mr. Greenfield were levelling the ground for a brick yard on the east bank of the Ontonagon River, half a mile above the village, in the year 1854, when they perceived some pieces of copper, which were well fashioned implements. They are said to have been found upon a bed of clay in a ravine, and covered about two feet with alluvial earth, a large cedar tree growing nearly over the spot. They consist of two implements, which may be described as spear or javelin heads, though more probably designed as miners' tools; and two cutting instruments that may properly be called chisels, as shown in the annexed sketches. These show the form and size better than any written description. The socket of the spear is small, and not of the best shape to give a good fastening to a staff, which may perhaps favor the idea that it was a weapon for the use of one hand, like a dirk. The blade is symmetrical and strong; it apparently had not been much bruised or injured by use. If it was to be thrown like a javelin, the stock or staff must have been fitted on around the shank and driven down over the blade some distance, to make the wooden attachment proportionally strong with the metal part.

The chisel also had not been used, since neither the cutting edge nor the head is battered. It is bent up longitudinally from near each end in the manner shown by the cross section in *c d*. The object in giving it this form must have been to stiffen it and thus save metal. This contrivance speaks well for the ingenuity of the maker. Those instruments have better proportions than similar ones found in Ohio. They were probably fresh from the hands of the workman when they were lost upon the banks of the river. Although I have myself examined these implements, I am indebted to Messrs. Emerson, Coburn, and Mullowney for facts respecting them. Both are represented to be more hard and less malleable than the native copper of the mines, from which it has been inferred that they have undergone a hardening process. Like those found at Marquette and elsewhere, I suppose the hardness is due only to prolonged hammering, by which the density is increased. The copper of the ancient inhabitants of Europe was hardened by alloying it with tin.

Copper Implements, Carp River. (Not on the Map.)—In August, 1854, while workmen were engaged for Mr. John Burt in making a dam across the Carp River near Marquette, signs of copper were discovered in gravel. They were wheeling earth from the banks of the stream, and did not at first preserve the remains that were visible in the form of spots of green carbonate, which on examination presented a core of unoxidized metal. Mr. Burt states that there were numerous thin chips of copper not entirely decayed, which appeared to have been cut from a piece of native metal by a sharp and thin tool. There was also found a rude copper knife, the shank two and a half inches, and the blade four and a half in length, making seven inches. The blade resembles in shape a short butcher knife very much worn. It has spots of native silver imbedded in it like those frequently seen in Lake Superior specimens of copper.

Another tool resembles a bodkin, with a socket for the insertion of a wooden handle. There were also arrow or spear heads of copper, which were probably made upon the spot. These relics were lying upon a bed of water-washed gravel, which Mr. Burt conjectures once formed the bed of the river, but the channel of this time is ten feet lower. Soil had accumulated over the tools to a depth of two feet, and on it were pine trees, considered to be at least one hundred years of age.

The knife was harder than the chips, and does not bend so easily. This hardness is probably due to the process of hammering which the mass underwent while it was in a cold state, and not to any tempering. If the bodkin-like implement had not been of this parcel the others might have been referred to the present race of Indians. They possessed knives and other implements made of copper when the French came among them, but these were very rude. Mr. Baily, of Eagle Harbor, has one which resembles somewhat the semilunar knife used by saddlers. There is a notch in the middle by which to attach a handle. Mr. B. thinks it was used in dressing and working skins. It was found in the gravel within the pickets at Fort Wilkins, Copper Harbor.

Fig. 15.

Rude Copper Knife.—Full size. Carp River. 1, 2. Spots of silver.

Fig. 16.

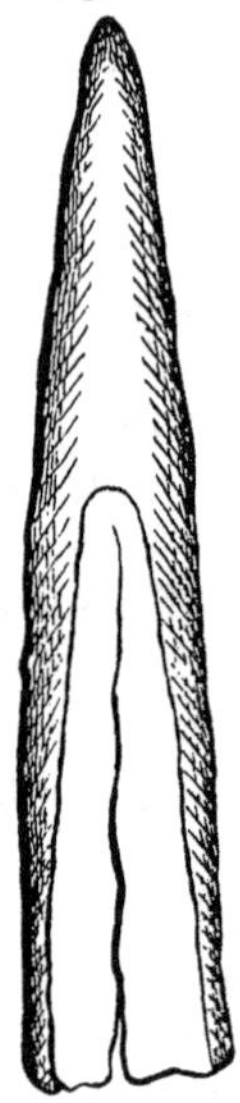

Pointed Tool with a Socket.—Full size. Carp River.

Near the mouth of Carp River there are remains of cabins, placed in a row like the houses of a village. This is shown by a line of heaps of stone and clay, like the remains of chimneys, and connected with them slight ridges of clay, resembling the low embankments around a log building after the timber has decayed. They may have been formed of clay which was used to daub the chinks. A forest of ancient growth covered these ruins. Although I know of no historical evidence illustrating the point, I should hesitate to give them a greater antiquity than the early French adventurers. It is about two hundred years since the Jesuits established themselves on Lake Superior. Traders may have preceded them thirty years, and constructed cabins at places not mentioned by the Jesuits.

I have seen the ruins of buildings on the west fork of the Ontonagon, near the old Copper Rock, the history of which has reached us, and which were erected in 1769. In 1845, eighty-four years afterwards, all the logs except such as were of cedar, had disappeared. Near a cabin which was used for a blacksmith shop, the outlines of a forge were quite distinct, with cinders, charcoal, and pieces of rusty iron lying upon it. There were also several pounds of corroded steel and brass, mostly the locks and guards of muskets, and

Fig. 17.

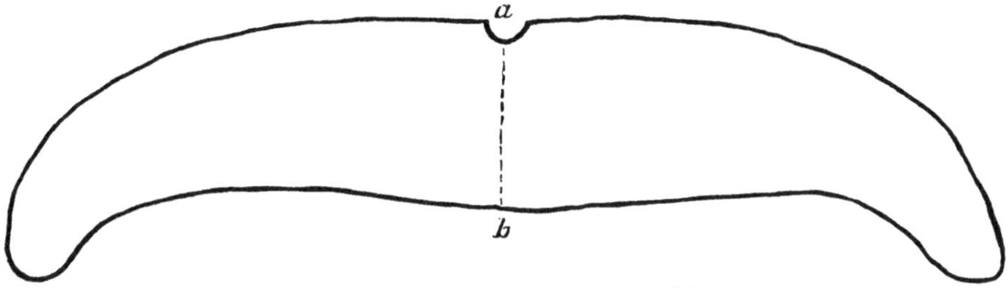

Copper Instrument.—Full size. Fort Wilkins.

Section through *a b*.

one gun barrel. On the forge a pine tree had established itself, which we cut down, and counted upon the stump sixty-one layers of annual growth.

In regard to the implements found at the mill on Carp River, I incline to the belief that they are not as ancient as the old mines. Mr. Henry, who has furnished us the account of the explorations just referred to on the Ontonagon River, and on the north shore, made by the English soon after the Treaty of Paris, says that the Indians beat out pieces of copper into bracelets and spoons. None of their implements are shown to have been so difficult to form as the chisels and spear-heads, which are found in the old pits. These required a state of mechanical skill apparently above the reach of Indians.

Mr. Burt has also furnished the following sketch of a *copper hook* found by himself in the excavation of the St. Mary's Canal.

Fig. 18.

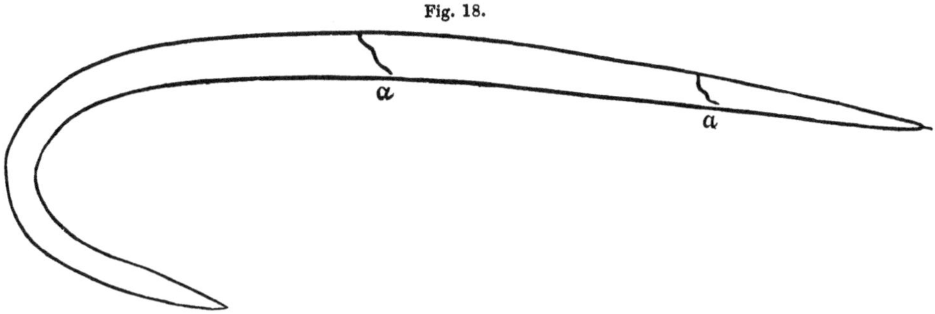

Copper Hook.—Full size. *a a*. Flaws in the metal. Sault St. Mary's.

It has the usual flaws which cold wrought articles exhibit, and doubtless belongs to the class of recently made implements.

On the Canada shore of the St. Mary's River, at Garden River, twelve miles below the Sault, an implement was discovered in the soil by a half-breed and presented to Mr. Burt. The horizontal and side views are sufficiently shown in the

Fig. 19.

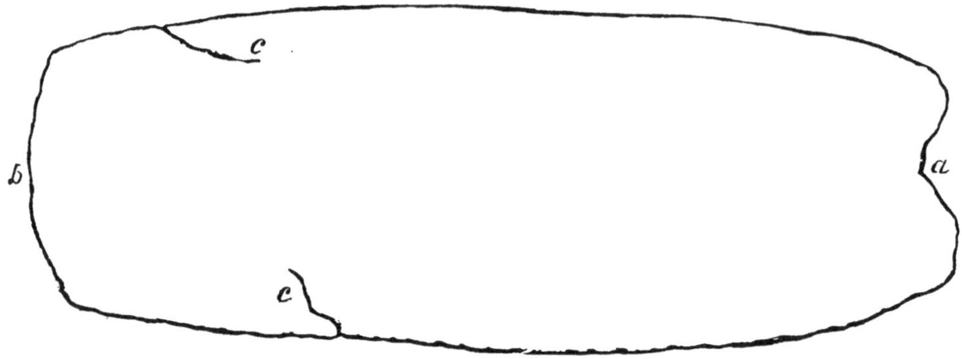

OUTLINE OF A COPPER TOOL. Full size. Garden River, Canada.—*a*. The head.—*b*. The edge.—*c c*. Flaws in the metal.

Longitudinal section.

Fig. 20.

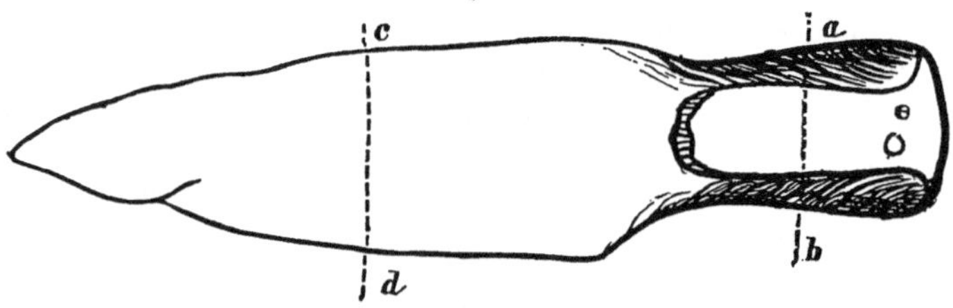

COPPER SPEAR-HEAD. Full size. Downward view.—*e*. Hole in back of shank. Oak Orchard, Oconto County, Wisconsin.

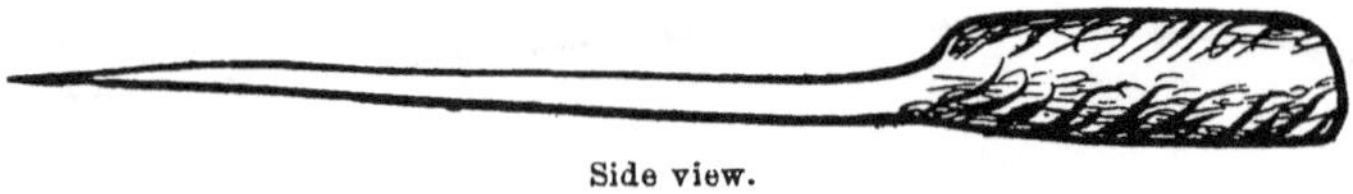

Side view.

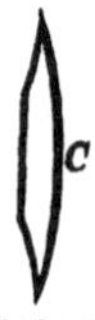

Section of blade through *c d*.

Section of shank through *a b*.

sketch to indicate its use, which was that of a cutting instrument like a chisel. Its bruised head shows the effect of blows from a mallet of wood or stone.

A rude knife and spear-head of copper were recently picked up by Mr. William Windross, at Oak Orchard, Oconto County, Wisconsin, on the western shore of Green Bay. They are in the possession of Lyman C. Draper, Esq., of Madison, Wisconsin, to whom they were presented by the Hon. C. D. Robinson, of Green

Fig. 21.

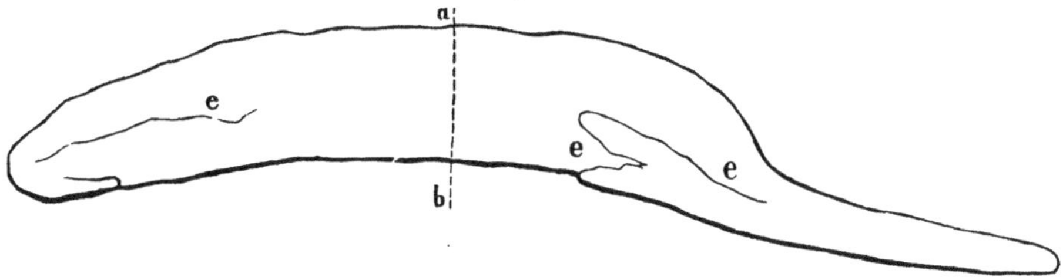

Copper Knife. Natural size.—*e e e.* Flaws.

Section of blade from *a* to *b*.

Bay. The spear or arrow-head differs from those of Lake Superior principally in the state of finish, and in having a hole *e* in the shank to fasten it to a handle or shaft. Both these specimens are roughly forged and apparently ground to a blunt edge. They are, with little doubt, recent, the work of some half-breed or Frenchman.

(Whittlesey, 1863, pp. 6-26.)

Daniel Wilson, who was a Professor of History and English Literature, at University College, Toronto, in the middle of the nineteenth century, was an avid student of ethnology and archaeology. He visited the Upper Peninsula copper area in 1855 and his records are valuable as those of an individual with some training in both observation and recording of prehistoric data:

The copper-bearing trap rock, after crossing the Keweenaw Lake, is traced onward in a southwesterly direction till it crosses the Ontonagon River about twelve miles from its mouth; and at an elevation of upwards of three hundred feet above the Lake. At this place the edges of the copper veins appear to crop out in various places, exposing the metal in irregular patches over a considerable extent of country. Here, in the neighborhood of the Minnesota Mine, are traces of the ancient mining operations, consisting of extensive trenches, which prove that the works must have been carried on for a long period and by considerable numbers. These excavations are partially filled up, and so overgrown during the long interval between their first excavation and their observation by recent explorers, that they would scarcely attract the attention of a traveller unprepared to find such evidences of former industry and art. Nevertheless some of them measure from eighteen to twenty feet in depth, and in one of them a detached mass of native copper, weighing nearly six tons, was found resting on an artificial cradle of black-oak, partially preserved by immersion in the water with which the deserted trenches had been filled, in the first long era after its desertion. This large mass had evidently been thus disposed preparatory to an attempt at removing it entire. It appeared to have been raised several feet by means of wedges, and then abandoned on account of its unmanageable weight; and probably portions had afterwards been detached from it, as its surface bore abundant traces of the rude stone implements with which the old miners seem to have chiefly wrought.

The stone hammers, or mauls, by which these ancient workers in metal carried on their operations, consist for the most part of oblong water-worn stones, weighing from ten to twenty pounds. Around the centre of these a groove has been artificially wrought, for the purpose of fastening a handle or withe of some kind, with which to wield them. Some of the specimens that I saw were worn and fractured as if from frequent use; many are found broken, and they are met with in such abundance in the neighborhood of the ancient Ontonagon diggings, that a deep well was pointed out to me, constructed, as I was assured, almost entirely of the stone hammers picked up in its immediate vicinity. (Wilson, 1856, pp. 227-28.)

The details of another, and in some respects more interesting discovery, than that which was brought under my notice at Ontonagon, were communicated to me in reply to the inquiries made while there. This took place, at a still more recent date, at a locality lying to the east of Keweenaw Point, in the rich iron district of Marquette. There, not far from the mouth of the river Carp, in what appeared to be the ancient bed of the stream, and about ten feet above the present level of its channel, various weapons and implements of copper have been recently found. Large trees grew over this deposit also, and the evidences of a remote antiquity seemed not less obvious than in that of Ontonagon. The copper relics included knives, spear or lance-heads, and arrow-heads, some of which were ornamented with silver. One of the knives was described as made, with its handle, out of a single piece of copper. It measured altogether about seven inches long, of which the blade was nearly two-thirds of the entire length, and of an oval shape. It was ornamented with pieces of silver attached to it, and was inlaid with a strip of silver from point to haft. Along with these relics were also found numerous fragments, or chips and shavings of copper, some of which were such as, it was assumed, could only have been cut by a fine sharp tool; and the whole sufficed to indicate even more markedly than those at Ontonagon, that not only was the native copper wrought in ancient times in the Lake Superior Regions: but along its shores, and on the banks of its navigable rivers, there existed manufactories where the native artizan fashioned the metal into tools and weapons for war and the chase. (Wilson, pp. 235-36.)

At the Bigelow House at Ontonagon, I had an opportunity of examining an interesting collection of copper relics found, a few months before in the neighborhood. These consisted of three copper spear-heads, one about fouteen inches, and the others about twelve inches in length; and two singularily shaped copper gouges (?) about fourteen inches long, and two wide, the precise use of which it would be difficult to determine. It was my good fortune to make the acquaintance, while at Ontonagon, of Captain Peck, whose knowledge of the native languages, and residence for years among the red Indians, have given him good opportunities of judging of their habits and arts; and his idea of the copper gouges was that they were designed for cutting holes in the ice for fishing, according to a method still pursued by the Indians for obtaining their winter supply of Lake fish. A different and more probable opinion, however, was advanced by a practical miner, who stated that he had been among the first who opened some of the ancient diggings found at the Minnesota mine, and the copper gouges seemed exactly adapted to produce the singular tool-marks which had then excited his curiosity. Subjoined is a representation of one of the spear-heads, sketched from the original [Pl. XXIII, Figs. 9 and 10]. Its form is singular, the blade being three-sided like that of a bayonet. The socket has been formed by hammering out the lower part flat, and then turning it over partially at each side. Precisely such a mode of fitting the blade to receive a haft is common in the more primitive forms of bronze implements found in Britain and the north of Europe. In the pure copper spear-heads of Lake Superior, it may be assumed, as a confirmation of the conclusion suggested by numerous other copper relics of this continent, that the ancient miners and mound-builders were ignorant of the arts of welding and soldering, as well as of that of smelting the metallic ores. An indentation made in the inner side of the rude socket closely resembles the device adopted for the same purpose in the class of bronze implements of ancient Europe, known as paalstaves; its object evidently being to present a point of resistance to the haft. The European implements, however, are made of a metallic compound, and mostly cast, thus proving a knowledge of metallurgic arts far in advance of the old workers of the metallic treasures of Ontonagon, and the copper regions of Lake Superior.

I was informed by Captain Peck, that a fourth spear-head had been found along with the above. The whole were discovered buried in a bed of clay on the banks of the river Ontonagon, about a mile above its mouth, during the process of levelling it for the purposes of a brick field. Above the clay was an alluvial deposit of two feet of sand, and in this, and over the relics of the ancient copper workers, a pine tree had grown to full maturity. Its gigantic roots gave proof, in the estimation of those who witnessed their removal, of considerably more than a century's growth; while the present ordinary level of the river is such that it would require a rise of forty feet to make the deposit of sand beneath which they lay. It is possible, however, that the original deposition of the relics may have been made in an artificial excavation, above which the pine tree struck its roots in later times, for along with the implements there were also found fragments of copper, the remains, as it might seem, of the operations of the ancient manufacturers, by whose skill these, or similar weapons and tools, were wrought on the spot. (Wilson, pp. 233-34.)

The Mesnard Mine in Keweenaw County was a location which did not turn out to be profitable. Mining was probably begun as the result of the finding of the large copper mass which is described below and illustrated in Plate XIII from a contemporary photographic record now in the Burton Collection in Detroit. This 18-ton slab was uncovered in 1862. The mine, as a producing unit from 1862 to 1883, only delivered a total of a little more than 41 tons (Swineford, 1884). It is one of the largest masses of copper that was worked by Indian groups. The Mesnard boulder has sometimes been said to have been dislodged and moved by Indians but Forster's statement below, given in an excellent review by R. S. Packard, does not support this interpretation.

> I am fortunate in being able to add to the foregoing the testimony of an eye-witness of some other discoveries in this district, viz, that of Mr. J. H. Forster, a well-known mining engineer who lived in the district many years. He was at one time superintendent of one of the mines, and was engaged on the Portage Lake Ship Canal as State engineer when the canal was opened, when he discovered some copper articles in an ancient grave at that point. He writes in regard to the discovery of old operations: "The largest mass of float copper found in modern times . . . weighed 18 tons, and contained very little rocky matter. When found in the woods, on the Mesnard location, it was covered with moss and resembled a flat trap bowlder. It had been manipulated by the 'ancient miner,' and much charcoal was found around it. Its top and sides were pounded smooth, and marks of stone hammers were apparent. All projections—every bit of copper that could be detached—had been carried away. . . . Subsequent explorations disclosed the spidote lode whence the mass came—torn from its matrix doubtless by the ice. The mass had been transported only about 50 feet and dropped on a ridge. When the lode was stripped of the drift the jagged edges of a mass in place were exposed. It was of the same length, thickness, and structure of the 'float.' It was observed at the time that if the 'float' could be set up on edge on the piece in place it would fit in exactly. A beautiful illustration of the power and direction of the glacier was thus afforded." (Packard, 1893, p. 182.)

Further reporting by Forster is given by Packard on locations in Houghton County:

> On the north side of Portage Lake, on the extension of the Isle Royale lode (opposite Houghton), the drift being shallow, "long trenches were dug on the back of the lode 3 feet wide and deep. There was much small mass or nugget copper (barrel work) released by the disintegration of the soft epidote vein stone." This was thrown out, while the earth was thrown behind the miner as he advanced, and the work resembled that of an expert "navvy." No evidence of deep mining could be found. As usual, stone hammers and charcoal were found in the trenches. A remarkably deep trench which was filled with earth and leaves was discovered at the South Pewabie [sic] (now Atlantic) mine, several miles west of the last locality, which extended 2 or 3 feet into the solid rock. At the bottom "was a well-defined transverse fissure vein of quartz, about 2 feet wide, containing here and there chunks of solid copper. By several pits sunk on the course of the vein, proof was had that it had been worked superficially several hundred feet in length. I walked through it a long distance. The surface of the formation was shattered and decomposed, hence the old miners could come at the quartz handily. They did not carry the rock out to the surface to dump it, but piled it up neatly on each side of the drift. At one point I found a handsome specimen of quartz and copper laid up carefully in a niche. It weighed several pounds. . . . As in other cases, we had proof that the ancient miner did not sink any shafts

and do real mining; he was only a surface gleaner." (Packard, 1893, pp. 182-83.)

As a short aside in this compilation of information on the discoveries of the work of the prehistoric miners, and as an indication of the dominance of the Lake Superior copper mining industry in the economy of Michigan in the middle of the nineteenth century, we add the following bit of information. In a popular magazine published in Boston in June, 1852, entitled *Gleason Pictorial, Drawing Room Companion* (Vol. II, No. 2, p. 337), there appeared the following article without an authors name:

Michigan Block

Herewith we give a fac-simile representation of a beautiful gift from Michigan for the Washington Monument, consisting of a massive block of copper, weighing upwards of 2100 pounds. It is three feet long, nineteen inches wide, and eight inches thick. On the surface embossed on plates of pure native silver, one fourth of an inch thick, is an inscription in these words:

"Michigan:
An Emblem of Her Trust in the Union."

The coat of arms of the State, beautifully wrought and standing in bold relief, are also engraven upon it, in connection with the motto "Si quoeris peninsulam amoenam circumspice." In one corner, engraved in the copper, are the words: "Native copper and silver from Lake Superior, 2100 pounds." The vein of silver running through it greatly adds to the effect. Both the copper and the silver are from the famous Cliff Mine on Lake Superior, and were presented to the State for this purpose by the "Pittsburgh and Boston Company," owning said mine, and by the State polished and fitted for its destination, as a portion of the Washington Monument now in progress at the Federal City. We have seen many larger—much larger masses of native copper, but none more beautiful than this. Through its polished face, specks of native silver imbedded in the copper are frequently visible, with larger and more abundant specks of crystallized quartz, while the primal ruggedness of the mass is not wholly polished away, and the five other sides are left rough and craggy as nature formed them. The block will be a very unique addition to the column which commemorates the father of his country, and doubtless will be an object of curiosity to all who behold it.

This Michigan Block is now to be found on the 19th landing of the Washington Monument (Harvey, 1903). It is fitting that the inscription is on silver, emphasizing the association of silver with copper which is such a striking feature of the native copper deposits of the Lake Superior basin.

One of the latest reports by an eye witness of specimens found in the prehistoric copper pits is given by West (1929, p. 52):

The writer, during his visit to the mining region on the South Shore in 1875, saw a ladder, two paddles and fragments of a birch bark receptacle, taken from one of the ancient pits. These were all in a good state of preservation, excepting that the birch bark when dried was very brittle. This ladder, like many others that were found in that district, was merely a trunk of a small tree with limbs cut away, leaving stumps of about six inches in length. This is the well-known form of Indian ladder. The one seen was cut off by hacking, with some instrument, clear around the portion to be cut and not cutting from two sides, as a white man does. The instrument used was reasonably sharp and might have been a copper or stone axe.

PREHISTORIC COPPER PITS ON THE EASTERN SIDE OF LAKE SUPERIOR

J. B. Griffin and G. I. Quimby

While many archaeologists are familiar with the location of prehistoric copper pits in the Keweenaw and Isle Royale areas of Michigan very few know of the sources of copper on the east side of the Superior Basin. In preparation for a 1956 summer survey with George I. Quimby, Griffin examined the publications of the Ontario Department of Mines and, among other papers, came across a recent study: *Geology of the Mamainse Point Copper Area* (Thompson, 1954) which included a map on which "Indian Diggings" were identified east of Hibbard Bay. "The existence of copper at Mamainse Point was known in very remote times, and the so-called "Indian Diggings" near Hibbard (Sand) Bay attest to the mining activities of the natives in this region. (*Op. cit.*, p. 4.)

The first accurate historic references to the Indian knowledge of copper in eastern Lake Superior was given by Champlain as has been pointed out above (p. 36).

In Carver's account of his travels in the interior parts of North America in 1766-69 he relates the attitude of some contemporary Chippewa regarding the copper deposits on the east side of Lake Superior:

> One of the Chipeway chiefs told me, that some of their people being once driven on the island of Maurepas, which lies towards the north-east part of the lake, found on it large quantities of heavy, shining, yellow sand, that from their description must have been gold dust. Being struck with the beautiful appearance of it, in the morning, when they re-entered their canoe, they attempted to bring some away; but a spirit of an amazing size, according to their account, sixty feet in height, strode in the water after them, and commanded them to deliver back what they had taken away. Terrified at his gigantic stature, and seeing that he had nearly overtaken them, they were glad to restore their shining treasure; on which they were suffered to depart without further molestation. Since this incident no Indian that has ever heard of it will venture near the same haunted coast. Besides this, they recounted to me many other stories of these islands, equally fabulous. (Carver, 1796, p. 85.)

In 1767, Alexander Henry, while moving north from Sault Sainte-Marie to Michipicoten observed native copper in the general area where the "Indian Diggings" are located.

At Point Mamance, the beach seemed to abound in mineral substances; and I met with a vein of lead ore, where the metal abounded in the form of cubical crystals. Still coasting along the lake, I found several pieces of copper ore, of that kind which the miners call gray ore.

From Mamance to Nanibojou is fifteen leagues. Nanibojou is on the eastern side of the Bay of Michipicoten. At the opposite point, or cape, are several small islands, under one of which, according to Indian tradition, is buried Nanibojou, a person of the most sacred memory. . . . This island lies no further from the main, than the distance of five hundred yards. On the opposite beach, I found several pieces of virgin copper, of which many were remarkable for their form; some resembling leaves of vegetables, and other animals. Their weight was from an ounce to three pounds. (Henry, 1901, pp. 204-7.) In 1771, Henry's exploring party "examined the coast of Nanibojou, and found several veins of copper and lead (*op. cit.*, p. 223).

Some thirty years after Henry, David Thompson provided another record of native copper in the Mamainse area:

> The same year (1798) on the survey, about 52 miles northward of the Falls of St. Maries, near Mahmaize, there were five, or six canoes of Indians, who informed me they were then at the old path of their grandfathers, who used to come here for pure copper for heads to their Lances, arrows, axes, knives, and other necessaries; by their description the place was about five miles in the interior. I requested to be shown the place, but they said they did not exactly know it, and dreaded the musquitoes. It appears that in those days, the first settlement of this country, the ornaments of the Churches of Rome came from these two mines, in pieces of pure copper. (Blue, 1894, p. 63.)

Writing of the copper deposits of the Mamainse area, Dawson (1857, p. 6) observed:

> On the summit of the ridge, the hard semi-crystalline trap is traversed by a narrow fissure, running nearly with the strike of the beds, or north and south. Its greatest thickness is about 6 inches, but in some places this has been found to be nearly filled with native copper. One mass weighing 600 lbs. has been extracted, and the whole yield of a shaft 27 feet deep and without galleries, has been about three tons. . . .The real Indian diggings are shallow holes, sunk at intervals along the courses of the veins, and surrounded by broken pieces of veinstone, along with which are occasionally found stone hammers. These hammers are merely beach pebbles, usually of trap, and having shallow grooves worked around them, to receive withes or thongs used as handles. Most of them are 5 or 6 inches in their longest diameter, but one, now in the collection of the Geological Survey, is about a foot in length.

In the *Geological Survey of Canada; Report of Progress from its Commencement to 1863* (Logan, 1863, pp. 700-707) there is a description of the native copper-bearing deposits along the east and north shore of Lake Superior as they were known at the time. The first quotation of these implies knowledge of either the "Indian diggings" reported above (pp. 51-71) or of similar ones. This report is also quoted in order to compare it with French knowledge of the Lake Superior deposits in 1670 which they had obtained from the Indians:

From the north side of Sand Bay to the south side of Mica Bay, along a distance of about twenty miles, bands of tufaceous rock occupy the greater part of the shore line. About mid-distance is the promontory of Mamainse, where explorations have been made on a considerable scale by the Montreal Mining Company. The following is a partial section of the strata at this place, as observed, in descending order, from the north-west extremity of the bay of Mamainse, inland. The dips are to the westward, at from 25° to 35°, and the rocks are very unevenly bedded. I. Alternations of trap and tufa, with a bed of conglomerate sandstone, the whole occupying a breadth of 300 yards. Large veins of calc-spar, quartz, and laumontite occur in the trap, and sometimes hold small portions of native copper and silver, with galena. Native copper is found in the vesicles of an amygdaloidal bed. II. Argillo-arenaceous beds, passing in some cases into a fawn-colored jaspery rock, and in other parts into mottled argillaceous sandstone, the whole occupying a breadth of 220 yards. III. Crystalline and amygdaloidal traps, with a bed of conglomerate, occupying together a breadth of 440 yards, and rising to an elevation of 300 feet; the lower parts being apparently tufaceous. This includes the workable deposit of copper. IV. A very coarse syenitic conglomerate, forming, like the last, a ridge, and having a breadth of 160 yards. The whole section probably represents a thickness of about 2000 feet. According to Dr. Dawson, to whom this description is due, the principal deposit of native copper occurs in a fissure running nearly north and south, along the summit of the ridge of hard semi-crystalline greenstone, III. The greatest breadth of this fissure is about six inches; and in some parts it is nearly filled with native copper, which occurs in a vein-stone of calc-spar and quartz. A shaft was sunk here to the depth of twenty-seven feet, without galleries, and yielded about a ton of native copper; the largest mass weighing 600 pounds. The shaft was sunk upon an excavation, which seems to have been the work of some aboriginal miners. A little to the west of this, the vein of native copper divides into two parts. These, like many other veins along this coast, are marked by depressions or trenches, resulting, according to Dr. Dawson, from the effects of erosion by the waters of the lake, at a former period, acting upon the soft materials of the veins. They are often regarded as excavations of ancient miners; but these, which are also frequently met with, are distinguished by being surrounded with broken fragments of veinstone, along with which are occasionally found stone hammers. These are merely rounded pebbles of hard rock from the beach, around which shallow grooves have been made, to hold the withes used as handles. Some of these hammers measure from five to twelve inches in their longest diameter.

Proceeding northward along the coast, at Cape Gargantua an amygdaloid containing native copper forms the projecting point; and in the older rocks near, small veins holding copper pyrites and vitreous ore are met with.

The island of Michipicoten may next be noticed. On the north side of this island there is a considerable mass of greenstone and amygdaloid interstratified with sandstones, the whole dipping eastwardly. Towards the west end of the island, the rocks present a low surface for a breadth of four or five hundred feet, and then rise into a cliff two or three hundred feet in height, in which the greenstone is marked by druses containing analcime and quartz. A soft amygdaloidal bed holding native copper, is traceable for some miles along the shore, sometimes beneath the surface of the water in the bays, and again running a little distance inland. In this bed in the North Bay, an attempt was made, a few years since, to work a remarkable deposit of native copper and silver, which were found disseminated in grains through a green hydrous silicate of nickel. At a point near the west end of the island, and about seven miles from the working just mentioned, the cupriferous stratum again appears, and fragments of the native metal are scattered along the shore.

The next region to be mentioned is the island of St. Ignace, to the south of Neepigon Bay, with the mainland to the west, and Simpson's Island to the east. Here, in 1846, explorations were made, and numerous locations taken up by the Montreal Mining Company. Instead of the older rocks of Laurential and Huronian age, which occur in the vicinity of the Black River, the Upper Copper-bearing series is met with, with its sandstones, greenstones, and amygdaloids, as on the south shore, and at Michipicoten Island and Mamainse. The strata are intersected by dykes of trap. . . .At the eastern extremity of St. Ignace Island, on the Chenal Ecarté, copper occurs in a vein cutting a thick mass of amygdaloidal trap, which lies conformably to the strata, here dipping south at an angle of nine degrees. The vein, which has an underlie of seventy degrees to the north, is four or five inches wide, and holds masses of native copper, occasionally more than one hundred pounds in weight, in a gangue of calc-spar, sometimes with native silver. About forty-seven feet to the south of this vein, is another about twelve inches wide, of which the veinstone is calc-spar, with a little quartz, including fragments of the wall-rock, and holding imbedded masses of vitreous copper ore, with native silver. The underlie of this vein is sixty degrees to the north, so that it should meet the former one at a depth of about twenty-five fathoms. In 1846, the Montreal Mining Company, to whom this location belongs, sunk a shaft about twenty-four feet, to the north of the vein of native copper, to the depth of ten fathoms. A drift to the southward then intersected the vein at a distance of about twenty feet, thus showing its continuance to a depth of ten fathoms. Having however directed their whole attention to the Bruce Mine, the company abandoned this working. The veins just described can be traced to the westward for nine miles, along the whole length of St. Ignace Island; carrying native copper and silver, with the vitreous sulphuret of copper, in greater or less quantity, the whole distance. Crossing Neepigon Strait, the same minerals are met with at two locations on the mainland opposite. Fluor Island, at the southern extremity of the Strait, consists of the same rock as the adjoining country; and it is traversed by numerous veins, in which vitreous copper ore has been found. It receives its name from the fluor spar which is said to abound in these veins. To the eastward of St. Ignace, the copper-bearing strata are traced across to Simpson's Island; where the vitreous and yellow ores, with native copper, have been found in several localities. The latter is often associated with laumontite, or imbedded in prehnite. These minerals, together with agates, are common in the amygdaloid, which is here interstratified with sandstone. Native copper has also been found on the Battle Islands. Specimens of the native copper from St. Ignace, and from the mainland opposite, gave, in several assays, from one fourth to one fifth of one per cent of silver. In other specimens from the same region, the quantity of silver was scarcely appreciable. It exists in the native state, and is irregularly distributed. Metallic silver likewise sometimes occurs in grains with the sulphurets of copper from this region.

Proceeding southwestwardly along the coast to Point Porphyry, at the entrance to Black Bay, is a mining location, which includes several small islands, the largest of which is known as Edward's Island. Here the amygdaloidal rocks are described as being traversed by numerous brecciated veins, containing yellow, variegated, and vitreous copper ores, in a gangue of quartz, calc-spar, and sulphate of barytes. Besides these, are veins of calc-spar, which are sometimes seven or eight feet in thickness, and often contain vitreous copper ore. Native copper is also met with here.

At least three prehistoric pits for mining copper are located on property of the Montreal Mining Company east of Highway 17 (59.1 miles), in the Sand Bay area a little over 1/2 mile east of the Lake. The pits are located on a high ridge of crystallin and amygdaloidal trap. They were briefly examined by Griffin and Quimby in 1956. Our elevation reading was 296 feet above lake level which conforms rather well with an elevation of 300 feet given by Canadian geologists for the height of the ridge. The first pit which we came across was cut at right angles to the north-south trend of the ridge carrying the native copper deposits. The size of the pit was 13 feet, 5 inches by 8 feet, 7 inches deep and there were between one and two feet of water in the bottom of the pit (Pl. XIV). The sides of this pit were almost vertical and the broken rock debris was thrown out on all sides of the pit. We saw no charcoal or other evidence of fire either in this or the other two pits we found later. We made no effort to clean or to otherwise disturb the pits as we had found them.

The second pit was located a short distance to the south and east of the first. It was 8 by 4 feet and was excavated along a north-south axis (Pl. XV, Fig. 1). The only hammerstone found was one hidden by moss on the east slope of the rock debris from this pit upon which Quimby tripped as he approached the pit. The third pit was long and narrow paralleling the ridge in which the copper vein is located. It was 21 feet, 5 inches long, 5 feet wide, and 4 feet deep (Pl. XV, Fig. 2). The three pits are approximately 100 yards apart.

In August of 1959, J. B. Griffin and M. L. Papworth revisited the pits in an effort to get satisfactory pictures. The pictures were taken by flashlight because of the dense foliage overhead. Better results were somewhat hindered by evidence of bear in the form of droppings, beds, a strong bear odor, and crashing sounds of a heavy animal in the nearby woods. The pits at this time were dry. These pits should be preserved by Canadian authorities. At no time did we disturb them.

The position of the "Indian diggings" at an elevation of 300 feet at Point Mamainse can be given a maximum age of possible prehistoric mining because of the changes in water level with relation to the rising land in the Superior Basin. The Nipissing isobase at the mine area would be at an elevation of about 668 feet above sea level so that the pits are well above that stage of Lake Superior about 2100 B.C. (Farrand, 1960, Pl. IV). In fact, Farrands' temporal alignment of the beach stages along the east side of Lake Superior, as worked out by Stanley (1932), would bring the amygdaloidal basalt ridge in which the pits are located out of water shortly before the Payette Beach was formed, that is, a short time before 7200 B.C. It might be possible as a result of careful excavation to obtain charcoal or preserved wood fragments from these pits, as was done by Drier and his associates from Pit 25 on Isle Royale, and thus obtain a firm date on them.

A word of caution about the age of the pits should be added. Even though "Indian diggings" are mentioned in the literature as early as 1857, we cannot be certain that the Hibbard Bay pits are prehistoric until they have been excavated, for it is possible that they are the result of early unrecorded attempts by Canadian or American miners. The statement has sometimes been made that William Logan, the Canadian geologist, had seen pits in the Mamainse area but he clearly indicates that his source is J. W. Dawson who did see "Indian diggings" in this area (see pp. 78-79).

THE PIC RIVER SITE

George I. Quimby

The Pic River site was found by Griffin and Quimby in the summer of 1957. It is located on the west side of the Pic River where it flows into Lake Superior south of Heron Bay, Ontario (Pl. XVI).

The lakeward portion of this site consisted of a dark cultural layer about four inches thick exposed in a wind-blown cut through a low sand dune. The black sand in this cultural layer was greasy to the touch and filled with grains and small pieces of charcoal, fire-cracked rocks, organic refuse, and cultural materials.

The dark occupation zone was not a soil horizon. It was a midden, or refuse layer, deposited by Indians in the course of the activities of daily living while camped at this spot. Beneath the dark layer was clean white sand deposited by wind and wave action. Above the cultural layer, about ten feet of clean white sand lay in a fore dune ridge, which had subsequently covered the site that lies about ten to twelve feet above the present level of Lake Superior.

The nature of the occupation layer, its thickness, and its position on a beach and under a sand dune proves that it represents a single occupancy over a relatively short period, perhaps one to ten years of summer camping. Moreover, under the conditions described it would be impossible for earlier-period materials to become mixed with later-period materials at this site. Everything found in the cultural layer of the site was once in the possession of the Indians who camped there.

Without attempting to remove the overburden of dune sand, we excavated the exposed area of the site, a strip about ten feet long and twelve inches wide on the west side of the cut through the fore dune ridge. Using trowels and scraping gently through the cultural layer we found the following objects: many small fragments of charcoal; fish scales; bones of sturgeon and other fishes; one beach pea *(Lathyrus japonicus);* bones of deer, porcupine, and beaver; bird bones; fire-cracked rocks; flint chips; a small trianguloid scraper of chipped flint; two sherds of rather thin, grit-tempered pottery with exterior imprints of a cord-wrapped paddle; one small, tubular bead of shell; four very small spheroidal beads of blue glass (seed beads); one melted blue-glass bead; a cut fragment of the rim of a brass or copper kettle or pot (Pl. XVII, Fig. 2); and a rolled pewter or tin pointed object like the metal part of a fish stringer.

In October of 1958 the site was visited by Quimby, James R. Getz, and Winston Elting. At that time the westernmost previously observed area in the lakeward part of the site where Griffin and Quimby had made test excavations in 1957 was covered by sand or destroyed by wind erosion; but the eastern part of this lakeward section was clearly exposed in a strip some thirty feet long and six to twelve inches wide in places. This cultural layer was excavated with trowels and brushes. Included in the object removed from this zone were additional flint chips; fire-cracked rocks; pieces of charcoal; bones of deer, porcupine, beaver, and sturgeon; a sherd of grit-tempered pottery with a cord-malleated or fabric-impressed surface that had been partly smoothed; a fragment of a greenish, iridescent glass bottle with whitish patination; and part of a forged nail of iron.

The archaeological remains recovered by our test excavations are not impressive but are, nevertheless, most significant because the food refuse and aboriginal artifacts were in direct association with trade materials from European sources. For instance, two blue-glass beads, the tubular shell bead, several flint chips, and one piece of cord-marked pottery were found with charcoal, fire-cracked rock, and food refuse in a shallow fire pit in the occupation zone. In another spot a similar pottery sherd, flint chips, and a fragment of a glass bottle were found together. This association proves that the Indians camping at this site still had cord-marked pottery and flint implements at some point within the historic period when white men's trade goods were reaching them.

The nature of the trade goods in addition to the presence of aboriginal artifacts indicates that the period is earlier than 1750. The evidence derived from the trade objects alone suggests a time around 1700.

Previous studies by Quimby (1937, 1938, 1939*b*) have shown that in the Lake Michigan and Lake Huron basins the assemblage of trade goods found in sites dating between 1750 and 1812 were different from the assemblages dating between 1700 and 1750. By 1750 the nonperishable items of Indian material culture were gone--brass kettles had been substituted for pottery, flintlock guns for bows and arrows, and iron tools for flint tools, although the social culture was probably little changed. For instance, they still placed the substituted items of material culture in graves lined with birchbark.

The absence of post-1750 trade objects at the Pic River site in addition to the presence of aboriginal pottery and flint chipping and types of trade objects that fit a pre-1750 context suggests a period between 1700 and 1750, and closer to 1700 than to 1750. It is possible that the date of the occupation of the Pic River site is earlier than 1700 but it seems virtually impossible that the date is later than 1750.

The native inhabitants of the north shore of Lake Superior in the seventeenth and eighteenth centuries of our era were for the most part the various bands and/or cultural divisions of the Chippewa (also called Ojibwa) but there were also small increments of Cree, Algonkin, Sioux, and Iroquois.

In considering the tribal affiliations of the occupants of the Pic River site the Iroquois can be eliminated at the outset. The cultural remains found there are definitely not Iroquoian. The Sioux also can be eliminated. Their homeland is to the west of Lake Superior and although bands of Sioux were trading and fighting in the Nipigon River area in the late eighteenth century, they were clearly foreigners in this area (See Carver 1796, Henry 1901, Long 1791).

The Cree were northern neighbors of the Chippewa and in the 18th century some groups of Cree came southward into Chippewa territory to trade with Upper Great Lakes traders and some Chippewa went northward into Cree regions to trade with Hudson's Bay traders. But the small numbers of Cree on the north shore of Lake Superior were completely outnumbered and dominated by the Chippewa with whom they were culturally similar.

There may have been some small groups of Algonkin Indians in the Lake Superior region. According to Jonathan Carver (1796, p. 138) who traveled in the area in 1767, "A few Indians inhabit round the eastern borders of this lake (Superior), supposed to be the remains of the Algonkins, who formerly possessed this country, but who have been nearly extirpated by the Iroquois of Canada." It is probable, however, that Carver refers to the Nopeming, a northern branch of the Chippewa who lived west of Lake Nipissing and north and east of Lake Superior.

The Nopeming, a term derived from No'pimingtashineniwug are the Opemens d'Acheliny of 1684 and the Nopemen d'Achivini of 1703 (Hodge, ed. 1912, II, p. 82). They undoubtedly are the "O'pimittish Ininiwac," "Wood Indians," "Men of the Woods," "Gens de Terre," and "Men of the Land" seen by Alexander Henry at Michipicoten in 1767, south of Sault Ste Marie in 1762, and near the Pic River in 1775 (Henry, 1901, pp. 62, 207, 208, 232).

All of these names have a connotation of rude people or people of the bush (in the sense of Canadian "bush"). The people of the Sapinerie mentioned in 1709-10 by Antoine Denis Raudot (see Kinietz 1940, pp. 364, 376) seem to have been Siouan people of the bush and by virtue of their location at the west end of Lake Superior are not relevant to this discussion.

In his letter of 1710 concerning the Chippewa, Raudot says:

> Of the Saulteur Indians and the Places Where they Live. . . .The Saulteurs live at the entrance to Lake Superior. . . .The Indians are divided into several families, who live along the shores of the lake. There are some at Kioueouenam. . . .Others dwell on the northern shore and live by hunting and fishing only. The latter are thieves and flock to pillage French canoes when they come alone. (Kinietz, 1940, pp. 371, 372.)

According to Kinietz (1940, p. 318):

> . . . . in 1670 Dablon reported that the principal and native inhabitants at the mission of Sainte Marie du Sault were those who called themselves Pahouitingwach Irini, and whom the French called Saulteurs. These numbered only one hundred and fifty souls, but united themselves with three other tribes which numbered more than five hundred and fifty persons. Visitors to the region of the Sault were the No-quets who came from the south of Lake Superior, and the Outchibous (Ojibwa), and Marameg, who came from north of Lake Superior.

Although it seems reasonably clear that there were Chippewa bands on the north shore of Lake Superior in the seventeenth century, it is difficult to make a direct ethnohistorical connection between them and a specific location such as the mouth of the Pic River.

The Pic River is shown on the Jesuit map of 1671 (Tucker, 1942, Pl. I) but the name "le Pik" was added to this map in the eighteenth century, probably by D'Anville (Tucker, 1942, pp. 1-2). However, the Coronelli map of 1688 (Tucker, 1942, Pl. X) shows the Pic River and gives its name as "Le Pik." The Franquelin map of 1688 (Tucker, 1942, Pl. XIB) also shows the Pic River and calls it "Le Pick." None of these maps provides any information about the native inhabitants of the Pic River or its mouth.

Turning now to sources of information concerning the Pic River in the eighteenth century, we can note the D'Anville map of 1700 to 1750 locating "le Pik" River (Tucker, 1942, Pl. III).

Jonathan Carver must have passed the mouth of the Pic River in 1767, but he did not record any specific information about it in his memoirs, nor did he leave a map.

Alexander Henry, the noted Indian trader may have visited the Pic River in 1775. He says that he was at the mouth of the

Pijitic which has been identified as the White River ten miles or less to the south of the Pic. But Henry's description of the river plus his statement that he crossed the bay "3 leagues in breadth" and landed on Pic Island better fits the Pic River than it does the White River. Here are Alexander Henry's own words about what he did and saw on June 20, 1775: "In the evening we encamped at the mouth of the Pijitic, a river as large as that of Michipicoten. . . .On the river are a band of Wood Indians, who are sometimes troublesome to the traders passing." (Henry, 1901, pp. 231, 232.)

Elsewhere Henry speaks of the "Wood-Indians" as "Men of the Woods", "Gens de Terre," and "O'pimittish Ininiwac." (Henry, 1901, p. 62). Henry found these Indians at Michipicoten in 1767. He wrote:

> On reaching the trading post, which was an old one of French establishment, I found ten lodges of Indians. These were Gens de Terres, or O'pimittish Ininiwac, of which nation I have already had occasion to speak. It is scattered over all the country between the Gulf of Saint-Lawrence and Lake Arabuthcow (Athabaska), and between Lake Superior and Hudson's Bay. Its language is a mixture of those of its neighbors, the Chippeways (Chippewa) and Christinaux (Cree). (Henry, 1809, Bain edition, 1901, pp. 207-8.)

John Long, an Englishman engaged in the fur trade traveled in the northern Lake Superior region during the years 1777-79. At Pays Plat on July 4, 1777 he found one hundred and fifty Indians "most of whom were of the Chippeway tribes; the rest were of the nation of the Wasses (Sioux). They gave me fish, dried meat, and skins, which I returned with trifling presents. The chief, whose name was Matchee Quewish, held a council. . . ." (Long, 1791, p. 45.)

Long left Pays Plat on July 21st and engaged twenty of the Chippewa to carry his goods over portages and arrived at Lake Nipigon where he "met another band of Savages of the same nation" (Long, 1791, p.50).

He may have visited the Pic River in 1777 or 1778, but his journal is not specific. He certainly had to pass the mouth of the Pic. He does describe a band of Indians at the mouth of the Pique River but his account of this river in relation to Pays Plat does not fit the Pic. He visited the Pique River in 1778. In his memoirs (Long, 1791, pp. 104-5) wrote:

> On the 15th of August I left Pays Plat, with four birch canoes, and the same men who wintered with me at Lac la Mort, and arrived at Riviére la Pique, which runs into Lake Superior. . . .On our landing, we found a large band of Chippeways, and some of the Rat nation, who

> immediately prepared a feast for us of dried meat, fish, etc. Among them was an Indian named Ogasby, or the horse; he was reckoned, even by his own tribe, a bad Indian, which put me on my guard during my encampment there. I traded for their skins and furs, and gave them some rum, with which they had a frolic, which lasted for three days and nights; on this occasion five men were killed, and one woman dreadfully burnt. When the fumes of the liquor had evaporated, they began, as usual, to reflect on the folly of their conduct, and all except Ogasby expressed great concern; he seemed rather to be pleased at the mischief which had happened, and before my departure, I was informed that he intended to destroy me, and plunder the property. To frustrate his villainous intention, I kept him in good humour, and made him sleep in my hut, a compliment he seemed highly pleased with, and which I believe for the time diverted him from his purpose; and though by no means fond of his company, I judged it most prudent to have my enemy in sight. In the morning I gave him a glass of rum, and promised him a two-gallon keg to carry off the ground, which, as the Indians express themselves, drove the bad spirit from his heart. When my men had prepared every thing for embarkation, I gave the chief of the band the liquor, and a single bottle of rum more than I promised to Ogasby, unknown to the rest, in which I had infused a considerable quantity of laudanum. Unsuspicious of what I had done, he put the bottle to his mouth, and shaking me by the hand, said to me, "Kee talinimanco negee," or, "your health, friend," and immediately took a hearty draught which soon stupified and lulled him into a profound sleep, in which, I was afterwards informed, he remained twelve hours, depriving him of the power of doing harm, and that soon after, an Indian who had an antipathy against him, and only sought an opportunity of gratifying his resentment, tomahawked him. His eldest son burnt him, and fixed his bones on a high pole, as he was the head chief of the tribe.

Although Long's descriptions of the land and its inhabitants do not specifically apply to the Pic River area they are indicative of nearby places and of the region in general. There is, however, a specific reference to the Pic River in a somewhat later source.

On a map of the north shore of Lake Superior made in 1794 and based on the journal of a coasting survey and remarks made by Lieut. Bennet and signed P. McNeff there is the following written notation at the "Rau Pic": "On this River dwells many Indians called by other Nations the Men of the Land" (Henry, 1901, facing p. 232). It seems likely that these Men of the Land or bush Indians were the Nopeming, one of the names for some northern Chippewa.

Conclusions: Various bands of Chippewa have lived along the north shore of Lake Superior since the dawn of recorded history in the area. Moreover, they seem to have been the dominant native inhabitants in the vast stretch from Lake Nipigon to Sault Ste Marie, Ontario. It thus seems most probable that the cultural remains found in association with trade objects at the mouth of the Pic River are those of some group of northern Chippewa (Quimby, 1958), perhaps the ancestors of the Chippewa who live there at the present time.

The Chippewa are such a vast group it is likely that significant cultural differences will be found among the tribal components. There seem to be considerable differences between the northern Chippewa who are closely related to Cree and Algonkin groups and the southern Chippewa who are closely connected with Ottawa and Potawatomi bands.

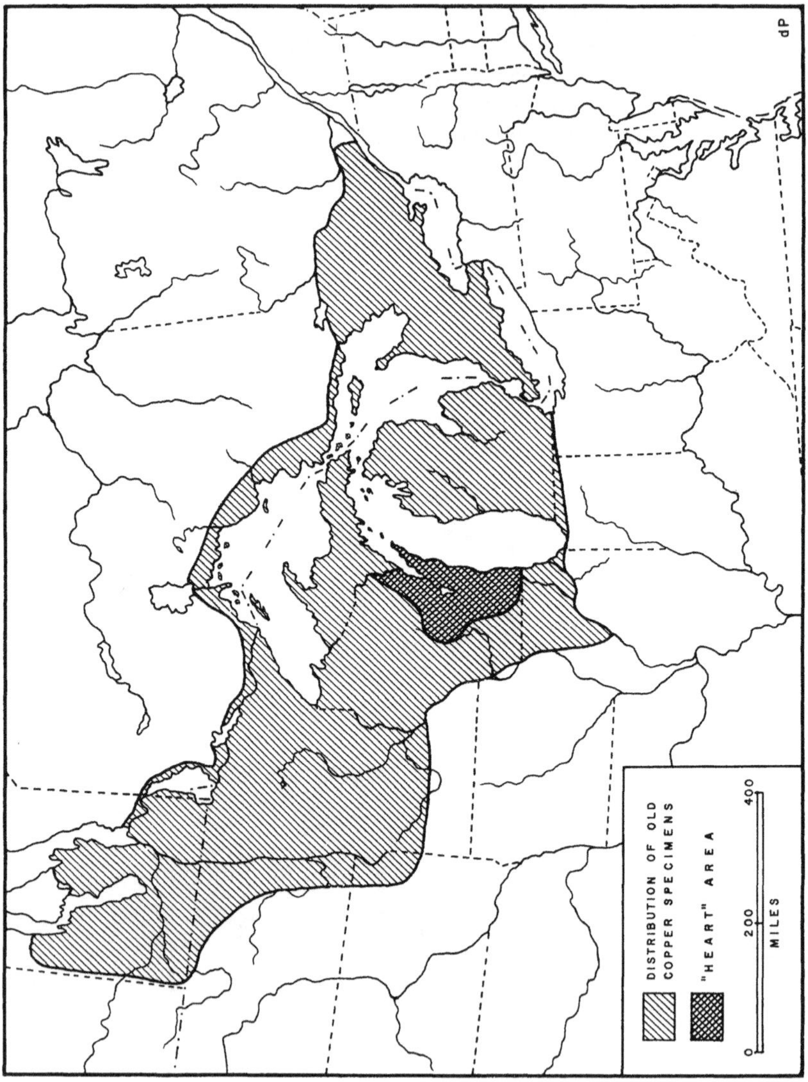

Map 5. This map showing the distribution of Old Copper specimens is somewhat arbitrary in its boundary line. For example, there are known copper specimens in central New York which have not been included. There are also some copper artifacts in the Southeast in Late Archaic sites which were, apparently, traded into that area. We are particularly indebted to Mrs. P. H. Stokes and P. W. Grant of Winnipeg, Manitoba, for their information including drawings, of the distribution of Old Copper artifacts in southern Manitoba. The Old Copper culture was in the Great Lakes area between 3000–1000 B.C.

THE McCOLLUM SITE, NIPIGON DISTRICT, ONTARIO

James B. Griffin and George I. Quimby

The McCollum site, locus of an Old Copper cache on a bay of southeastern Lake Nipigon, produced one of the most interesting Old Copper finds of recent years. It is north of the region where most of the Old Copper finds have been made and certain features of the materials suggest a late date for this site within the time span of the Old Copper culture (Map 5).

The McCollum site is situated on the shore of Pijitawabik Bay about 25 miles north of the town of Nipigon on Trans-Canada Highway No. 11 and about 2 miles south of the hamlet of Orient Bay. This location is very close to 40° 20' N. and 88° 8' W. Pijitawabik Bay is a part of southeastern Lake Nipigon and is the remnant of a former glacial channel that connected with the basin of Lake Superior. William McCollum, owner of the site, has developed a tourist resort and fishing camp on the east side of the Bay where it is crossed by the Canadian National Railways tracks. The railway bridge a short distance east of the site with a milepost sign of 44.2 is the means of reaching the site on foot from the McCollum resort (Pl. XVIII, Fig. 2).

Our attention was first called to this site in the summer of 1955 when Quimby received from Dr. Warren L. Wittry a news clipping and picture from the June 17th *Port Arthur News Chronicle*. A similar account was seen by Quimby in the *New York Times* of July 7, 1955. This information was filed until the summer of 1957, when we were conducting our second season of archaeological survey of the Lake Superior basin, at which time we visited the McCollum site, made test excavations, studied the artifacts, and obtained the following information from the McCollum family who were most co-operative.

In the fall of 1954, Mr. William McCollum had a bulldozer brought down the bay on a barge to provide a sloping beach so that his boats could conveniently be brought out of the water at the close of the summer season. The bank at this spot faces north and was about 5 to 9 feet above water level (Pl. XVIII, Fig. 1). The bulldozed area was about 100 feet east and west and about 80 feet from the water's edge toward the south. On Friday, May 13, 1955, Billy, the owner's six-year old son was playing in the sand some 2 to 3 feet above the then level of the lake and found one of the copper specimens. Their curiosity aroused, the McCollum family, continued to dig and in an area about 8 feet square recovered 13 thin copper discs; 4 copper bracelets; 3 small, rolled tubular beads; 1 long, tubular bead; 3 chisel-punches; 2 long, thin pieces; a small, rounded needle without an eye; an adze; socketed lance heads; 4 beveled blades; socketed spear heads; two beveled blades; socketed knives; a spike-like punch; a small ladle-shaped implement with a tiny bowl at one end and a hook at the other end of the handle; 4 native copper unworked pieces; a large, thin, flattened ovoid blade of taffy-colored flint; 2 corner-notched projectile points of gray flint; a long flake scraper of what appears to be Knife River flint; and a large flake scraper of bluish-gray flint.

The McCollum's agree that fragments of cord were present in the short tube sections of copper and Mrs. McCollum states that there were wood fragments in the socket handles. Mr. McCollum, however, does not believe that any wood was preserved. Three of the specimens, the copper adze, the large, ovoid blade of taffy-colored flint and the large, gray flint scraper still have small particles of red ochre adhering to them; but none of the excavators recall noticing any reddish discoloration of the soil, or on the other artifacts.

Billy McCollum claims he found nine teeth in, or very near, the area of the copper finds. Mr. and Mrs. McCollum did not recall such a find. In our subsequent excavations of this area we did not find any evidence of human or animal bone, charcoal, or red ocher. A search was made by boat of the exposed banks along Pijitawabik Bay and along the railroad cuts but no signs of Indian occupation were noticed. None of the people interviewed in the immediate area had ever heard of other finds.

DESCRIPTION OF THE FINDS

The Copper Discs

The thirteen perforated copper disks are made of very thin sheet copper, 1 mm thick and are flat to slightly curved (Pl. XIX). Ten are circular, two are heart or pear-shaped, and one is almost diamond-shaped. The disks had apparently been nested, for on the upper surface of some of them are areas of markedly less patina and the carved arcs of less discoloration match the arc of other disks. The disks were hammered into very thin sheets, cut out, and the edges ground. Twelve of the disks have a single perforation while one has two perforations 5 mm apart.

The perforations vary in size from 2 mm on the larger disks to 1 mm on the smaller ones. The measurements are as follows:

No. 1 . . . . 3.2 cm
No. 2 . . . . 3.3 cm
No. 3 . . . . 3.9 cm
No. 4 . . . . 4.0 cm long by 3.4 cm wide (diamond-shaped)
No. 5 . . . . 4.9 cm
No. 6 . . . . 5.4 cm by 5.1 cm wide (pear-shaped)
No. 7 . . . . 6.3 cm long by 4.6 cm wide (pear-shaped)
No. 8 . . . . 6.0 by 6.1 cm
No. 9 . . . . 6.1 by 6.4 cm
No. 10 . . . . 6.4 by 6.4 cm
No. 11 . . . . 7.0 by 7.2 cm
No. 12 . . . . 7.1 by 6.9 cm (the two-hole specimen)
No. 13 . . . . 7.7 by 7.6 cm

Several of the disks, No. 10 particularly, have a brownish incrustation which might be either leather or bark.

The Bracelets

The bracelets are paired, in that there are two small ones and two large ones (Pl. XIX). They are all made in the same way and are formed from thin strips of copper of the same thickness as the thirteen disks. Bracelet No. 1 is 7 cm long and 5.8 cm wide. There is a gap of 8 mm between the two arms. The greatest width of the band is 1.6 cm and is opposite the band opening. There are perforations 8 mm from each end in the midline. Along the midline of the band there are 17 *repoussé* bosses punched from the inside with a depression 3 mm in diameter. One of the bosses on this bracelet is punched through. The bracelet is almost broken through at the weakened section, five bosses form one end.

Bracelet No. 2 is 6.4 cm long and 6.2 cm wide. The greatest width of the band is 1.5 cm opposite the gap and 1.5 to 1.4 cm wide at the gap. There are two perforations in the midline of the band, placed 1 cm from each end of the gap. Instead of a single continuous line of bosses as on bracelet No. 1, this bracelet has two bosses opposite the opening spaced 1 cm apart and two groups of three bosses which are placed opposite each other. These are spaced from 1 to 1.4 cm apart. One of the punches forming the bosses has perforated the thin copper plate. The gap between the arms is 1.3 cm.

Bracelet No. 3 is 4.9 cm long and 4.4 wide. The gap between the arms is 1.4 cm wide. The greatest width of the band is 1.4 cm and is opposite the gap. The band width gradually tapers toward each tip and is only 6 mm wide at this point. There are two perforations 8 mm from the tip of the arms, one on each side. This bracelet has a single continuous line of twelve small bosses, spaced 7 mm to 1 cm apart, and six of these are perforated through the band.

Bracelet No. 4 is 4.8 cm long and 4.5 wide with a space of 2.2 cm between the tips. Like bracelet No. 3, this one is 1.4 cm wide opposite the gap, and the sides are gradually constricted to the tips which are only 6 mm wide. There are the same two perforations near the tip of each arm. These are only 5 mm from each tip, and one of them was made by two closely spaced punches. This bracelet has paired bosses and there are ten such pairs spaced 8 mm to 1 cm apart around the bracelet. Six of these bosses are perforated through the band.

The Copper Beads

The bead sections are all rolled, thin-sheet copper (Pl. XIX). The three small beads are badly worn and eroded. The tube diameter is 5 mm and the three beads are 1.5 cm, 1.7 cm, and 2.4 cm long. The long tubular "bead" is 11.4 cm long.

The Copper Adze

This fine specimen is 17.3 cm long, 4.8 cm wide at the bit, and 1.9 cm wide at the poll (Pl. XXI). The thickest part of the blade is 1.3 cm while at the poll it is 8 mm thick. One face of the blade is flattened and on that surface at the cutting edge there is a short, beveled area 2 to 3 mm wide. There are no indications of hafting visible at this time. Two small areas on the blade are reddish in color and are suggestive of red ochre discoloration.

There are six spear or pike heads which have a rectangular outline on the blade to a rolled almost circular socket (Pl. XXI). Four of these have a very similar pattern though differing in size.

The last two specimens in Table III have the same rectangular section but differ markedly in the length of the socket compared to the blade length.

Lance No. 6 is also the only one with a tang like those on some antler projectile points of the Archaic into the Hopewell period.

TABLE III
DIMENSIONS OF McCOLLUM SPEAR HEADS
(In Centimeters)

Number	Length	Socket Length	Socket Thickness	Width Above Socket	Thickness Above Socket	Socket Breadth
1. . .	22.7	1.5	.9	1.8	1.3	5.5
2. . .	23.2	1.6	1.0	2.1	1.5	5.6
3. . .	19.5	1.2	.6	1.1	.9	2.7
4. . .	13.5	.5	.3	.7	.5	2.5
5. . .	15.9	1.3	.6	1.6	1.2	5.8
6. . .	13.5	1.3	.9	1.8	1.8	7.3

Socketed, Beveled-Blade Spear Points

There are four beveled spearheads with rounded sockets (Pl. XX). The blades are beveled along the blade on each side and on each face. They are slightly "hollow ground," while the rest of the blade face is slightly convex:

TABLE IV
DIMENSIONS OF SOCKETS OF BEVELED BLADE SPEARS
(In Centimeters)

Number	Length	Length of Socket	Maximum Breadth of Blade	Width of Socket	Thickness of Socket	Blade Thickness
1. . .	14.3	5.4	2.9	1.3	1.2	.4
2. . .	13.7	6.3	2.9	1.5	1.3	.4
3. . .	9.6	3.5	2.2	1.3	1.0	.3
4. . .	6.7	3.4	1.8	1.3	1.0	.25

Socketed, Beveled Knives

These large blades are "hollow ground," beveled on one side and on one face only (Pl. XX). The rest of the upper surface of the knife is slightly convex. The under surface of the knife is flattened. The blades do not come to a point but are curved as in a modern table and case knife. The beveled edges are thinned to a knife edge which is worn and serrated. The sockets are well rounded:

TABLE V
DIMENSIONS OF SOCKETED BEVELED KNIVES
(In Centimeters)

Number	Length	Length of Socket	Width of Socket	Socket Thickness	Width of Blade	Thickness of Blade	Width of Bevel
1. . .	22.8	7.	2.4	1.6	.3 to 1.3	.4 to .05	1 to .5
2. . .	20.4	5.9	2.1	1.5	2.7 to .6	.3 to .05	1 to .5

Miscellaneous Objects
(Plate XXI)

There are two long, narrow, thin sections of copper of which the use is unknown. They are eroded along the edges. They are 5 mm wide and 1 mm thick. One is 17.9 cm long and the other is 12 cm long. There is one short, 5.5 cm needle with rounded cross section. According to Mrs. McCollum there were originally two such needles.

There are three specimens which have flattened blades and awl-like points. Two of these are about the same size, 7.8 and 7.9 cm long. One has a maximum breadth of 1.7 opposite the tip while the other is only 1.3. Both have sharp edges along the sides. One has the point formed by hammering it into a rounded projection. The third is 13 cm long and has a spatulate-like end with rounded tip opposite the awl-like point which projects from a rectangular section. The greatest breadth of this awl is 1 cm. A "railroad spike" copper awl has a hammered head and is 12.3 cm long. The shaft is roughly rectangular in cross section 1.2 x 1 cm near the head and comes to a rounded point.

The spoon or ladle-like object has a total length of 10.9 cm and is made from a long, thin, narrow copper bar which is flat for 9 cm of its length and then expands laterally and is deepened to form a cone 1 cm deep. The end opposite the cone-shaped cup is hooked. The cone has two small perforations placed opposite each other near the lip of the cone. The cone has a diameter of 1.8 cm. It is a unique specimen and its function is unknown.

There are four irregularly shaped pieces of copper which would have been suitable for working into implements. They are 4.8 x 1.8 x .5 cm; 5.6 x 2.3 x .3 cm; 5.1 x 2.1 x .2 cm; and 4.3 x 3.4 x .6 cm.

Comments on the Copper Artifacts

Most of the copper tools and weapons from the McCollum site seem to be typical Old Copper styles. The beveling of the blades on knives and spearpoints, although pronounced, is similar to that on specimens from sites near Menominee, Michigan (see Quimby, 1957, p. 38 and Spaulding's collection in the Museum of Anthropology, University of Michigan). There is, however, an unusual, if not unique, attribute of all of the socketed artifacts from the McCollum site. The sockets are all rounded in section rather than oval. None is angular or squared. Since all of these sockets are open types none is a complete circle in section. They range from half circles to three-quarter circles. The sockets on similar kinds of copper tools and weapons from sites in Wisconsin and Michigan (observation by Quimby) are either angular or obviously oval. We have emphasized this attribute of circularity of sockets on artifacts from the McCollum site because it may well be of use in future studies of temporal and spatial distributions of Old Copper artifacts types and modes. Quimby suspects that the circularity of sockets is a criterion of late age within the time span of the Old Copper culture, but that tools and weapons with this attribute are older than the leaf-shaped copper blades and the copper harpoons with multiple unilateral barbs that are associated with the Red Ocher culture.

The only copper discs similar to those from the McCollum cache which have come to our attention are those from Wisconsin briefly described by Charles E. Brown (1904, p. 114):

> In the illustration forming our frontispiece is shown a fine, almost circular, sheet copper gorget about 3-1/4 inches in diameter and 1/16 of an inch in thickness throughout, which was also formerly in the Ellsworth collection, and came from the banks of Silver Lake, Kenosha County. One face of this beautiful specimen is handsomely oxidized in varying shades of light and dark green, the copper color of the metal showing through here and there in flecks and spots. The other is worn quite smooth, as if through long contact with the person or dress of its owner. It is provided with two perforations.
>
> Specimens of this form, but possessing a single perforation, have been collected by Prof. Lewis at Prairie du Chien, Crawford County; Wyalusing, Grant County; Aztalan, Jefferson County; Jefferson, Jefferson County; near Madison, Dane County; Portage, Columbia County; Menasha, Winnebago County; Green Bay, Brown County, and Lake Chetek, Barron County.

There are also similar-looking discs in the American Museum of Natural History in New York from the Great Lakes area, but on close inspection they were identified as circular cutouts from European trade pots and are thus not the same as the McCollum specimens.

The ornaments from the McCollum site are important because very little is known of Old Copper ornament types. Ornaments have not been present in cache finds made previously and they have been rare in graves. The interpretation favored in this paper is that these ornaments are a reflection of the increasing use of copper for ornamental forms which begins in the Early Woodland cultures and reaches its culmination in the north central United States in the Hopewellian cultures of 200 B.C.-A.D. 200. Red ochre in graves and/or caches is a trait that may have considerable antiquity in the Great Lakes area but is most commonly associated with the Late Archaic to Early Woodland burial complexes. W. H. Jensen suggested that Browns Valley Man was associated with red ochre (Jenks, 1937, p. 7), but his description is not completely satisfactory in establishing this point.

THE FLINT ARTIFACTS

Five flint implements (Pl. XXII) were found by the McCollums. These forms are of some assistance in determining the cultural relations and temporal position of the copper forms. Outline drawings, notes, and photographs were taken by Griffin and this data was later supplemented by photographs taken by James V. Wright. The following description of the flint specimens has been prepared by Lewis Binford based on the above data. The descriptive nomenclature is presented in some detail in a forthcoming paper by Binford (no date). The lamellar blade or flake knife was made from a mottled, translucent brownish chalcedony which many archaeologists in the midwest would call Knife River flint from North Dakota. This is what we called it in 1957, when we studied the material. Subsequently, however, James Wright has informed us that this flint type is found in some quantity in the northern part of the Lake Superior Basin. This raises the question as to the origin of similar flint which has been found in Hopewell sites in Wisconsin, Illinois, and Ohio, and which has been attributed to the North Dakota deposits. A further association of apparently this type of chalcedony and copper artifacts is reported from the Farquar Lake cache in Haliburton County, Ontario (Popham and Emerson, 1954, p. 6).

Projectile Points

Raw Material.—Both specimens were manufactured of a light, taffy-colored chert which appears to be massive in structure and to lack inclusions and cavities.

Blade Element.—Shape of the blade: Both ovate and contracting ovate blade shapes are represented. Judging from a specimen excavated by James Wright of the National Museum of Canada, from the McCollum site, cross sections are biconvex and longitudinal sections are also biconvex and quite symmetrical.

Chipping of the Blade.—Primary scars are diminutive and expanding. Hinge fractures do not characterize the terminus of chip scars yet the definition in terms of ridges between scars is quite pronounced. Secondary retouch is not continuous along the lateral edges, but where present it is represented by short expanding and lamellar scars.

Base Element.—Shape of the base: Straight to only slightly subconvex.

Chipping of the Base.—Chip scars originating on the basal edge tend to be diminutive and do not dominate the face of the specimen. Well-defined longitudinal scars are absent. Chip scars are expanding and lamellar in form. The basal edge is ground to an even, well-defined edge.

Haft Element.—Shape of the haft element: Juncture is normally lateral-coincidental, however, the placement of the "notches" may be slightly asymmetrical resulting in one side having lateral-coincidental juncture while the other has lateral-basal juncture. The distal point of juncture is normally acute and slightly circular. Failure in chipping and breakage however, may result in right angles, and/or obtuse forms at the distal point. Medial points may be either single or double. When double medial points of juncture are present the distal point is normally right angled, while the proximal point is obtuse, resulting in roughly parallel expanding tang. The proximal point of juncture of the haft element is acute with circular articulation.

Chipping of the Haft.--The notches were produced by the multiple removal of diminutive chips from both faces. Scars originating on both the lateral and basal edges showing that the production of the notches was the last step of the manufacturing process. No information is available concerning the presence or absence of grinding within the notches or along the tang.

TABLE VI
METRICAL ATTRIBUTES OF THE McCOLLUM POINTS

Specimen	Base Width	Tang Width	Shoulder Width	Axial Length	Tang Length	Notch Length
A	2.1	1.5	2.8	6.7	1.2	.90
B	2.1	1.3	2.8	5.7	1.1	.80

Comments.— Specimens very similar to those from the McCollum site, have been recovered from the Stroebel site in Saginaw County, Michigan, associated with a burial in the flesh, and powdered hemitite. Another specimen, sharing with the McCollum specimens the same pattern of flaking and general size but differing slightly in the placement of the haft, was recovered from feature Number 6, at the Riverside cemetery, Menominee County, Michigan, which was excavated by Albert C. Spaulding in 1956. These four known specimens almost certainly represent a distinct type of projectile point that is distinguished from many other Late Archaic forms by the fact that they were not manufactured on Meadowood point blanks (Ritchie, 1961, p. 35).

Other Chipped-Stone Materials

"Flake Knife."—A large (9.2 cm) lamellar "blade" with lateral edges parallel to the axis of percussion and pronounced concavo-convex longitudinal section showed evidence of having been utilized as a tool. Fine marginal retouch was present along one lateral edge of the distal half of the specimen. Retouch was on the external face (face opposite the cleavage face). The external face exhibited longitudinal scarring indicative of the flake having been removed from a prepared core of the "blade" type. The pronounced concavo-convex longitudinal section may be indicative of removal from some form of pyramidal core. Retouch along the lateral edge suggests either a cutting or scraping function. The specimen was manufactured of a raw material quite similar to "Knife River flint."

"Flake Scraper."—A massive (9.3 x 5 cm) decortication flake of a gray chert had been reworked into a "scraper." Primary and secondary retouch on the external face had largely removed the original cortex of the flake. Retouch was absent on the internal face. The orientation of the working edge with respect to the axis of percussion was not observed. A single convex edge showed secondary retouch suggestive of a scraping function.

"Blank."—A large (10.7 by 7 cm) roughly oval bifacially chipped artifact was manufactured from the same taffy-colored flint as the projectile points. It is quite similar to artifact forms from Early and Middle Woodland assemblages commonly designated as "blanks." The specimen is 10.7 cm long, 7.1 cm wide, and 1.0 cm thick with convex base and ovate blade shape. The points of juncture between the basal edge and the lateral edges as well as the tip are all articulated with gently curving arcs giving the specimen a disk-like appearance. The basal edge is obliquely orientated with respect to the longitudinal axis of the specimen. Chip scars are massive and expanding in form frequently terminating in hinge fractures. This particular form is not commonly found in Archaic assemblages from the Great Lakes region. Its presence suggests a very late date in the Archaic period or contemporaneity with Early Woodland complexes in the Illinois and Ohio River valleys.

EXCAVATIONS

A series of very small test trenches and pits were made at the McCollum site in August of 1957. The excavations were undertaken by Griffin and Quimby, who directed the work of James C. Griffin, Edward Quimby, and Billy McCollum. Techniques used were shoveling and trowling and, in some instances, the washing of sand through screens with the aid of a jet of water forced through a hose by a centrifugal pump and gasoline engine. The latter system was essentially a hydraulic mining technique.

The site lay within the area bulldozed by McCollum. This area was about 100 feet east and west by 70 feet north and south. The north side of the site was at the water's edge. The present elevation of Lake Nipigon is 855 feet above sea level. At the time of the bulldozing and prior to the use of a system of dams between Lake Nipigon and Lake Superior the elevation of the water was 852 feet above sea level.

Before bulldozing, the surface of the McCollum site was about 8 to 10 feet above the old water level. The locus of the Old Copper artifacts was 5 or 6 feet beneath the surface and, when this spot was struck by the bulldozer blade, the artifacts and surrounding sand were pushed into the water. The artifacts, when found, were in the water and in an area 8 feet square adjoining the water.

Our excavations into the waterward sloping surface of the McCollum site produced no artifacts after it had been bulldozed; but they did provide us with a number of small, round concretions of copper salts and sand. All of these concretions were confined to an area 60 feet east and west and 30 feet north and south from the water's edge.

The concretions were found sparingly throughout this area. There was no specific concentration. On the other hand, we did not find any of them in the sand outside of this area. We concluded that these concretions of copper salts and sand were in some way related to the Old Copper cache (or possibly burial) found by the McCollums and that the original find had been, before probable dislodgement by the bulldozer, within the area of the distribution of the concretions.

Geology of the Site

The McCollum site is situated on the floor of a former glacial channel cut through high rock hills. The floor of this valley, in the vicinity of the site, is composed of a layer of water-deposited sand on top of an apparently undulating surface of gray clay. The copper specimens were in the sand.

If we knew when this sand was deposited and available for a burial pit, we would have a maximum limit to the age of the Old Copper culture at the McCollum site. Dr. John Elson (1957, p. 1001) has suggested that Lake Agassiz II discharged into Lake Nipigon and thence to the Lake Superior basin. Although this event is postulated for early post-Valders times, the specific period and its duration are unknown. But this event, if dated, could provide a maximum estimate of age for the Old Copper culture at the McCollum site because the site undoubtedly would have been under water during the postulated period of Lake Agassiz discharge to the Lake Superior basin via Lake Nipigon.

Dr. Farrand's preliminary study of the Lake Helen to Pijitawabik Bay terrain caused him to propose that:

> "The abundance of sediment in the Pijitawabik Bay canyon implies the presence of the ice sheet either in Pijitawabik Bay itself or at least in the Lake Nipigon basin. These facts lead to the conclusion that the Nipigon basin was ice-filled (or nearly so) in Minong times. As lake levels fell in the Lake Superior basin and the ice sheet retreated from the Lake Nipigon basin these basins apparently contained separate water bodies connected only by the ancestral courses of the Nipigon and Black Sturgeon rivers. In other words, there appears to be no validity in the assumption generally made that the Nipigon and Superior basins were occupied at any time by one continuous lake. (Farrand, 1960, p. 82.)

VARIOUS FINDS OF COPPER AND STONE ARTIFACTS IN THE LAKE SUPERIOR BASIN

George I. Quimby and James B. Griffin

There are a number of finds of single copper and stone artifacts in the Lake Superior basin. In the museum of the Historical Society of the 49th Medium Anti-Aircraft Regiment, R.C.A. of Sault Ste Marie, Ontario, there is a leaf-shaped knife with a broad flat tang. This specimen is about 10 inches long and was found on Batchawana Island, Algoma District, Ontario.

This specimen, according to Quimby, is not a type indicative of the Old Copper culture, but is a form found in the somewhat later Red Ocher culture and related Late Archaic and/or Early Woodland contexts, in general, similar to knives shown in Plate XXIX.

We visited Batchawana Island in July, 1956. It was a low-lying, densely wooded spot of land that had an outline somewhat like a Rorschach ink blot. As measured by Paulin altimeter readings the crest of the island was 25 to 30 feet above the level of Lake Superior.

Also on display in the Historical Society Museum of the 49th (Sault Ste Marie) Medium Anti-Aircraft Regiment, R.C.A. were some interesting copper finds from the Ontario coast of Lake Huron southeast of Sault Ste Marie, a short distance from the Superior basin.

A copper spear point or knife about 8 inches long was found near Desbarats 10 feet beneath the surface of the ground. This point is leaf-shaped with a socket that is angular in cross section (variant of Wittry's type J. (Wittry, 1951.) The land around Desbarats has an elevation of about 595 to 600 feet above sea level and is about 18 feet or less above the level of Lake Huron.

A leaf-shaped point or knife with rolled socket (Wittry's type B1) came from Portlock Harbor. This specimen is about 6 inches long. The land around Portlock Harbor stands at an elevation of about 600 feet above sea level or less. This is about 18 feet or less above Lake Huron.

Two copper projectile points or knives were found in a washout 2 feet beneath the surface along the Thessalon River about 10 miles above Thessalon, Ontario. One of these points was about 5 inches long, the other about 6 inches. Both were leaf-shaped with flat tangs, and, according to Quimby, were types typical of Red Ocher and other Late Archaic cultures rather than of the Old Copper culture.

The lake from which the Thessalon River flows has an elevation of 636 feet and at a point just west of Thessalon it has an elevation of 626 feet. It would seem reasonable to assign an elevation of 630 to 640 feet for the Thessalon River copper find. This is about 48 to 58 feet above Lake Huron.

On the north shore of Lake Superior Joseph Lecours of Heron Bay, Ontario, found a copper blade or point in 1951 on the terrace along the west bank of the Pic River opposite the mouth of Black River. In August of 1957 we examined this blade. It was leaf-shaped, 9 cm long and 2.3 cm wide, and had a lenticular cross section. This style of point or blade is not typical of the Old Copper culture, but has been noted in Late Archaic and Early Woodland assemblages. The terrace where the point was found is about 45 feet above the level of Lake Superior.

A copper awl and a somewhat similar blade, apparently with a broad tang, were found by Norbert Lemolin in a sand blow on what appears to have been the same terrace. We do not have all of the details because at the time we interviewed Lemolin he was riding a boom of logs down the Pic River and we were on the shore.

A remarkable copper find made in 1884, and reported by Bell (1928, pp. 51-54) was made one mile east of the Heron Bay station along the right of way of the Canadian Pacific Railway, the account of which was located by Griffin in the Spring of 1957 as part of our preparation for a second joint field trip to the Canadian shores of Lake Superior.

In the course of making a cut 600 feet east of the Pic River a workman for the Canadian Pacific Railway unearthed a copper, hook-shaped implement or gaff 17 inches long (Pl. XXIII, Fig. 8) and a number of fragments of charcoal and charred wood. The find was immediately drawn to the attention of W. H. D. Armstrong, C.E., divisional engineer in charge of construction, who after a critical examination of the location, made a ground plan and cross section of the cutting and forwarded the material to Dr. Bell:

> The railroad cutting which revealed the presence of the implement was made directly through a roll of rock which is raised above the level of the immediate surrounding uninhabited country and was situated on the east bank of Pic River and about 600 feet distant therefrom. On the centre top of this rock a deep cavity existed and this being filled up with clay and gravel it was first supposed by the engineers that the summit or

> top was a solid mass with a gravel surface imposed thereon, but the stripping of the gravel at once revealed that in fact a deep hollow or depression was in position between four walls or sloping sides. This is clearly shown in the plan and cross section which Mr. Armstrong made for me. The hook was found at the bottom of the cavity on the sloping rock side under about twenty-five feet of drift clay topped by a layer of gravel. The elevation of the spot by actual measurement was about one hundred feet above the present normal surface of Lake Superior.
>
> It seems apparent that there would necessarily be a depth of water over the adjacent country before the surface could flow over the surrounding rock walls and fill the enclosed pocket or basin with the drift clay and gravel deposit which actually was found there covering the copper implement, for the Pic River being within such a short distance, 600 feet in fact, and as it runs in a deep rock valley it seems practically impossible that the clay deposit could have been washed into the pocket (by runoff from surrounding surfaces).
>
> The hook was found, as stated, amidst a number of fragments of charcoal and charred wood, some pieces of which were one and one-half inches in diameter, but the deposit covering this old camp fire of some prehistoric man did not show any layers of vegetable mould or remains, the strata being entirely of clay with a topping of drift gravel characteristic of the neighborhood. No human remains were found. The bottom of the pocket was fairly level and there is no elevation in the immediate vicinity so situated as would cause a local flood to wash the clay and gravel into it from an opening. Any local flood would pour its waters around the base of the rocks directly into the deep valley of the Pic. Indeed the cross section drawn to scale by Mr. Armstrong shows a ravine of about twenty-five or thirty feet in depth on the eastern side of the mound or rock wall. The slope of the Pic Valley is immediately from the west side of the mound into the Pic River. . . .The general contour of the country here south from the Canadian Pacific line follows a series of irregular steps, evidently of old lake beaches, down to Lake Superior.

(Bell, 1928, p. 52.)

We were interested in examining the area, although the railroad cutting made in 1884 destroyed the locus of this find and changed the surrounding terrain. We discovered that we could reach the spot by walking across the ties of the long single-track railway bridge high over the gorge of the Pic River. From the station agent at Heron Bay we learned that, although there was a definite schedule for passenger trains, there was no such schedule for freight trains. One could cross the bridge at almost any time of day without adequate warning. So after ascertaining that there was not room for us and a train on the trestle at the same time and after reviewing the numbers of our dependents and financial obligations, and the like, we decided not to visit the site.

In the following summer, however, Dr. William R. Farrand, then a graduate student in geology at the University of Michigan, crossed the bridge and took kodachrome pictures of the area 600 feet east of the Pic River. At a subsequent date he kindly allowed Dr. Griffin and myself to see his kodachrome slides projected. We were thus able to see that the locus of the find is now quite level and the raised projection of rock, where the copper was found, is no longer there.

Dr. Bell, in his article, concluded rightly that the clay and gravel on top of the copper was deposited by water. He also provided evidence that local runoff could not account for the deposit of clay topped with a layer of gravel. Dr. Bell conjectured that the site was: ". . . within a measurable distance of the great northern glacial face, which, under some extraordinary circumstances sent down a vast volume of water and drift thus covering to a great depth the district of country where this copper article lay securely in its pocket in a high rock." (Bell, 1928, p. 53.)

Dr. Bell's conjecture is at variance with facts of postglacial geology not known to him. The series of old lake beaches he noted between the site and Lake Superior continue on inland to elevations much higher than the site. Griffin and Quimby noted what appear to be beach gravels at 520 feet above Lake Superior (measured by Paulin altimeter) inland from Heron Bay. West of this spot at Jackfish Bay, Lawson (1893, p. 275) found a delta plain at 420 feet above Lake Superior. From upwards of 400 feet down to the level of Lake Superior there is a series of old beach lines, and the rock cavity containing the copper hook and charcoal was at the level of one of these fossil beaches.

The bottom of the rock cavity was about 100 feet above the level of Lake Superior. Most glacial geologists assume that the beach at this particular spot with an elevation of about 110 feet is the Nipissing stage beach (Leverett and Taylor 1915, p. 460, Hough, 1958, p. 257-58).

It is now known that the Nipissing beach was formed by waters rising from a low-water stage to a high-water stage (Hough, 1958, pp. 248-51).

Quimby is inclined to the view that the water-laid clay, topped with a layer of gravel, is a deposit of the Nipissing stage and that the copper hook and charcoal and charred wood beneath the clay and gravel date from some period prior to the Nipissing stage deposits at the Peninsula—Pic River locality.

Quimby and Spaulding (1957, p. 200) had suggested earlier that the gaff of copper found on the east side of Lake Superior is pre-Nipissing in age, but if Farrand is correct this does not now seem to be as likely as it did when Griffin ran across the original report (Bell, 1928) in 1956. While W. L. Farrand was making his study of the post-Pleistocene sequence of the Lake

Superior basin he was requested to examine the location of the find. The following statement is quoted from his thesis:

> Another discovery of prehistoric copper artifacts was reported by Bell (1928). A hook-shaped implement of beaten copper was found during a railroad excavation on the east side of the lower Pic River opposite Heron Bay Station. This hook, some charcoal and charred wood were lying in a bedrock cavity and covered by 18 to 25 feet of clay topped by gravel. A construction engineer determined the elevation of this discovery to be about 100 feet above Lake Superior.
>
> The writer visited this site in 1958 in order to verify the geology of the original report, but cut-and-fill work along the railroad right-of-way had obscured the deposits. However, the rock cavity, directly through which the railroad now passes, was observed and its elevation verified. If the artifact lay about 100 feet above Lake Superior, then it was coincident with the broad clay terraces which border the Pic River at this place. The rock cut itself, however, rises above this terrace and the clay which originally filled it must have had a surface elevation of 725 feet or slightly higher. The Nipissing beach at this same place occurs at 725 feet also. Although the gravel which capped this deposit might be Nipissing in age, the underlying clay (18-25 feet thick) is not a shore-line deposit. Furthermore, the Houghton low stage is not a "low stage" in this part of the Superior basin. The Houghton beach occurs nearly 100 feet *above* the Nipissing beach because uplift in the Houghton-Nipissing interval greatly exceeded the rise of lake level. This corner of the basin was covered by the ice sheet or submerged by the lake from the onset of Wisconsin glaciation right down to the time of the Nipissing Great Lakes.
>
> Quimby and Spaulding (1957, p. 200) have suggested that Nipissing deposits overlie this copper hook, but an alternative explanation is required by the facts presented in the preceding paragraph. It is suggested, therefore, that this rock cavity served as a shelter or wind-break for prehistoric man along the shore of Nipissing Lake Superior or a later lake and that it was filled with clay which slumped from the higher slopes just above the site. This clay was originally deposited in pre-Nipissing time. The presence of charcoal and wood precludes the alternative that these materials and the copper hook were dropped into the waters of a former lake. (Farrand, 1960, pp. 107-9.)

Griffin is impressed with Farrand's conclusion that this copper gaff is of Nipissing age. Quimby, on the other hand, would still argue that the copper artifact was beneath clay that was topped by Nipissing gravels and that the artifact is therefore pre-Nipissing in age.

There are at least three possible solutions to this apparent impasse. It is possible, but unlikely, that the gravels that topped the clay are not Nipissing. If they are not of Nipissing age then the copper hook and charcoal can belong to some post-Nipissing interval of time. However, the elevation of the gravel topping at about 125 feet above Lake Superior, the identical level of the Nipissing beach in this area, is an argument against this solution to the problem.

The second possibility is that the rock cavity served copper-using Indians as a shelter early in the Nipissing stage and that it was filled by clay that slumped from higher slopes and then was covered by beach gravels deposited at the maximum water plane (605 feet or even slightly higher) of the Nipissing stage. This hypothesis would account for all of the alleged facts in the case and should produce agreement between Griffin and Farrand on one side of the argument and Quimby on the other side.

The third possibility is that there may have been a low-water stage in the Lake Superior basin some hundreds of feet lower than the Houghton stage described by Farrand. At the present time there is no direct geological evidence in support of this idea. There is, however, some zoological evidence on the basis of the following interpretation by Quimby.

Hubbs and Lagler (1949, pp. 73-134) writing on the fishes of Isle Royale state in substance that the high lakes on the island are inhabited by warm-water-type fishes. Outlets to these lakes are too small to serve effectively as channels by which such fishes can ascend to these lakes. Moreover, the cold waters of the deep trenches surrounding Isle Royale would be a barrier to the movement of such fishes which are of kinds that are seldom or never collected around the Lake Superior shore and are not even represented in Lake Superior by closely related types. In addition, the richness of the fish fauna increases with elevation so that the higher lakes of Isle Royale have the richest fauna.

The situation of the fishes on this large island suggest that they arrived there at a time when they could move through shallow waters that were warm. Such conditions would have existed only if the waters of the Lake Superior basin had been lowered some hundreds of feet beneath the present level. If this were the case, Isle Royale would have been either part of a peninsula joined to the present Bayfield peninsula or part of an archipelago running from Bayfield peninsula to Isle Royale. In either instance the warm-water-type fishes could easily have reached the island where they subsequently were isolated by the rise of land in relation to the water level of the Superior basin.

If one accepts all of the preceding argument, then there is a very strong suggestion of former water levels so low in the Superior basin that their strand lines were obliterated by the subsequent rise to the Nipissing level. And the copper find at Pic could date from some interval of time between the Minong stage and the Nipissing stage.

On the other hand, some ichthyologists (Dr. Reeve M. Bailey, personal communication) believe that the presence of warm-water fishes on Isle Royale does not necessarily demand either a markedly lower level in Lake Superior or an appreciably warmer water temperature in that lake. All fishes of the Lake Superior arca are physiologically adapted not only to withstand the cool temperatures of the present lake, but to maintain normal activity within it. A few of the present Isle Royale fishes could not reproduce in the main lake. Waifs from streams or small inland lakes can and do enter large bodies of water such as Lake Superior, especially at times of storms or severe flooding. The aimless wandering of such stragglers would bring some into contact with protected areas such as Isle Royale and set the stage for colonization of these areas.

In the summer of 1957 we learned of some copper and stone specimens found in the vicinity of Nipigon village on the northwest shore of Lake Superior. E. C. Everett, of Nipigon, who is interested in such matters, informed us that a copper spike-like object, perhaps a punch or chisel and a number of pieces of raw copper were found on top of the high hill by the bridge crossing the Nipigon River. The find was made in 1933-34 in the course of highway construction. These copper objects were reported to have been found 8 feet beneath the surface of the hill.

The hill in question was examined by us in August of 1957 and appears to be part of the formation identified as a former bar by Lawson (1892, p. 268) with an elevation of about 200 feet above Lake Superior.

Everett also reported that a grooved axe or maul of stone was found in a clay bank topped with gravel when the highway construction crew was working at Cavers about 35 miles east of Nipigon village.

At the government dock in Nipigon we were told that the pictographs on the face of a sea cliff on one of the Islands in Nipigon Bay were in poor condition caused by weathering of the rock face.

Thomas E. Lee, then of the National Museum of Canada, reported to us in the summer of 1957 that a commercial fisherman named McLeod had pulled up a copper gaff in his nets while fishing off Geikie Island in northern Lake Nipigon. Another gaff was brought up in a net off Pic Island southeast of Fort William, Ontario. A picture of this hook (Pl. XXIII, Fig. 7) and the circumstances of the find are reported on page 54 of the *Thirty-sixth Annual Archaeological Report of the Ontario Provincial Museum* (1928). Additional copper gaffs from the same area are illustrated in Plate XXIV.

In the Historical Museum at Fort William, Ontario, there are displayed some artifacts found in the vicinity (Pl. XXV). These include two gaffs of copper, about three and six inches long respectively; a socketed conical point of copper; a copper spatulate form; and a spud-like object of copper with a pointed blade (Pl. XXV, center left). This unusual form is about 10 inches long and was found at Cloud Bay south of Fort William.

Also displayed in this museum are some chipped-stone artifacts found near Kakabeka Falls. These include a leaf-shaped blade of brownish flint about 8 inches long, 3 fragments of large blades, 3 large ovid scrapers of flint about 5 or 6 inches long and 4 inches wide, and a stemmed blade of chipped taconite about 5 inches long.

These chipped-stone implements of flint and taconite seem to have been found in the higher grounds adjoining the old lake plain extending westward from Fort William and Port Arthur. They are reminiscent of chipped taconite and flint materials from the Brohm site near Pass Lake about 20 miles northeast of Port Arthur (see MacNeish, 1952). At the present time this is the oldest known site in the Lake Superior basin and it seems to be associated with the Minong stage (see MacNeish, 1952, Quimby, 1959) of postglacial lakes in the Lake Superior area.

We visited the Brohm site in the summer of 1957 and made surface collections. In October of 1958, Quimby returned to the Brohm site and obtained some additional materials. Some of these which are indicative of traits not found in the MacNeish excavations have been illustrated by Quimby (1960, Fig. 16, p. 39).

Between 1872 and 1918 there were some interesting finds of copper artifacts made at Fort William (see Tanton, 1931, pp. 83-84), and reported to the Geological Survey, Canada, by Peter McKellar. This information is as follows:

> A discovery of relics was made in 1872 in the McKellar garden on Island No. 1, Fort William, about 150 feet back from the junction of the Kaminstikwia and McKellar Rivers. The plough turned up 7 or 8 copper tools in a bed of ashes. The tools were much eroded and covered with green carbonate of copper (Tanton, 1931, p. 84).

Unfortunately these "tools" are not described. They may or may not be types indicative of the Old Copper culture.

> In 1914 relics were discovered on Mountain Avenue, Westfort (section of Fort William, about 3,480 feet north of the turning basin). . . .Here the skeleton of a man was found 4 feet below the surface of the ground, in a sitting position. . . .Near him were . . . three square copper chisels each a foot long, and one flat and one half round chisel. Also a copper adze (Tanton, 1931, pp. 83-84).

The objects described above could be Old Copper artifacts or equally well could be representative of other cultures belonging to the Late Archaic and Early Woodland periods.

> Relics were discovered July, 1918, in an excavation made by the Canada Car and Foundry Company about 80 feet north from the turning basin, Westfort. About 12 bones of a mammal and a finely made copper spearhead were found together, about 40 feet below the surface of the ground (Tanton, 1931, p. 82).

The materials found at this locus were submitted to the Geological Survey and Harlan I. Smith, archaeologist, reported the results of examination as follows:

> According to Mr. Lawrence M. Lambe, vertebrate paleontologist of the Geological Survey and Mr. Sternberg, preparator of paleontological specimens, the bone marked B 11 . . . is of a cloven footed animal, possibly a buffalo or a specimen of domestic cattle. . . .Bones marked B 1 and B 10 and B 12 to B 13 inclusive, Mr. Lambe and Mr. Sternberg both pronounce to be those of the horse and not petrified. Mr. Sternberg is convinced that most of them belong to the same individual. The point with the flanged tang made of copper marked C 1 is characteristic and typical of prehistoric Indian handiwork. . . . (Tanton, 1931, p. 84.)

The copper spearpoint described by Harlan I. Smith as having a "flanged tang" is obviously a socketed point or blade and thus is almost certainly an artifact of the Old Copper culture.

Some years ago, Quimby (1954, pp. 169-70) raised the possibility that the horse and bison or cow bones found near Westfort turning basin were those of extinct animals. In 1953 Bryan M. Patterson, then at Chicago Natural History Museum, and now of the Museum of Comparative Zoology at Harvard University, informed Quimby that the present status of paleontological studies of horses does not permit a specialist to distinguish the larger American Pleistocene and postglacial horses from modern horses on the basis of such fragmentary material and that a similar situation obtains for fragmentary bison or cattle bones. Thus the paleontological evidence alone in this case cannot tell us whether the bones are those of historic cow and horse or of prehistoric bison and horse. The question would have to be settled by the geological context of these bones.

As already indicated, the mammal bones and the copper point with flanged tang or socket were found about 40 feet below the surface of the ground.

> A discovery of relics was made, in 1913, about 680 feet north of the turning basin, Westfort, in the Stanley Street sewer, at a depth of about 40 feet. They appeared to rest on clay, the same geological horizon as that of (the previously mentioned copper point and mammal bones)

. . . .Many copper tools were found. Unfortunately the many copper tools were not described.

The geological context of these two finds 40 feet beneath the present surface has been described by Tanton (1931, p. 82-84) and discussed by Quimby (1954, pp. 169-70). The copper artifacts are alleged to have been found on the eroded surface of a bed of blue clay and covered by cross-bedded sands from 4 to 40 feet in thickness filling up the inequalities on the clay surface and forming the plain at its present elevation of 638 feet above sea level. (The Westfort turning basin area was briefly examined by Griffin and Quimby in August, 1957.)

The geological situation requires a period of low-water level during which the blue clay was eroded and channeled and during which were cut the subaqueous channels on the bottom of Lake Superior off Fort William. This was followed by a period of high water during which the cross-bedded sands were deposited on top of the eroded blue clay. The latest known major rise of water level in the Lake Superior basin marked the Nipissing stage, and if the copper artifacts found beneath the cross-bedded sands were actually *in situ* they antedate the Nipissing stage (Table I, p. 12).

The mammal bones could be contemporaneous with the copper artifacts or they could have washed out of an older locus and have been redeposited on top of the blue clay prior to the rise of water level that marks the Nipissing stage. If the mammal bones could be proved to be of the recent historic period we would have to conclude that the copper was not found *in situ* and had somehow worked its way downward from a higher level. Griffin, however, feels that available evidence is so indecisive that both the animal bones and the copper implements could have fallen from the upper four or five feet and that the association of copper, bovid, and horse is fortuitous and that they cannot be ascribed to the level of the blue clay.

There are some interesting finds of copper and stone artifacts along the south shore of Lake Superior. Quimby and Spaulding (1957, pp. 189-201) have described the remains of the Old Copper culture along the Keweenaw waterway that crosses the Keweenaw Peninsula in upper Michigan. They noted that a number of finds of Old Copper artifacts were from levels that were beneath the water plane of the Nipissing stage and that the Garnell and other sites in the vicinity had characteristics suggesting that they had been submerged:

> The salient feature of these sites is the presence of a few comparatively heavy tools and a nearly complete absence of ordinary campsite debris such as flint chips, bone scraps, and charcoal. It seems quite possible that the slight reworking of shallow cultural deposits by the advancing and retreating water might produce this effect. The tools do not exhibit a heavily rolled or battered appearance, but this is not a fatal objection to the theory. The Garnell site would have been situated on a relatively quiet inlet. . . .(Quimby and Spaulding, 1957, p. 200.)

It seems possible, indeed probable, that the Old Copper sites along the Keweenaw waterway antedate the maximum level of the Nipissing stage water plane in this area.

Recent evidence on the Houghton low-water stage of Lake Superior and the climatic conditions in immediately pre-Nipissing time has been presented by Peter A. Hyypio of the University of Michigan and Farrand (no date) and is briefly described by Farrand (1960). In connection with the construction of a new bridge now in use between Houghton and Hancock, borings "disclosed a thick sequence of unconsolidated materials overlying bedrock and a very deep bedrock channel which bisects the Keweenaw Peninsula." A layer of red organic silt which contains an appreciable quantity of organic matters occurs near the top of the unconsolidated sequence and extends across Portage Lake between Houghton and Hancock and is about 6 feet thick. It lies about 60 feet below the water level of Portage Lake and Lake Superior. This organic silt layer is at the top of the sedimentary sequence but is overlain in places by red sand and silt with traces of wood fragments. Below the layer is a complex sequence of sand, gravel, boulders, and clay in the form of poorly sorted outwash and probably till over 40 feet thick.

The pollen studies by Hyypio were from five samples from four test holes and were from depths from 60 to 70 feet below the present water level of Portage Lake and Lake Superior. Two samples from one hole at 60 and 65 feet afford some stratigraphic control. The two samples studied (as were the other three) were of red silt and contained 106 and 218 grains, respectively, of arboreal pollen. Hyypio interprets the percentages as indicating the lower sample at 65 feet was deposited during a pine-birch-hemlock period with small percentage of fir, alder, tamarack, spruce, willow, elm, and basswood. The upper sample at 60 feet in the small core contains no elm, basswood, or fir; shows a decline in birch, alder, willow, and spruce; a marked decline in hemlock and a very strong rise in pine. This is interpreted as indicating a shift from a relatively warm period to one of increased cold. Since the Nipissing beach at Houghton of about

2200 B.C. is at an elevation of 628 feet, the location of the peat is at a position of 85 to 90 feet below the Nipissing beach. The time period then must be before 2200 B.C., and may be about equivalent to the age of a peat deposit from near one of the Apostle Islands to the west.

Samples of peat from a location one and one-half miles west of Sand Island, Bayfield County, Wisconsin, were studied by L. Wilson (1935) both macro- and microscopically. The samples were obtained beneath fourteen feet of lake bottom sand and under forty feet of water. The level of the peat bed is about 60 feet below the Nipissing beach which has an elevation of 609 feet in this area of Lake Superior. Since one large section of the peat was about 4 inches thick it was arbitrarily separated into three levels which do show significantly different pollen percentages. Wilson interpreted the sequence as beginning with a high proportion of spruce, relatively low in pine and fir, birch slightly higher than fir and with minor counts of oak, maple, and alder. The middle level has a marked drop in spruce and fir and a marked rise in birch, while pine shows a relative rise. The top layer has a pine maximum, a rise in spruce and a marked decline in birch; white oak and alder are not represented. Wilson recognized the plant assemblage as typical of the Canadian zone and that the peat deposit he had to study was not the pioneer vegetation of the area.

The Sand Island peat has been dated at 5000 ± 150 (L-605), (personal communication, W. R. Farrand). Both pollen profiles, at Sand Island and Houghton bridge indicate minor climatic shifts which occurred before the period of maximum warmth of the rise to the Nipissing stage. The exact correlation and interpretation of these fluctuations in the pollen profiles is not clearly understood and additional pollen cores closely dated by C-14 is indicated.

In Packard's (1893, pp. 183-84) paper on Pre-Columbian Copper Mining he has a most interesting quotation from a letter by J. H. Forster on the discoveries made in connection with the building of the ship canal during the latter part of the nineteenth century:

> In connection with these last remarks by Mr. Houghton, I beg to state that while I was State engineer on the Portage Lake and Lake Superior Ship Canal, the superintendent in laying water pipes opened a very old grave. The grave was in the yellow sand, in a grove of Norway pines, near Lake Superior. At the bottom there was an exceedingly thin layer of mold, darker than the sand. Some human teeth were found and a string of copper beads strung on sinews. The sinews, much decayed, still held

the beads in place. The copper bead was a small thin piece of copper about one-fourth of an inch long. It was rudely bent into a cylinder for the string to pass through, but was not welded; the edges were in contact, but not fastened together. This grave was at the Grand Portage or carrying place.

In dredging, the dipper brought up from the bed of the ship canal where the sand drift had originally been at least 25 feet deep, several perfect stone hammers and a copper implement which I pronounced to have been the head and ferule of a pike pole. It was about 18 inches long, tapering, sharp, and solid for two-thirds the distance from the small or lower end. At the upper or pole-end the copper had been flattened out and then bent round to form a socket for the pole. There was a slight opening between the two edges of the curved copper; it was not joined or welded. The pike was bright and shining like a clean copper kettle.

I saw it, and it was dredged from the bottom of the canal, and its position, as regards strata, was under the drift or dune sand and on the hard gravel and clay underlying. I know of no other finds in that section. The gravel and hard pan found in the bottom of the dredged canal I regarded as the bed of the ancient stream or estuary, now filled up with drift sand blown in from Lake Superior. How much the glacial drift had to do in filling up the ancient gorge in which the present canal is only a line, I can not say. In some of the marshes cut by the canal were found three distinct forests, one growing on top of the other, to a depth of 14 feet.

In October of 1958, a brief archaeological reconnaissance of the Huron Mountain Club land in Marquette County, Michigan, was undertaken by Quimby, Winston Elting, and James R. Getz. The Lake Superior shorelines at Pine River, Conway, and Salmon Trout Bays were searched for sites without success. However, Mr. William P. Harris, Jr. kindly allowed us to examine a spearpoint, or knife, of chipped stone, that he had found previously in the Lake Superior beach sands near his cottage by the mouth of Pine River.

This knife, or point, is about 9 cm long and about 3.5 cm wide in its broadest part. It has a wide stem and weak shoulders. The point is made of yellow-brown flint or chalcedony that is translucent and contains opaque inclusions. On typological grounds the point seems representative of Late Archaic or Early Woodland culture and probably belongs to some time interval between 1000 B.C. and 300 B.C. It is possible that this artifact is somewhat younger because the type of flint or chalcedony of which the blade or point was made was popular and apparently traded rather extensively in Middle Woodland times about 300 B.C. to A.D. 400. The form of this artifact, however, suggests the earlier period.

Although this point or blade was found on an eroding beach it does not show signs of wear by water, so probably it had not been long exposed when collected by Harris. The locus of the point and its probable age implies that when it originally was deposited the Lake Superior shore was much farther lakeward than now.

The absence of protohistoric and historic sites along the shores of Pine River, Conway, and Salmon Trout Bays suggests that relatively recent erosion has destroyed the old shore line. Some confirmation of this idea is offered by the present position of the shore line in relation to the ruins of the old E. J. Rasmussen homestead in Conway Bay. Wave action there has cut the terrace right into the foundation ruins of the old house. Mr. Winston Elting remembers that, when he was a boy, the homestead was at least 50 feet from the edge of the terrace. It looks as if the shore line in Conway Bay is cutting back into the land at a rate of about 100 feet per century and probably this, or a similar rate, holds for many places on the south shore of Lake Superior.

The most interesting find in the Huron Mountain Club area was a crude scraper found by James R. Getz on the crest of the Nipissing beach ridge on the west side of the Salmon Trout valley near the road leading into the Huron Mountain Club. The elevation is 630 feet above sea level. This crude artifact is a core-type scraper made of massive quartz. It is ovate in outline and lenticular in section, about 5.5 cm long, 4.5 cm wide, and 2 cm thick. On typological grounds this scraper seems to be representative of Late Archaic or Early Woodland.

Within twenty-five feet of the locus of the quartz scraper there was a hearth manifested by fire-cracked rocks. Excavation around and beneath these rocks revealed sections of burned earth and flecks of charcoal, but no artifacts.

In the summer of 1955, Dr. Albert C. Spaulding visited the locus of an interesting find of copper near Grand Marais, Alger County, Michigan. The find is significant because it included a leaf-shaped copper point with tang and a somewhat similar bone point with a longer tang.

The locus of this find is 95 to 100 feet above Lake Superior at the level of a cobble beach and old cedar swamp. Most of this level is now covered by active sand dunes but some small areas near the brink of the wave-cut, 100-foot-high cliff have been windswept of sand.

In the summer of 1959, G. I. Quimby assisted by Edward Quimby dug some small test pits into the cedar swamp level where it was exposed by shifting sands. The upper two feet of this level is a dense, peaty mixture of silt and sand interspersed with roots and twigs. It would probably be easy to obtain pollen samples from this brownish soil. The beach cobbles seem to lie on top of this deposit.

J. B. Griffin and M. L. Papworth also visited the site of this find (Section 2, or 3, township 49 N, Range 14 W) in the summer of 1959. From Charles Mattson of Grand Marais they obtained the artifacts found here and deposited them in the Museum of Anthropology of the University of Michigan (Pl. XXVII, Fig. 1).

The copper knife is 10.4 cm long and 2.3 cm wide. One edge is less concave than the other, and the short tang comes to a point. The greatest thickness is in the midline and is .5 cm. The bone point is now 13.3 cm long, 2.4 cm wide and .5 cm thick. The point has suffered severely from exposure on the sand dune. This bone point is one of the few such forms preserved. It is the type of bone artifact which has been regarded as a prototype of the copper rat-tailed points. It was made from a rib section of a large herbivore. Mattson also kindly turned over two fragmentary flint points to the Museum of Anthropology—both are highly polished from sand blasting, including the surfaces where sections were broken away from the points. The side-notched point with the broken tip has a markedly thinned and convex basal edge with some retouching.

OLD COPPER SPECIMENS FROM NEAR BROCKVILLE, ONTARIO

One of the easternmost finds of Old Copper implements, and also one of the earliest to be called to the attention of archaeologists, are those illustrated in Squier and Davis (1848, p. 201) from near Brockville, Ontario. The most complete description of this find is given by Reynolds (1856). His account follows. The drawings of the implements are based on those in the above-mentioned sources and from Wilson (1865):

> In excavating the St. Lawrence Canal, at Les Galops Rapids, in the year 1847, a curious collection of Indian relics was brought to light, at one of the beautifully picturesque points on the River St. Lawrence, at the head of the first rapid, or cascade, met with in descending that river. Thus situated at a point where the free navigation of the upper part of the river is first interrupted, this place is likely to have been frequently visited in former times, as a spot where both Indians and voyageurs would be tempted to rest, or camp for the night, before venturing their canoes upon the rapids; and this may perhaps have had to do with the deposition of the relics, discovered in the process of excavating the Canal destined to overcome the impediments which nature had there opposed to the free navigation of the noble river.
>
> The following description of such of the relics as have come into my possession, will serve, with the aid of the accompanying illustrations, to convey some idea of their various forms and special characteristics. The most massive of the copper implements, figured here, is an instrument in which will be observed a hollow or socket for a handle: the back, which is here represented, being convex, corresponding to the opposite concavity. [Pl. XXIII, Fig. 4.] The chisel-shaped termination is now blunt, but it retains sufficient indications of its having originally had a sharp edge. This instrument might perhaps answer the purpose of a chisel or gouge for hollowing out wood; but I was struck at first sight of it, with the resemblance it bears to the coulter, or point, of the old Jewish plough. The precise use for which it was designed can now only be surmised; and this might be an interesting matter for further inquiry, as one means calculated to throw light on questions in connexion with the origin of the native American tribes. The subject has been reverted to in relation to another discovery of copper relics found about the same time as those now described, at Penetanguishene, and the speculations thus originated, even if they lead to no very definite or practical results, are at least curious, and suggestive of interesting reflections.
>
> The dimensions of this ancient implement are six inches in length, fully two inches in breadth at the edge, and two and four-fifths at the broadest part of the socket. A second object may be described as a copper knife, of full size, with the edge still tolerably sharp, and bearing marks of considerable use. The point was broken off when it was first discovered; and the handle, which must have been of wood or some other material less durable than the metal blade, had yielded to the ravages of

time. In its present mutilated state this instrument measures five inches and three quarters long, and when the blade was perfect was probably not less than eight inches in length. [Pl. XXIII, Fig. 3.]

A third implement, figured here, may be described as a knife, or small dagger, nearly five inches long, and with a hooked extremity, as represented in the annexed wood-cut, designed to serve some unknown purpose of Indian domestic economy, or convenience in war or the chase. This, it may be assumed, was used without any handle attached to it, whatever may have been the purpose to which it was applied. (Pl. XXIII, Fig. 5.]

The fourth copper instrument is a knife or dagger upwards of seven inches in length, including the narrow end for insertion in the haft [Pl. XXIII, Fig. 2]; and the fifth, which is here figured, is a spear head, rudely hammered out of the native copper, and presenting unmistakeable evidence of its having been brought to its present shape by the hammer, and entirely without the agency of fire. After being wrought, by means of the hammer, into the rude form of a spear-head, the broad end has been overlapped as shown in the wood-cut, and roughly hammered to the desired shape, so as to provide it with a short narrow prolongation intended to fit into a handle, or to be secured to it by means of a cord or ligature, though it must have very imperfectly answered the purpose [Pl. XXIII, Fig. 1]. This spear-head is of considerable thickness, and not much corroded. It is still pointed, and tolerable sharp on both edges; and, imperfect as it seems, was probably a weapon of no slight importance and value among the braves in olden times.

In addition to these weapons and implements of copper, I have in my possession a small pipe mouth-piece, found along with them, measuring an inch and a quarter in length, made of the celebrated Indian red pipe-stone; and also a miniature clay mask, figured here, (though with less minute accuracy, than would have been desirable) about one half the diameter of the original [Pl. XXIII, Fig. 6]. It is in some respects a tolerably fair representation of the Indian skull, from which one might fancy it to have been copied. In its shape it struck me as resembling the appearance presented by the skulls found in the same place; and the hollow sockets of the eyes, though doubtless designed only to imitate the Indian masks, were assumed, on its being first found, to prove that it was meant as a representation of the bony structure of the head, and not the fleshy or living subject. This relic I presume is the head of an Indian idol or household god, modeled by the warrior-artist as a charm or protection in battle, or in the other trials and dangers to which he might be exposed. It is imperfect, having been broken off, some additional piece of workmanship, to which it was attached by the piece partially shown in the wood-cut, projecting behind; but it has no perforation or other indication such as would have shewn its use had it originally formed part of a pipe, which the Indians frequently shaped into a human or animal's head. . . .

All these relics were found at a depth of about fourteen or fifteen feet below the surface, in a soil composed of clay and sand. The shore at the point of land, which is considerably washed by the action of the rapid stream, presents a face of large granite boulders with quartz conglomerate—a fitting resting place for the stalwart forms of a score of skeletons, which were found inhumed in a circular space with their feet towards the centre. Some of the skeletons were of gigantic proportions. The lower jaw of one is in my possession, and is sufficiently large to surround the corresponding bone of an adult of our present generation. The condition of the bones furnished indisputable proof of their great antiquity. The skulls were so completely reduced to their earthy constituents that they were exceedingly brittle and fell in pieces when removed and exposed to the atmosphere. The metallic remains however, of more enduring material, as also, several stone chisels, gouges made of the same durable material, and probably designed for tapping the sugar maple, and some flint arrow heads, all remain in their original condition, and furnish evidence of the same rude arts which we know to be still practiced by the aborigines of the far west. A few yards distant from this spot, and at about the same depth from the surface, another circular place of sepulture was exposed to view; but here the organic remains had been subjected to the action of fire, and the charred and partly consumed bones, with the charcoal ashes, bore testimony to the fact that the decomposition which time and the action of their mother earth would have produced, had been anticipated by the hand of man and his use of the fiery element.

In another section of his article Thomas Reynolds expresses the opinion that his specimens seem to confirm: "that the Indians possessed the art of hardening and tempering copper, so as to give it as good an edge as iron or steel. This ancient Indian art is now entirely lost." As a result of this belief, to which Daniel Wilson of the University College, Toronto, did not subscribe, the implements were turned over for analysis to a chemist, Henry Croft, also of University College. His report, quoted below, is one of the earliest to be made on Old Copper specimens. It should be noted that the myth of the Indian art of tempering copper is still with us today:

A collection of ancient copper implements, dug up on the banks of the River St. Lawrence, in the vicinity of Brockville, having been transmitted, by Dr. Thomas Reynolds, for exhibition before the Canadian Institute, along with various other relics of native art found at the same time; that gentleman accompanied them with a communication, containing remarks on the peculiar condition of the copper, as indicative of a supposed art of hardening and tempering the metal, which is assumed to have been in use by its ancient native workers, but to be now lost. From the allusions made to this same lost art of native metallurgy in a previous communication, the subject was remitted to me to report upon, with special reference to the Brockville relics, which were put into my hands for the purpose of experiment and analysis.

The object of the following experiments, accordingly, was to ascertain whether the metal of which these implements are made is identical with the native copper of the Lake Superior Mines, or whether it had been subjected to some manufacturing process, or mixed with any other substance, by which its hardness might have been increased. A careful examination establishes the conclusions here stated:

1stly. No perceptible difference could be observed in the hardness of the implements, and of metallic copper from Lake Superior.

2ndly. The knife or small dagger, with a hook at the end, was cleansed as far as possible from its green coating;

It weighed	32.440 grammes.
It lost in water	3.741 "
Hence its specific gravity is	8.66 "

A small fragment, broken off the end of the broad, flat implement, described as a "copper knife of full size," having been freed from its coating, was found to have a specific gravity of 8.58.

During the cleaning of this fragment, a few brilliant white specks became visible on its surface; they appeared to be silver, from their colour and lustre. The structure of the metal was also highly laminated, as if the instrument had been brought to its present shape by hammering out a solid mass of copper, which had either split up or had been originally formed of several pieces. These laminae, of course, contained air, and the metal was covered with rust, which could not be removed,—hence the specific gravity would naturally be less than if the metal had been dense.

It is probable that the structure of the dagger previously referred to, is the same; but as the coating of oxide, which could not be removed, would have more effect on the small fragment, which weighed only about three grammes, than on the larger dagger blade, the specific gravity of the latter was found to be rather higher.

A portion of very solid copper, from Lake Superior, of about the same weight as the fragment, was weighed in water, and its gravity found to be 8.92; in this piece there were no cavities perceptible.

The specific gravity of absolutely pure copper, varies from 8.78 to 8.96, according to the greater or less degree of aggregation it has received during its manufacture;

Hooked dagger	8.66	
Fragment	8.58	
Native copper	8.92	
Pure copper	8.78	8.96

The small differences between these numbers would lead to the conclusion that the implements were made of pure copper.

The fragment was completely dissolved by nitric acid; and the solution, on being tested for silver by hydrochloric acid, gave a scarcely perceptible opacity, indicating the presence of an exceedingly minute trace of silver. The copper having been separated by hydro-sulphuric acid, the residual liquid was tested for other metals. A very minute trace of iron was detected.

The native copper from Lake Superior was tested in the same manner, and was found to contain no trace of silver, but a minute trace of iron, the quantity being apparently about the same as in the fragment.

From this, it appears that the implements are composed of copper almost pure, differing in no material respect from the native copper of Lake Superior, and not of an alloy of that metal, with any other substance.

It is not by any means probable, from the conclusions resulting from the experiments detailed above, that these implements could have been hardened by any mechanical means; and no process is known at present by which copper can be rendered harder, although its density may of course be increased to a small extent by pressure and hammering. (Croft, 1856, pp. 334-36.)

This find is important not only because of its geographic location in eastern Ontario but also because the account by Reynolds indicates that these Old Copper pieces were in association with stone woodworking tools, projectile points, and burials of what would now be regarded as a Laurentian or "Boreal Archaic" complex. This association with stone gouges, and with cremations (?) is significant in terms of the probable period of 2000 to 1000 B.C. when the "Les Galops Rapids" finds were deposited.

There are some unusual features to this early recovery of Old Copper implements. The first is the depth beneath the surface which was stated to be from fourteen to fifteen feet. It is supposed here that some amount of this overburden was alluvial deposit over an old land surface into which the burials had been intruded. The small pipe mouthpiece of "Indian red pipe-stone" can be interpreted as a section of a tubular pipe of Ohio pipestone and not Minnesota catlinite which is not known to have been used at the time period of the copper implements. This supposition is strengthened by the finds downstream north of Massena, New York, where three blocked-end tube pipes of Ohio pipestone were excavated in 1881 (Ritchie and Dragoo, 1960). These pipes, however, were associated with a later burial complex of an estimated age of approximately the beginning of our era. The real puzzle, however, is the clay head reported by Reynolds. If it is clay, it must be presumed to have been fired in order to have been preserved. If such is the case it would be the earliest known effigy head of clay. If both the clay head and tubular pipe were valid associations with copper specimens it would mean that the copper forms would be near their minimum age.

Another possibility is that the clay head is an Iroquoian piece for it seems to be stylistically Iroquoian. If that is the case, then the pipestem may be catlinite of the early historic period. We would then have to assume that the collection obtained by Reynolds was not from one deposit and that the pipe and effigy were not found with the Old Copper forms. It is not likely that an Iroquoian group would have come across the copper pieces and reburied them.

This find is also of importance because some of the archaeologists in the northeastern United States have felt that the copper artifacts found in New York and New England were made from local copper sources. These specimens, however, with their striking similarity to Old Copper forms of the Upper Great Lakes and because of the presence of silver in the copper were probably traded or carried from that area to the upper St. Lawrence Valley.

COPPER ARTIFACTS FROM MANITOBA

The location and distribution of copper artifacts in Manitoba is one of the important areas for reasonable interpretations of the temporal position of the Old Copper culture and for its correlation with other cultural complexes. The information given below and the illustrations in Plates XXVIII and XXIX have been provided by a number of Canadian students of archaeology. Some ten years ago Mrs. P. H. Stokes of Winnipeg began a correspondence with me about the important excavations and collections of a group of amateur archaeologists in the Winnipeg area. The work of this group provided the background and stimulus for a publication on this area by the National Museum of Canada (MacNeish, 1958). Mr. and Mrs. Stokes came to Ann Arbor in 1957 and were asked to gather data on copper finds in Manitoba. On their return to Winnipeg they enlisted the help of Peter Grant, who, in turn, had the valuable co-operation of R. W. Sutton, Curator of the Manitoba Museum. Grant sent to me, in July, 1957, the information he had obtained, with outline drawings of the artifacts, some measurements, and some provenience data. The outline drawings in this publication are copies made from those sent by Grant.

It is unfortunate that a comprehensive analysis of the Lake Agassiz-Lake Winnipeg Basin has not been published which could form the physiographic background against which to interpret the time period at which it would have been possible for Indian groups to enter the area. Elson (1957) has provided a valuable summary of his interpretations of the post-Pleistocene history of the area. He observes that the upper beach of Lake Agassiz I was probably formed during the retreat of the ice from the Port Huron-Mankato moraines of about 10,500 B.C. Lake Agassiz I was drained during the Two Creek interval of about 9500 B.C., during which time the Agassiz I basin was invaded by praire flora. Lake Agassiz II was formed by the Valders ice advance which blocked the eastward drainage outlets and the water level rose until it found an outlet over the alluvial fan at Browns Valley. This fan was formed during the Agassiz I-II interval. When the Browns Valley alluvial fan was eroded, the level of the lake reached an equilibrium to form the lower Campbell beach and the presence of Agate Basin and Plainview points, which have been found in association with this stand (Elson, p. 1001), suggest an age for it of approximately 8000 to 5000 B.C. There followed a series of eastward outlets into Lake Nipigon and from there to Lake Superior. With the continuing ice retreat to the northeast of Lake Agassiz II, lower outlets were opened into "incipient" Hudson Bay, and finally Lake Agassiz II was drained by way of the Nelson River Basin into Hudson Bay. Elson has dated this final drainage to roughly the present Lake Winnipeg-Lake Manitoba stand as taking place before 1600 B.C., partly because the earliest projectile forms on the former Agassiz II Basin are of the same type as those found in the early levels of Signal Butte in western Nebraska and the McKean points of the Dakotas (MacNeish, 1958, p. 78).

The preceding resumé is pertinent to the dating of the Old Copper complex and its associations. While we do not have sufficient controls on the location or elevation of the copper finds in Manitoba it seems to be obvious that most of the points identified as being from the Lake Winnipeg-Lake Manitoba area could not have been in the area until some time after Lake Agassiz II was drained. The exact time at which this occurred is not known but it could have been between 5000 to 2000 B.C. Elson's interpretation and the dates available to him would have placed the final drainage close to the 2000 B.C. figure, but recent developments in the study of the Hudson Bay marine intrusion suggests that this occurred about 5500 B.C. (Lee, 1959, 1960). This could mean that the drainage through the Nelson River of Lake Agassiz II into Hudson Bay could have taken place substantially earlier than Elson postulated. The archaeological evidence, so far obtained, indicates that hunting bands did not occupy the area of southern Manitoba in the Lake Agassiz II Basin until 2000 B.C., or slightly later. The intrusion of peoples with McKean-style projectile points suggests that this was done from prairie areas to the south, into a prairie vegetation zone which occupied the old lake basin. Since the Old Copper culture is primarily associated with a forest ecology the appearance of the copper forms may be associated with the westward and northern spread of the forest into the former Lake Agassiz II basin. According to the interpretation favored by Griffin, the Old Copper culture, while possibly in existence between 3000-2000 B.C., did not reach its height until between 2000-1000 B.C. The interpretation adopted here, therefore, is that the copper points from Manitoba represent a movement or dispersal of socketed forms into the area around 1500 to 1000 B.C., and that the flat points probably came into the area between 1000 to 500 B.C.

In addition to the finds illustrated on Plates XXVIII and XXIX, Peter Grant wrote that a copper point 10 inches long had been found near Swan River, Manitoba, which is on the river by that name west of Lake Winnipegosis, and near the Saskatchewan border. It is the most northern reference now available. A copper point from Lac du Bonnet, northeast of Winnipeg was also mentioned by Grant. These finds are all apparently the result of surface collection or accidental finds. None of them are the result of excavation so that there are no associated materials from which to form a judgment as to the probable temporal placement of the copper.

In September, Mrs. Stokes wrote that she had visited the Riding Mountain National Park Museum at Wasagaming, Manitoba, and had seen a copper axe there with a badly battered butt. This axe is catalogued as specimen No. 291 and, according to the Museum records, was found at the town of Riding Mountain. The axe is illustrated on Plate XXVI, Fig. 1. In an earlier letter, July, 1957, Mrs. Stokes mentioned "a copper tool" found near Wawanesa in southwest Manitoba about 15 miles east of the Pembina ridge. Like all other surveys of the distribution of prehistoric artifacts this one is probably incomplete. For example, Rithzenthaler (1960) has published an illustration of an Old Copper crescent knife from 150 miles north of Calgary, Alberta. It may be expected, however, that the spatial coverage now indicated would include forms found earlier, but for which no record is available, and objects to be found in the future. Through the efforts of Mrs. Stokes and Grant the western extension of prehistoric copper forms is published for the first time (Map 5).

INTERPRETATION OF TECHNOLOGY AND CULTURAL LEVEL FROM THE COPPER PITS AND INCLUDED MATERIALS

Any attempt to assess the cultural level of the peoples who engaged in prehistoric mining in the Lake Superior deposits is made unusually difficult because of the numerous factors. Copper mining apparently was carried on from about 3000 B.C., at least, to close, or up to the historic period—roughly 4500 years. During this long time period the cultural equipment and cultural level of the Indians in the Lake Superior area changed in a number of significant features. The cultural complexes of Indian groups to the south in the United States changed even more. As is indicated in the accounts of people who have surveyed the Keweenaw and Isle Royale areas, there were thousands of copper pits but only a score or so were investigated by individuals who have reported on what they saw and found. Some of the writers, such as Whittlesey, Davis, and Winchell have provided fairly adequate descriptions and, in some cases, illustrations of what they found. We do not, however, know the time period at which many of these reported objects were produced, whether they are 4000 years old, or 400 years old. There is also no reason to believe that the objects and culture traits annotated below are contemporaneous. We are not, therefore, presenting items from a single group of people who conducted mining within a short period of time.

The water-logged condition of many of the pits allowed the preservation of a number of wooden implements which were briefly described and some illustrated. None of these are now available for comparative study. From the Keweenaw area Whittlesey described a 3 1/2-foot-long wooden paddle or shovel made of white cedar and reported that several of these had been found on the property of the Waterbury Company. There was a wooden paddle or shovel reported from the McCargoe Cove area on Isle Royale. Although only a foot length remained of its handle it was apparently similar to those from Keweenaw. Additional wooden shovels or paddles came from the Owl Creek mine on Keweenaw. A large wooden bowl or scoop was found in a pit in the Minong area of Isle Royale and other wooden bowls were taken from pits on the Keweenaw Peninsula. These were apparently used in bailing water from the pits.

Gilman reports finds of copper knives in the debris thrown out of pits on Isle Royale, and copper "arrowheads" from the vicinity of pits and "scattered over the island." One of his references is to a copper sheet "bowl-like utensil" which he did not illustrate and remains a unique reference. From the mainland area, copper spearheads, knives, and chisels were found associated with mines and mining debris. The forms of these copper implements are those of the Old Copper culture. Some were found under trees with an estimated age of 700 to 800 years.

There are a few references to leather-working. One is to rawhide strands, perhaps from caribou, and even to a leather bag. Whittlesey speaks of axe marks on timbers used as skids for a large copper mass which were about 2 1/2 inches wide. Some of these timbers were of "Spanish" oak. One oak timber is spoken of as a rude ladder with the branch stumps for steps. Other timbers were used as levers.

Hammerstones were the most common implement, as might be expected. These vary considerably in size, type of rock used, and in whether they had been grooved. Some proportion of those from the Keweenaw area were grooved, and at least one was found which was double grooved. Still another was recovered with a cedar root twisted around the groove as a handle. Only a very few of the hammerstones on Isle Royale were grooved. Some individuals who have examined the Isle Royale hammerstones have suggested that they were transported by man from the north shore of Lake Superior. The inference being that the Isle Royale miners must have come from the north shore, transported a considerable tonnage of rocks from there, and were a "different" group from the miners on the south shore of the Lake. The opinion of other scholars, such as Dustin, is preferred, however, for they have demonstrated that the Isle Royale hammers were obtained from local sources of ice transported and water-rolled stones.

From such evidence as we have, it can be said that during the mining activities of some of the prehistoric Indians they utilized some skill in woodworking. This was evidenced by trees which were cut down, the use of timbers for a variety of purposes, the shaping of paddles or scoops, the manufacture of wooden bowls, the production of spear projectile point shafts, the probable development of boats which were most likely of the canoe type rather than the dugout. In the gradual development of prehistoric technology in the Eastern United States the appearance of grooved axes, adzes, and gouges is part of the Late Archaic cultural complex of about 3000 to 1000 B.C. Such large woodworking tools had their main development during this period in the area south of the Great Lakes and south of the St. Lawrence.

It is a reasonable assumption that the Old Copper complex in the Lake Superior Basin is a regional representative of this Late Archaic period. As has been indicated above (pp. 13-14) the trees which are represented in the pits by leaves or wood fragments include spruce, cedar, red oak, oak (sp?), maple, Norway pine, and birch. The hardwood trees, part of a mixed coniferous-hardwood forest, would probably not have reached the Keweenaw area in their northward migration until shortly before 3000 B.C., according to current interpretations of pollen diagrams for the Wisconsin, Michigan, Isle Royale area. They would have reached and developed in the Lake Superior area at the same time as the development of the Late Archaic culture complex.

COMMENTS ON CURRENT AND RECENT "FOLKLORE" AND MISCONCEPTIONS ABOUT THE LAKE SUPERIOR PREHISTORIC COPPER AND THE AREA IN GENERAL

There are an unknown number of ideas which have either been presented in print or by word of mouth about the use of copper by prehistoric and historic Indians which deserve special treatment in this compilation. This is not presented with a naïve hope that such misconceptions will thus be completely eliminated, but perhaps some of the people now, and in the future, will be able to make a choice between reasonably sound data and clearly erroneous, sometimes fraudulent, and otherwise unsound interpretations.

1. The Indians, or a vanished prehistoric "race" of non-Indians, had the "secret" of tempering copper so that the copper implements were harder than steel, or iron.

This would indeed be a "secret." Copper can not be "tempered." In metallurgy, particularly in the steel industry, the term "temper" may refer to the process used to bring steel to a proper hardness or toughness, to the amount of carbon included in the steel, or to the physical state of the metal. Temper is also employed for a variety of other meanings, such as an alloy added to a metal to procure certain changes, or foreign particles added to clay in pottery manufacture. The utilitarian copper artifacts of the Great Lakes area were hardened by the Indians by means of forging.

2. The copper projectiles, knives, and axes were cast, indicating an advanced metallurgical technique.

No competent metallurgist who has worked with a respected or competent archaeologist has ever reached this conclusion. This idea is almost always brought out or supported by individuals who have other "axes to grind" than the prehistoric copper axes. Such ideas usually appear in the writing of individuals who are trying to prove that European, "Phoenicians," or some other "civilized" and usually, "white men" must have visited North America and passed on their metallurgical skill to the Indians. It will probably be a long time before such myths completely die out. While this subject has been raised, a few more observations will be made along this general line.

For many years the known contact of the Norse along the east coast of North America during the Middle Ages has helped spur a welter of unsound claims of Norse settlements, armor, mooring holes, words introduced into Indian dialects, stone towers, and the genuineness of curiosa such as the Kensington Stone. It can be categorically stated that there are no Norse, or other European settlements, artifacts, boat landings, or runic inscriptions known to have preceded the soundly documented arrival and penetration of North America during the sixteenth and seventeenth centuries. A recent superb comprehensive review of the Kensington Stone (Wahlgren, 1958) makes clear that what originally started as a relatively innocent operation by local Scandinavians in Minnesota in the 1890's was later turned into thousands of words of misdirected scholarship and has misled those people who were either anxious to believe or to have faith in the printed word. The Beardmore find of Norse armor north of Lake Superior excited considerable interest some years ago; but it is now known to have been a complete "plant" by the individual who "found" them (Olson, 1957). There are claims made by individuals, and even organized groups in the United States, that elements of high achievements in culture were introduced into Middle America by voyagers from the Mediterranean which account for the striking development of prehistoric Mexican culture and for the northward spread of such introduced ideas (Verrill and Verrill, 1953). This is a complex and complete fabrication which has no support from competent interpreters of American archaeology.

3. The "Mysterious Mound Builders" were an ancient, civilized group of people who occupied the Mississippi and Ohio Valley's, journeyed to Lake Superior, mined the copper, and then returned to their homes to the south.

The myth of the "Mound Builders" as a superior group of non-Indians who were driven out by the barbarous historic redskins developed during the nineteenth century in popular and even in scientific literature. By the end of the last century, however, it was clearly demonstrated by archaeological research that there were a number of different prehistoric cultural groups who built a variety of earthen mounds, that these groups were the ancestors of the historic Indians and that many historic Indian tribes were building and occupying certain types of mounds. More recent archaeological work and more precise means of dating indicate that the earliest known burial mounds were built about 1000 B.C., reached their height of complexity about 2000 years ago and that the earthen platform mound used as a base for important building construction is known from about A.D. 700 to 1700. Much of the copper mining and most of the Old Copper culture clearly precedes, in time, any prehistoric builders of mounds. The cultural items found in the Lake Superior area, either in association with the pits or on the known village sites are not those of more advanced prehistoric groups to the south, but are representative local complexes of several different time periods.

4. The concept of metallurgy and the copper implement forms were introduced from Northeast Asia as part of a circum-boreal or circumpolar culture spread.

This interpretation depends on rather specialized knowledge and so is not found very often in popular accounts. It is occasionally found in anthropological writings in little-read journals or other publication form comparable to this paper. There are some general, but never very precise, formal similarities between some Asiatic bronze forms and some American copper implements or ornaments. Bronze spread into southern Siberia from the west and southwest by about 2000 to 1500 B.C. (Loehr, 1956, p. 112). A further eastward penetration of metallurgy into the Lena Valley is considerably later and is, by that time, clearly connected to the developing Chinese metal complexes. There are no clear indications of a northward and eastern spread of either copper or bronze forms into northeastern Asia or into northwestern North America which would account for the development of the Old Copper complex in the Great Lakes area.

The only possible intrusion from Asia of a copper (bronze?) ornament into Alaska is a double-ended spiral form from Dixthada, Upper Tanana Valley, Alaska (Rainey, 1939, p. 367). From time to time over the last ten years I have called this to the attention of various archaeologists who were interested in the Arctic area. No one, however, seems to be particularly excited about it. Rainey referred to it as being made of copper and as being a nose or ear ornament. The double-ended spiral is a specific artifact form which is common in Danubian II and other cultures of Europe about 2500 B.C. It reaches the Upper Yenisei Valley in south-central Siberia during the Andronovo intrusion to the east which is dated to about 1500 B.C. (Gaul, 1943, p. 162; Gimbutas, 1957, p. 166). This movement, or diffusion of metal artifacts of copper-bronze into southern Siberia is the first time such items appear. The known beginnings of copper forms and mining in the Lake Superior basin thus precedes the southwestern and central Siberian metals, and also precedes the known use of metals in western South America. It is clearly an independent development.

5. Isle Royale native copper is distinctive in the Lake Superior area because it is combined with silver.

Actually, silver is associated with copper from various localities in the Lake Superior area, and Isle Royale is not at all distinctive in this respect. Copper and silver artifacts from Illinois or Ohio cannot be identified as being specifically derived from Isle Royale deposits.

6. Copper from the Lake Superior area was traded to the American Southwest and to Mexico.

There is no proved occurrence of Lake Superior copper in either the Southwest or Mexico. Metallurgy was not known in Middle America until it was introduced in an advanced form from South America about A.D. 700. From western Mexico cast copper ornaments were traded into the Southwest. None of these forms are known to have reached the Mississippi Valley. There is no contact between these two quite different types of utilizing copper.

7. The Indians would not have been able to canoe to Isle Royale.

There are early French accounts, by eyewitnesses, that they did paddle across the lake from the Keweenaw Peninsula to the Island. Much of this volume is devoted to demonstrate that the Island was occupied periodically by Indian groups for about 5000 years. By the late prehistoric period the variety of Indian pottery shows that Indians from both Canada and Michigan were on the Island.

8. The early historic Indians knew about the copper but were too superstitious to go near the copper deposits and would not mine it.

While there are such accounts in the historic literature there are others which clearly state that the Indians not only knew of the deposits in the main copper formation around Lake Superior but there are also indications that some mining was being done. The presence of copper artifacts in the village sites of very late prehistoric and early historic Indian groups in the Michigan, Superior, and Huron basins is adequate testimony that such groups were obtaining copper. The "market" for copper which developed among the Indians in the Mississippi Valley and in the Southeast from A.D. 900 to 1500 was destroyed by the marked changes in population density and social structure which took place between A.D. 1500 to 1700 as a result of European commercial and military influences, and by disease. This probably had an effect on mining activity around Lake Superior between A.D. 1630 and 1700 when the French were writing about the area.

ARCHAEOLOGY AND SOME METALLURGICAL INVESTIGATIVE TECHNIQUES

Roy W. Drier [1]

Experience has indicated that cross fertilization of archeological techniques with analytical and investigative techniques of other disciplines is constructively fruitful in many instances. The success of carrying the Carbon 14 dating method over into the archeological fields was such that it encouraged further attempts to apply other techniques to archeological problems.

Chemical methods have frequently been used to attack archeological problems. William Foster (1934) used chemical analysis to investigate Grecian and Roman stucco, mortar, and glass. The *Journal of Chemical Education* describes chemical disiplines used in the study of Mayan cements (Manuel, 1935, p. 579). The results of many chemical-archeological cross fertilizations indicate the desirable applicability of this method of attack. Geological dating, using such information as lake levels, and botanical dating by means of annular rings in trees, have been of great assistance in archeological dating.

Root (1949*a*) mentions metallographic examinations being made of samples of Peruvian gilding, but adds, "much yet remains to be done." His report on the southern coast of Peru includes chemical analyses and metallographic examinations (Root, 1949*b*).

Some years ago, an attempt was made to identify potsherds found on Isle Royale with pottery of known Indian cultures (Drier, 1939). The Island sherds were found by an expedition of the University of Michigan, and the comparator sherds of identifiable cultures were obtained from the excellent collection of the Milwaukee Museum, through the courtesy of W. C. McKern. X-ray diffraction, micrometallographic, and spectroscopic methods were used in the attempted correlation and identification.

No success attended the efforts to identify the Island sherds.

1. Professor Emeritus, Department of Metallurgical Engineering, Michigan College of Mining and Technology. This chapter was initially prepared during 1956-57 and submitted to the Museum of Anthropology for publication. It was accepted for publication in 1960. This work was sponsored in part by the Wenner-Gren Foundation for Anthropological Research and the Michigan College of Mining and Technology.

By comparing patterns of various Wisconsin clay deposits with sherd patterns, it was possible to correlate sherds with clay sources and thus develop the hypothesis that certain cultures used certain clays for their pottery, and to show that some pieces of pottery thought to be related to one culture were actually the products of another culture and were possibly the results of trade or intermarriage or of some manner of physical penetration of one culture by the other. It is very possible that these prehistoric copper miners were of a prepottery culture and that the sherds found on the Island were left there by a more recent culture. In recorded descriptions of the excavation of these old mines, no mention has been made of pottery; and inasmuch as water was a deterrent to deep mining, it is logical to assume that, if the miners were of a pottery-making culture, pottery vessels would have been used for dewatering.

An attempt to apply a metallographic technique to an archeological problem was reported in *American Antiquity* in October, 1935. In this work, Wilson and Sayre (1935) used micrometallography in their investigations of initial grain conditions in native copper "nuggets" to draw definite conclusions regarding the history of primitive copper work. Subsequent investigation at the Michigan College of Mining and Technology has shown that Wilson's basic assumption, that these "nuggets" had no grain structure as taken from the ground and, even if cold-worked, showed no grain structure until subsequently annealed, is entirely erroneous. In a study of the native copper-arsenic diffusion couple, I have polished and etched hundreds of samples of the native copper "nuggets" and have never found one without grain structure; in fact, modern metallurgical theory precludes such a possibility.

Leonard Frank (1951), on the basis of some metallurgical data, has concluded that the old copper artifacts were formed by hot or cold forging and annealing. H. Mallery (1951) in *Lost America*[2] uses the presence of the copper-cuprous oxide eutectic as a criterion to indicate that copper artifacts of the Great Lakes Copper Culture were formed by melting and casting.

It is a metallurgical fact that copper melted and cast by ordinary methods does contain the eutectic (Pl. XXX, Fig. 3), but to prove the necessity of its absence in copper artifacts formed only by working, eutectic-free masses of native copper (Pl. XXX, Fig. 2)

2. Professor Drier refers to this publication for metallurgical reasons. Otherwise such a curious volume would not have appeared in the References.

were heated in a charcoal fire and formed to shape by hammering. This required as many as fourteen reheatings and forgings and cross-section reductions as much as from 2 inches by 1 inch down to 1/4 inch square. Copper-cuprous oxide eutectic structures were almost invariably present in the grain boundaries and in the grains themselves in the completed forging, even though the incandescent charcoal was highly reducing. This was dependent, of course, on the amount of heating and reheating required. Normally the eutectic would increase with increasing time and temperature. Twins were present in all samples inspected. Twins are due either to the sudden application of a mechanical force or to cold-working followed by annealing. This is particularly true of face-centered cubic metals such as copper. The red copper oxide mentioned by Mallery in *Lost America* as being found in some so-called "Old Copper" artifacts might easily be the oxide that copper forms at its freezing or solidifying temperature (1083°C). The temperature of a charcoal (wood) fire (higher than 1083°C) is high enough to melt copper which it no doubt does to thin sections, but the high thermal conductivity of the metal interferes with the rapid melting of a mass of copper even though thin sections do reach the melting temperature. This may very well be the source of the red oxide found in the non-eutectic structure of some copper artifacts.

It would seem that the mere presence of the copper-cuprous oxide eutectic, and the presence of the red cuprous oxide not in the eutectic, might be indicative of previous melting and casting or previous heating and forging, but they definitely cannot be used to differentiate between the two methods of forming. On the other hand, the amount of oxide present, as estimated visually, might indicate the direction which the investigation should take; that is, twinning and little or no oxide, which is the condition of the Old Copper artifacts, would lead one to suspect forging as the method of forming, whereas the presence of much oxide would lead one to suspect the artifact was formed by casting.

A micrograph of a Hohokam copper bell (Museum of Anthropology Collection, University of Michigan) from Arizona micrographically showed the presence of a great amount of the eutectic. X-radiographs of the bell showed evidence of gas bubbles in the interior of the metal. Dendrites were detected in the micrograph, and no annealing twins were present. To forge an artifact, the shape and dimensions of the bell would require numerous annealings and much hammering, which would definitely result in the presence of annealing twins. (The lack of columnar structure was possibly due to the thinness of the section.) The hardness of the bell was greater than cold-worked copper which would indicate that it was an alloy, as was corroborated by analyses showing the presence of zinc. All these conclusions indicate formation from the molten condition. The amount of eutectic corroborated this (Pl. XXX, Fig. 3). This also indicated the relative amount of the eutectic to be expected in artifacts formed by casting. In all instances the amount of eutectic in the "Old Copper" artifacts was small.

Moreover, if native copper containing native silver is melted, the copper and silver form solid solutions and the silver loses its individual identity. Many copper artifacts, particularly of the jewelry or adornment type, have been found which contain silver in the native state. These definitely could not have been melted at any time. No finds have been recorded of any of the refractories used in the processes of melting and casting.

Some artifacts show the presence of overlapping of the metal, which is the result of formation by forging rather than by casting. (Pl. XXXI, Fig. 3; Pl. XXXII, Fig. 6.)

A 6-inch-long copper spud from the Michigan College of Mining and Technology Collection was cut in two from the cutting blade to the open socket end (Pl. XXXII, Fig. 5). Hardness values were taken along the entire long axis, along the cross section where the blade end was thickest, and also along a cross section at the midpoint of the socket. The thick section of the blade end would require upsetting to form and from there to the cutting edge would require much hammering or forging to form. As would be expected, this section of the spud was harder than the rest of the artifact. (If it were cast, this would not be true.) The thin section of the socket which possibly required a little more forging was found to be slightly harder. The ratios of comparative hardnesses were AA-70:BB-54:CC-50 (Table VII).

The variation in the hardnesses of the spud would indicate that various parts of the metal had been subjected to different amounts of cold-working. The amount of work done where the hammer struck would be greater than in nearby areas. This difference in hardness of nearby areas is corroborative of the conclusion that the forming is by cold-working.

The hardnesses of the float-copper specimens do not show as great a variation as do the artifacts. The work done by the glacier on the float specimens would be in the nature of a generally distributed pressure which would cause a general hardening or straining of the specimen rather than a differential hardening. This, too, is evidence for the cold-working hypothesis of artifact formation. Casting of pure (native) copper from the

TABLE VII

HARDNESS TEST ON SECTION OF PREHISTORIC SPUD*

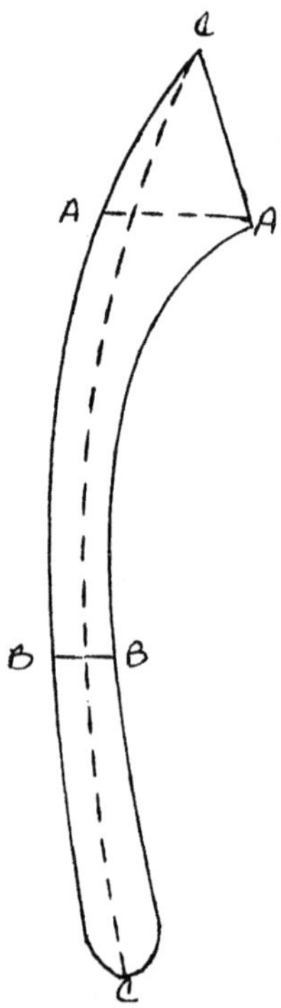

Section C-C	Section A-A	Section B-B
90	70	53
49	74	56
53	50	53
41	74	56
31	75	52
30	73	50
34	68	54
40	70	53
32	69	55
44	73	50
55 (cross B-B)	69	65
48	70	Average 54.2
48	72	
46	72	
46	70	
48	73	
48	68	
47	Average 70.6	
51		
57	Float	Float
58	Specimen A	Specimen B
55	65	73
56	65	65
56	68	74
61	71	73
72	73	79
58	76	82
60	75	Average 73
62	79	
68 (cross A-A)	70	
70	72	
73	54	
72	72	
72	79	
77	74	
Average 50.6	76	
	73	
	75	
	Average 73	

* Rockwell Superficial Hardness Tester, 15 kg load. Spud was sectioned, polished, and etched.

molten state would not result in hardness differentials as indicated in Table VII.

Masses of native copper, which had been recently cold-worked and were similar in size to artifacts, in general, were harder than "Old Copper" artifacts and about the same as float copper. (Float copper is mass native copper torn loose from a vein by a glacier and dragged along, bent, squeezed, and so forth, resulting in the copper being exceedingly cold-worked.) Two pieces of float copper, about the size of the tested spud, and free from gangue indicating much glacial cold-work, had an average comparative hardness of 73, which is not a striking difference, but would seem to indicate that postglacial time was not sufficient to result in complete stress relief and to anneal. Annealing--softening after cold-work—of some metals is thought to be the result or product of temperature and time; that is, a long time at a low temperature. In general, the term "annealing" refers to any heating and cooling operation applied to induce softening. It is believed that the softness of the artifacts is due in part to at least one anneal being a part of the forming process.

The fact that these artisans knew that heating (annealing) softened the copper after cold-working is evidenced by the charcoal found around the Ontonagon Boulder—and many other large masses left by the prehistoric miners—and the fact that protuberances had been removed, would indicate that they would include annealing in their forming technique. Artifacts, in general, do not contain cracks or splits that are due to overworking the metal while cold. One example of such splitting, observed by the author, was a piece of copper pounded out flat to such an extent that there were radial splits on the edges. This piece (N 21 of Tables VIII-X) was found near the prehistoric mine which I excavated. It was located near McCargoe Cove, Isle Royale, and apparently was the place where the miners were liberating the copper metal from the mined rock by stamping or crushing with stone boulders or hammers (cold work).

Micrographic examination of cross sections of a larger artifact—a spud; as much as 5/6 of an inch in thickness (Pl. XXXII, Fig. 6) showed no signs of columnar crystallization. The columnar structure would be definite evidence of forming by casting. Usually very little oxide is present. All this is indicative of forming by forging.

I have tried to identify copper from copper artifacts with native copper from various sources (see list on pp. 140-43 and Pls. XXXI-XXXIII). Tables IX and X indicate the great difficulty in such differentiation and correlation.

The following list and Table VIII indicate the diversity of samples of native copper and of artifacts which were subjected to optical spectroscopic analysis. As indicated in Table IX, all samples showed the presence of silicon, magnesium, silver, and iron. In Table X, an attempt is made to classify the samples according to composition. The overlapping of districts differentiated by the presence of any one element interposes a serious difficulty to individual differentiation, as do the sources of various artifacts and samples of native copper; though, where no particular source is indicated for a native copper sample, it came from somewhere in Michigan's Copper Country.

LIST OF COPPER ARTIFACTS TESTED BY OPTICAL SPECTROSCOPIC ANALYSIS

A1 Copper gorget from Hastings, Barry County, Michigan. R. W. Drier Collection. Not illustrated.

A2 Copper gorget from Hastings, Barry County, Michigan. R. W. Drier Collection. Not illustrated.

A3 Awl from Isle Royale in the R. W. Drier Collection. Length about 13 cm. Pl. 31, No. 1.

A4 Earspool fragment of Hopewellian type. From Tennessee and now in the R. W. Drier Collection. Pl. 31, No. 2.

A5 Spear point. Michigan College of Mining and Technology Collection. Not illustrated.

A6 Copper knife with ovoid to rounded socket and handle perforation from the Michigan College of Mining and Technology Collection. Length about 21 cm. Pl. 31, No. 6.

A7 Copper axe or spud. M.C.M.T. Collection. Not illustrated.

A8 Celt with hammered butt end from Houghton. M.C.M.T. Collection. Length about 27.5 cm; bit width 12 cm; poll width 5.4 cm. Pl. 31, No. 7.

A9 Chisel with mushroom shape butt end from Houghton, M.C.M.T. Collection. Length about 10 cm. Pl. 31, No. 3.

A10 Projectile point with ovoid to rounded socket. M.C.M.T. Collection. Length 11.3 cm. Pl. 31, No. 4.

A11 Projectile point of simple conical form. M.C.M.T. Collection. Length 5.2 cm. Pl. 31, No. 5.

A12 Projectile point with ovoid perforated socket. M.C.M.T. Collection. Length about 14.5 cm. Pl. 31, No. 8.

A13 Knife with badly eroded socket edges and handle perforation. M.C.M.T. Collection. Length about 20 cm. Pl. 31, No. 9.

A14 Socketed knife handle with perforation and simple decoration on upper socket edge. M.C.M.T. Collection. Length about 17.7 cm. Pl. 32, No. 1.

A15 Unsocketed knife. M.C.M.T. Collection. Length about 22 cm. Pl. 32, No. 2.

A16 Socketed projectile point with perforation. M.C.M.T. Collection. Length about 21 cm. Pl. 32, No. 3.

A17 Spud split lengthwise. The small holes along the cut edge of the right-hand section were measured for hardness by Professor Drier. M.C.M.T. Collection. Length about 16 cm. Pl. 32, No. 5.

A18 Spud. M.C.M.T. Collection. Length 17 cm. Pl. 32, No. 6.

A19 Long projectile point with perforated socket. M.C.M.T. Collection. Pl. 32, No. 4.

A20 Earspool fragment from Louisiana (Mississippi period style?). R. W. Drier Collection. Pl. 32, No. 7.

A21 Rolled sheet copper bead from Knoxville, Tennessee. R. W. Drier Collection. Not illustrated.

A22 Copper fragment from Knoxville, Tennessee. R. W. Drier Collection. Not illustrated.

A23 Large cast copper bell fragment from Hohokam site in Arizona. U.M.M.A. Collection. Not illustrated.

A24 Copper piece from "Indian Mound," Lake Mendota, Dane County, Wisconsin. Keweenaw Club House Collection. Not illustrated.

A25 Copper piece from Newport (?), Wisconsin. K.C.H.C. Collection. Not illustrated.

A26 Bipointed copper awl or point, Portage County, Wisconsin. K.C.H.C. Collection. Length about 9.2 cm. Pl. 32, No. 8.

A27 Socketed spear point from Dane County, Wisconsin. K.C.H.C. Collection. Length about 9.2 cm; maximum width of blade 1.7 cm; length of socket 2.7 cm; width 1.2 cm. Pl. 32, No. 9.

A28 Stemmed projectile point from Shawano County, Wisconsin. K.C.H.C. Collection. Length 7.2 cm; width of blade 1.7 cm; length of stem 1.8 cm; stem width .8 cm. Pl. 32, No. 10.

A29 Open socketed projectile point from Manitowoc County, Wisconsin. K.C.H.C. Collection. Length 12.2 cm; maximum blade width 2.2 cm; length of socket 4.1 cm; socket width 1.6 cm. Pl. 32, No. 11.

A30 Open socketed projectile point from Middleton, Dane County, Wisconsin. K.C.H.C. Collection. Length 11.8 cm; maximum width of blade 2.6 cm; length of socket 3.2 cm; socket width 1.8 cm. Pl. 32, No. 12.

A31 Long socketed projectile point with triangular blade from Portage County, Wisconsin. K.C.H.C. Collection. Length 11.4 cm; maximum width of blade 2.6 cm; socket length 4.6 cm; socket width 1.5 cm. Pl. 33, No. 1.

A32 Stemmed projectile point from Williamson Farm, Madison, Dane County, Wisconsin. K.C.H.C. Length 11.3 cm; maximum width of blade 2.4 cm. Pl. 33, No. 2.

A33 Short stemmed, broad bladed point from Ottawa County, Michigan. K.C.H.C. Collection. Length 12.5 cm; maximum width of blade 4.3 cm; stem length 1.5 cm. Pl. 33, No. 3.

A34 Short stemmed point from Marquette County, Michigan. K.C.H.C. Collection. Length 7 cm; maximum width of blade 2.4 cm. Pl. 33, No. 4.

A35 Long cylindrical stemmed point from Jefferson County, Wisconsin. K.C.H.C. Collection. Length 18.5 cm; maximum width of blade 2 cm; stem length 8 cm. Pl. 33, No. 5.

A36 Open socketed point from Durrop Farm, Middleton, Dane County, Wisconsin. K.C.H.C. Collection. Length 13.3 cm; maximum width of blade 2.2 cm; socket length 3.5 cm; socket width 1.5 cm. Pl. 33, No. 6.

A37 Celt with almost parallel sides from shore of Fox Lake, Dodge County, Wisconsin. K.C.H.C. Collection. Length 11.7 cm; width of bit about 5.5 cm; width of poll about 4.1 cm. Pl. 33, No. 7.

A38 Long socketed point from northern Dane County, Wisconsin. K.C.H.C. Collection. Length 19.6 cm; maximum width of blade 2.8 cm; socket length 5.8 cm; socket width 1.8 cm. Pl. 33, No. 8.

A39 Long socketed spud from Bassantee Farm, Dane County, Wisconsin. K.C.H.C. Collection. Length 17.6 cm; length of socket 10.1 cm; maximum width 4.6 cm. Pl. 33, No. 9.

A40 Long stemmed point from near Plainfield, Waushara County, Wisconsin. K.C.H.C. Collection. Length 15 cm; maximum width of blade 3.3 cm; stem length 5.7 cm; stem width 1.9 cm. Pl. 33, No. 10.

A41 Long narrow celt from near Madison, Dane County, Wisconsin. K.C.H.C. Collection. Length about 18 cm; width of bit about 3.7 cm. Note recurved poll end. Pl. 33, No. 11.

A42 Contracting sided celt from Baraga County, Michigan. K.C.H.C. Collection. Length about 21.2 cm; width at bit 6.2 cm. Note poll narrowed and recurved. Pl. 33, No. 12.

A43 Long socketed point with broken tip from Baraga County, Michigan. K.C.H.C. Collection. Length about 22.7 cm; maximum width of blade 2.5 cm; socket length 8.7 cm; socket width 1.8 cm. Pl. 33, No. 13.

A44 Awl from Haliburton, Ontario. Not illustrated.

A45 Awl from Great Falls, Manitoba. Not illustrated.

A46 Bead from Melita, Manitoba. Not illustrated.

A47 Spear point from Great Falls, Manitoba. Not illustrated.

A48 Celt from Point Peninsula, Ontario. Not illustrated.

A49 Copper Mine River, Northwest Territory, Canada.

A50 Pine Falls, Manitoba.

A51 Alexander, Manitoba.

A52 Awl from Nipigon, Ontario.

This list was submitted by Professor Drier. The editor is responsible for the measurements, for the plate arrangements, and for observations which are based on the photographs which Drier furnished in late January, 1961.

TABLE VIII

CATALOG OF NATIVE COPPER SAMPLES TESTED BY OPTICAL SPECTROSCOPIC ANALYSIS

Number	Source
N1	Griggstown, New Jersey
N2	Arizona
N3	Arizona
N4	Michigan—Supposedly very pure
N5	Point Mamainse, Ontario
N6	Freda Mill, Michigan—high arsenic
N7	Michigan
N8	Michigan
N9	Michigan
N10	Michigan (float)
N11	Michigan (float)
N12	Michigan (float)
N13	Michigan (conglomerate)
N14	Michigan (float)
N15	Michigan (float)
N16	Michigan—Ahmeek Mine
N17	Alaska
N18	Found in New Mexico (looks like float)
N19	Michigan (float)
N20	Minnesota—Soudan Mine
N21	Isle Royale, Prehistoric Pit
N22	Isle Royale, Todd Harbor
N23	Isle Royale, Minong Mine
N24	Newfoundland, West Coast

An interesting instance is found in the case of samples A1 and A2 of Table IX. Both of these, and also several pieces of metallic lead in the form of rings, were dug up on a farm near

TABLE IX

RESULTS OF OPTICAL SPECTOGRAPHIC ANALYSIS OF SAMPLES OF NATIVE COPPER AND ARTIFACTS

Number	Pb	As	Others	Number	Pb	As	Others
N1....	x	x	Ti, Na, Mn	A13...	...	...	......
N2....	x	...	......	A14...	...	...	......
N3....	...	...	......	A15...	...	...	Z_7
N4....	x	...	......	A16...	...	x	Z_7, Mn
N5....	...	x	......	A17...	...	...	......
N6....	x s	x	......	A18...	...	...	......
N7....	...	...	......	A19...	...	...	......
N8....	x s	...	Z_7S, Mn	A20...	x s	...	Z_7
N9....	...	...	Mn	A21...	...	...	......
N10...	x	...	......	A22...	...	...	......
N11...	x	...	......	A23...	...	...	Z_7
N12...	...	...	......	A24...	x	...	V, Ti
N13...	x	...	......	A25...	...	...	......
N14...	x	...	......	A26...	x	...	V
N15...	...	...	......	A27...	x	...	......
N16...	x	x	Z_7	A28...	x	...	V, Ti
N17...	...	x	Mn	A29...	x	...	......
N18...	x	...	Z_7S	A30...	x	...	......
N19...	...	...	......	A31...	x s	...	V, Ti
N20...	...	...	......	A32...	...	...	......
N21...	x	...	......	A33...	x	...	V, Ti, Mn
N22...	x	...	Mn	A34...	x	...	V, Ti, Mn
N23...	x	...	Mn	A35...	x	...	Mn
N24...	...	...	......	A36...	x s	...	......
21 old	...	...	......	A37...	x	...	......
22 old	...	...	......	A38...	x s	...	......
Soudan	...	...	......	A39...	x	...	Mn
				A40...	x	...	......
A1....	x s	x	Sb, Bi, Ni, Mo	A41...	x	...	......
A2....	x s	...	Z_7, Sn	A42...	...	...	......
A3....	x	...	......	A43...	...	...	......
A4....	...	...	......	A44...	x	...	V, Ti
A5....	...	...	......	A45...	x	...	V, Ti
A6....	...	...	......	A46...	x	...	Al
A7....	...	x	......	A47...	...	...	......
A8....	...	...	......	A48...	...	...	......
A9....	...	...	......	A49...	...	...	Al
A10...	...	...	......	A50...	...	...	......
A11...	...	...	......	A51...	...	...	Al
A12...	...	...	......	A52...	...	...	......

All showed Si, Mg, Ag, Fe.

TABLE X

GROUPED SAMPLES OF NATIVE COPPER AND ARTIFACTS

Number	Source		Group
Ni	New Jersey		Arsenic
N5	Ontario		
N6	Freda, Mich.		
N16	Ahmeek, Mich.		
N17	Alaska		
N21 old.	.4 per cent As ?		
A1	Hastings, Mich.		
A7	?		
A16	?		
N8	Amygdaloid	much	Zinc
N10	Float	trace	
N13	Conglomerate	trace	
N15	Float	trace	
N16	Ahmeek		
N18	Santa Fe, N.M.	much	
A2	Hastings, Mich.		
A15	?		
A16	?		
A20	Louisiana		
A23	Southwest U. S.		
N6	Freda, Mich.		Strong Lead
N8	Amygdaloid		
A1	Hastings, Mich.		
A2	Hastings, Mich.		
A20	Louisiana		
A31	Portage Co. Wis.		
A36	Jefferson Co. Wis.		
A38	Dane Co. Wis.		

Number	Source	Group
N1	New Jersey	Weak Lead
N2	Arizona	
N4	?	
N10	Float	
N11	Float	
N13	Conglomerate	
N14	Float	
N16	Ahmeek	
N18	Santa Fe, N.M.	
N21	Isle Royale	
N22	Isle Royale	
N23	Isle Royale	
A3	Isle Royale	
A24	Kew. Co. Wis.	
A26	Portage Co. Wis.	
A27	Dane Co. Wis.	
A28	Shawano Co. Wis.	
A29	Manitowoc Co. Wis.	
A30	Dane Co. Wis.	
A33	Ottawa Co. Mich.	
A34	Marquette Co., Wis.	
A35	Jefferson Co. Wis.	
A37	Dodge Co. Wis.	
A39	Dane Co. Wis.	
A40	Waushara Co. Wis.	
A41	Madison Co. Wis.	
A44	Haliburton, Ont.	
A45	Manitoba, Can.	
A46	Melita, Can.	

Lines found in all samples Si, Mg, Ag, Fe.
Other lines found in a few Al, V, Ti, Mn, Ca, Na, Sn.

Sample Al showed As, Sb, Pb, Bi, Ni, Mo, Si, Mg, Ag, Fe.
Sample A2 was brass with much Pb and Zn and little Sn.

Hastings, Michigan. Sample A1 was a copper artifact differing from any of the other artifacts in shape and composition. It was about 7 inches long, 2 inches wide, and 1/16 of an inch thick. In shape it resembled a long tongue, one end being rounded like a cross section of a long paraboloid of revolution and the other end square. The edges were thin, but it did not seem to be an edged instrument like a knife or a double-edged spear point. It could be quite readily differentiated from any of the other samples by its impurities. Sample A2 was definitely an alloy of copper, probably a brass which contained tin and lead as well as zinc. This undoubtedly was the result of smelting, but the presence and amount of tin would indicate that this piece was of foreign origin, possibly European.

Results of optical spectroscopic analysis so far do not indicate the possibility of correlating with certainty any one artifact with any one deposit or mine. Glaring differences as in the case of A1 and A2 are somewhat rare, as are instances of the presence of native silver. It was hoped that trace elements might be present in sufficient amounts to identify the copper in an artifact as originating in a certain deposit, or even in a certain mine.

Vanadium and titanium were found in a number of artifacts from such widely scattered sources as Wisconsin, Michigan, Ontario, and Manitoba, though the copresence of manganese was found only in two artifacts, from Ottawa and Marquette Counties in Michigan. Aluminum seemed a little more critical, it being present in artifacts from Manitoba and the Copper River District of Canada. Zinc was present in four artifacts--from specimens of unknown source, from Louisiana, and in a bell from Arizona. Manganese was present in five artifacts, which again were from widely scattered sources. As Table X shows, arsenic and lead were also widely scattered, as were silicon, magnesium, silver, and iron.

In the native coppers, titanium was present only in the sample from New Jersey. Neither aluminum nor vanadium was indicated as present in any of the native copper samples. Literature on copper metallurgy frequently states that bismuth is not found in American native copper. Analysis of native coppers corroborated this statement and the presence of this element in sample A1, which likely is foreign, is further substantiation. It is hoped that a similar criterion can be found which will differentiate between American native coppers.

It is realized that the acceptance of forging (hammering) as the method of forming certainly admits the possibility of the presence in the artifact of some of the contiguous matrix rock-forming elements. Hammering will force rock particles into the copper and folding or lapping will trap some rock in the artifact, and accurate analyses will indicate their presence. Likewise, because of the roughened and irregular surface of the artifacts, greatly aided by corrosion, the analyses will very likely indicate the presence of elements in the soil in which the artifact was found. This would be true even if the artifact sample were cleaned. An analysis which indicated the presence of an identifying atom from the rock matrix originally surrounding the copper metal would be almost as valuable as though it were in the metal itself. Perhaps more and larger samples and more exhaustive trace element chemical microanalysis, or correlation based on differential isotopic ratio or X-ray spectroscopy, will throw some light on the problem. All of these methods are being investigated.

CONCLUSIONS

It is agreed that the difficulty of forming the sockets on the various artifacts would seem to require a casting technique or a high degree of artisanship to form by forging, but all metallurgical evidence to date indicates that the copper artifacts of the Old Copper culture of the Great Lakes Region were formed by a forging technique which included cold-working, and possibly some hot-working, and annealing or softening. The same is true of the artifacts without sockets.

If native silver is present in an artifact, it can be safely concluded that the Lake Superior Region was the source of the copper, but various analytical methods which have been tried, to date, have not been developed sufficiently to otherwise definitely differentiate between native copper from different sources.

Certainly the Old Copper culture was a metallurgical culture, and as such it should be amenable to further analysis and study based on metallurgical disciplines.

METALLURGICAL EXAMINATION OF FIVE COPPER ARTIFACTS FROM SOUTHERN MICHIGAN

William C. Root

In December, 1954, Dr. William C. Root of the Department of Chemistry, Bowdoin College, wrote to J. B. Griffin as follows:

> I have available this year a small sum I can use for having metallographic sections made, so I would like to use part of it on the problem of whether the Indians of the Central States did or did not cast copper axes and other specimens. Do you have some suitable specimens that I can have sectioned, or can you refer me to someone at Wisconsin that might have some? I would like to cut small pieces from the ends of two or three objects that look like they might have been cast and have polished sections and photo-micrographs made at M.I.T. so we can tell what happened during their manufacture.
>
> Perhaps this has already been done. I am not very familiar with this field, but last time I talked to James Ford he seemed to think it was something that should be done.

As a result of this request seven copper specimens were sent to Dr. Root in January, 1955. Root sent two axes to W. F. Flanagan, a metallurgist, at Massachusetts Institute of Technology, who made thin sections and reported to Root in September, 1955. In June, 1957, I received a copy of the Flanagan report given below and in August, 1958, a short statement by Root on his spectroposcopic examination of four of the other specimens.

The first of the two axe heads or celts examined by Flanagan (U.M.M.A. cat. No. 27651, Pl. XXVII, Fig. 2, No. 5) is one of two copper celts from Denver Township, Isabella County, Michigan, which had been in the collection of Dr. W. B. Hinsdale since before 1928. They were accessioned as part of the Museum collection in October, 1944. It is presumably, but not certainly, an Old Copper specimen. The axe is 13.6 cm long, 4.8 cm wide at the beveled bit, 2.2 cm wide at the poll, and is 1.1 cm thick. The second axe studied by Flanagan is from the Converse Mound group of the Hopewell culture, from Kent County, Michigan (Pl. XXVII, Fig. 2, No. 4). It was formerly in the Chicago Natural History Museum. This is a small, almost dainty form. It is 8 cm long, 3.4 cm wide at the bit, 2.4 cm at the poll and .6 cm thick in the midline.

Axe 27651. (Analysis 1490) Michigan.

> Both ot the axeheads were very soft, and it was difficult and not expedient to polish them scratch free. This does not affect the caliber

of the information one obtains from them. Figure 1 is of the large axehead. The very large twinned crystals, or grains, indicate that the final treatment has been a high anneal after previous mechanical working. Since both time and temperature, as well as purity, enter into the grain size one obtains, it is impossible to say what the temperature of this final anneal has been, except that it was above the recrystallization temperature (approximately 200°C). The slight bending of the twins indicates a little working after this anneal, but its effect on the mechanical properties would be slight. The picture was taken at the surface where this latter effect would be more evident.

(Figure 1 (Pl. XXVII, Fig. 2, No. 5) was etched with H_2O_2, NH_4OH, H_2O mixture at a magnification of 100.)

Axe 52238. (Analysis 1492) Michigan.

Figure 2 is of the small axehead. Its treatment has been similar to that of the other axehead except that its final grain size is much smaller, indicating a lower temperature or shorter time of final anneal, or a different purity. Some forging laps are indicated in the picture which were formed during some previous working cycle when the surface of the specimen had been folded over on itself.

(Figure 2 (Pl. XXVII, Fig. 2, No. 4) was etched with a H_2O_2, NH_4OH, H_2O mixture at a magnification of 150.)

Dr. Root examined four specimens spectroscopically. These include the Isabella County axe discussed in Flanagan's report. U.M.M.A. Cat. No. 22191 is one of two copper spear points probably from Montcalm County, Michigan, which were collected by Dr. G. E. Dakin and were received in the Museum in May, 1939, from Mr. and Mrs. F. Earle Lyman (Pl. XXVII, Fig. 2, No. 3). It is 9.8 cm long and the blade is .3 cm thick. The socket is 1.3 cm wide and .8 cm from front to back. This is almost certainly an Old Copper point as are the other spear points. A socketed copper point (U.M.M.A. Cat. No. 30464) is from Eaton Rapids, Eaton County, Michigan (Pl. XXVII, Fig. 2). It was received by the Museum in March, 1952, from Mrs. Mary E. Goheen. This point is 13.3 cm long and is .4 cm thick. The socket handle is 1.5 cm wide and 1.1 cm thick. Another socketed point (U.M.M.A. Cat. No. 39001) is from Scott Lake near Rosebush, Isabella County, Michigan (Pl. XXVII, Fig. 2, No. 1). This was received by the Museum in March, 1952 as a part of the Dr. R. M. Kempton Collection. It is 16 cm long, .4 cm thick and the socket is 1.7 cm wide and .7 cm thick.

SPECTROSCOPIC ANALYSIS BY DR. W. C. ROOT

In his letter of August, 1958, Dr. Root wrote: "These results confirm the view that Lake Superior Copper is pure, except for a trace of silver. . . .I think there is now no question about the casting of copper. There is not any evidence for it at all. It seems to me unnecessary to make any more tests on axes or the like." His analysis is listed below:

TABLE XI

SPECTROSCOPIC ANALYSIS OF FOUR COPPER SPECIMENS FROM MICHIGAN

Analysis	Cat. No.	Au	Ag	Sn	Pb	As	Sb	Bi	Zn
1490—Denver Twp., Isabella Co. This is one of the axes that was sectioned .	27651	. .	x	. .	. .	. .	. .	. .	. .
1491—Montcalm County	22191	. .	x	. .	. .	. .	. .	. .	. .
1493—Isabella County	39004	. .	x	. .	. .	. .	. .	. .	. .
1494—Eaton County.	30464	. .	t	. .	. .	. .	. .	. .	. .

TRACE ELEMENT AND METALLOGRAPHIC STUDIES OF PREHISTORIC COPPER ARTIFACTS IN NORTH AMERICA: A REVIEW[1]

Tyler Bastian

To arrive at the truth archaeologists and technologists need to work together, lest they separately go astray. (Read, 1934, p. 389.)

Archaeologists frequently call on specialists for elucidation of particular problems. The results are incorporated into the archaeologist's monograph, or, as is more frequently the case, they are relegated to an appendix. If the archaeologist is unfamiliar with the specialist's field, he may have a tendency to accept the report as authoritative and final. On the other hand, it is left to the archeologist, as it properly should be, to integrate and interpret the data, because the specialist usually has neither the interest nor the time needed to carry out exhaustive research involving archaeological problems. Examination of the available literature on trace element and metallographic studies of North American archaeological remains suggests that no integration of the data in this field has been attempted, probably because they are so conflicting that interpretation is difficult. This situation has not been viewed as a major problem, because the few available studies are widely scattered and their conclusions, despite the inconsistencies of the data, are usually compatible with other archaeological evidence.

Trace element and metallographic research have been applied to two archaeological problems. Trace elements (elements occurring in very small amounts) may, by the analysis of copper from natural deposits and artifacts, suggest the sources of copper used by the Indians. Metallography (the study of the structure

1. This paper would not have been written without the encouragement and advice of the specialists who have been kind enough to read and comment on sections of various drafts. Dr. David M. Pendergast, Assistant Professor of Anthropology, and Dr. James A. Whelan, Assistant Professor of Mineralogy, University of Utah, have been especially helpful. Dr. H. Edward Flanders, Professor of Metallurgy, University of Utah, has shaped some of the viewpoints expressed in the section on metallography. The final responsibility for the paper as it now stands is, of course, my own. (Mr. Bastian did not have available the papers by Drier or Root included in this publication. Ed.)

of solid metals and alloys) may suggest the techniques used to work the copper.

The emphasis of this paper is on the identification of sources of native copper north of Mexico through trace element analysis. In summarizing the available studies on this subject, discussed below in chronological order, an attempt is made to show that the data are inconsistent, and that some of the analyses do not meet modern standards of analytical technique and sensitivity. This latter problem has been noted for South America by Caley and Easby (1959, p. 63).

A brief summary of the methods of metallographic studies of copper artifacts from North America is also included. The available information presents a fairly consistent pattern, but it is not extensive for North America.

"Lake Superior," "Upper Michigan," and "Michigan" are used interchangeably in this paper.

TRACE ELEMENT STUDIES

The earliest trace element studies of copper archeological specimens from North America were largely concerned with demonstrating that the copper found in precontact Indian sites is of American origin, and that European metals occur only in postcontact sites. Clarence B. Moore (1894, pp. 213-41) had specimens of American native copper (naturally occurring and chemically pure except for trace elements), European smelted copper; and Indian copper artifacts analyzed for trace elements by several specialists using the gravimetric method (separation of components and their quantitative estimation by weight). In this pioneering study he says: "In the investigation of copper found within the limits of the United States, for some reason, analysis has been hitherto entirely overlooked, and we shall now endeavor to throw some light upon copper from a chemical point of view." (Pp. 220-21.) Actually, Moore was not the first to employ these methods, for E. G. Squier and E. H. Davis in their classical study, *Ancient Monuments of the Mississippi Valley*, note that some copper axes from eastern United States: ". . . were found, upon analysis, to be *pure copper*,—unalloyed, to any perceptible extent, by other metals." (1848, p. 202 [italics theirs].)

Moore concluded from the analyses that native copper is distinguished by a purity of 99.65 to 99.994 per cent and the absence of lead, while European commercial copper averaged about 99.5 per cent pure. Electrolytic copper is purer than 99.65 per cent, but it was not produced until the 1860's (Kroll, 1957, p. 227).

According to Moore (1894, p. 221), European refined copper of the early post-Columbian period was usually not over 99.0 per cent pure. He notes that: "It is evident, then, that a copper purer than the average of that produced under modern methods of smelting cannot have been derived from Europe during the sixteenth or seventeenth centuries." (P. 221.)

Moore assumed that the Europeans would not have brought European native copper, which is probably of about the same purity as American native copper (Voce, 1948, p. 20), to America when refined copper, in the form of tools and utensils, was readily available to the Europeans, and was in great demand among the Indians. Although Moore's argument may be essentially valid, it has since been pointed out that copper smelted from some ores may be as pure as native copper (Coghlan, 1951, p. 92; F. Thompson, 1958, p. 1).

Very close similarity was found by independent investigations of some of Moore's archaeological specimens (pp. 222, 235). Nevertheless, some of the trace elements tested for, which recent analyses have shown to be occasionally present in native copper, were not detected in any of Moore's samples. Voce (1948, p. 19) has previously noted this deficiency in Moore's data. The failure to detect lead in any of his American native copper samples is particularly surprising, because most subsequent analyses have shown that it is usually present. In fact, Bergsøe (1938, p. 17) says: "Lead is always found in varying amounts in copper." Elements present in the gangue (the matrix of a metal) may become mixed with the associated copper. It is clear that Moore is aware of this (p. 221), so it seems a paradox for him to deny that lead is present in American native copper, and at the same time to state that "Lead *ore* may exist in the same gangue." (Italics his.)

Subsequent analyses made for Moore (1903, p. 412; 1910, p. 258) conform to his earlier data. Lead was detected in one sample, but the analyst, H. F. Keller, states that: ". . . this must be regarded as due to local contamination from an external source, for other parts of the same plate are absolutely free from lead." (Keller, in Moore, 1900, p. 329.)

Despite the questionable validity of Moore's data, no subsequent study of trace elements in North American metal archaeological specimens rivals Moore's systematic selection of materials to be analyzed, his extensive discussion, or this archaeologist's involvement with the chemical data.

A year after Moore's work appeared, James Douglas (1895), a geologist, published an article based on Moore's data and presenting essentially the same viewpoint. A series of discussions on the European versus American origin of the copper used by the Indians, in which Moore repeats some of his earlier data, was published in 1903.

N. H. Winchell (1911, p. 503) submitted a copper object from Minnesota, and of unknown cultural affiliation, to C. F. Sidener for analysis. Of the nine elements tested for, Sidener found only a "very slight trace" of iron. Winchell concludes from this analysis that "The absence of those impurities which characterize metallic copper derived from the smelting of copper ores, shows that this disk was made of pure metallic copper, and that it was from the Lake Superior region." The analysis may indicate that the specimen was made of native copper, but it is not indicative of the source of the copper.

George B. Phillips (1925*a*), in an article published separately in London and in Menasha, restates the problem of the origin of the copper used by the Indians. He presents analyses by the United States Bureau of Standards of trace elements in Lake Superior native copper and in copper from "European sources." The method of analysis used is not stated, but it may have been gravimetric, because the spectrochemical method (chemical analysis of a substance by observation of its spectrum) was just becoming popular at this time (Meggers and Scribner, 1941, p. 3). These analyses show that nickel, silver, iron, arsenic, antimony, and lead are present in copper from both sources. Phillips had three copper artifacts analyzed (two from near New London, Waupaca County, Wisconsin, and one with no provenience). The analyst(s) who studied these archaeological specimens is not named, but it may have been D. L. Wallace of the University of Pennsylvania, who analyzed some other specimens for Phillips (1922, p. 143; 1925*b*, p. 552; 1928, p. 466). The only trace element found was iron. Despite the analyses, Phillips concluded that American copper is 99.9 per cent pure with traces of silver and iron; and that foreign copper is rarely 98.0 per cent pure, and always contains a number of trace elements. Appended to the London publication of this article is an analysis of one of the same Wisconsin artifacts by C. O. Bannister (1925) who found four elements besides iron. In a later publication, Phillips (1926, p. 106) states that an analysis of a specimen of native copper from the Keweenaw Peninsula of Upper Michigan detected no iron or silver.

T. A. Rickard (1934, p. 271), a mining engineer and metallurgist, repeats Phillips' (1925*a*) conclusions, but in reprinting Phillips' analyses of American native copper by the Bureau of Standards, Rickard omits antimony and lead. Apparently little known to Americans, Rickard's article is a wealth of information on the mining, working, and use of copper by the North American Indians in early contact times.

A later discussion by Eli Lilly (1937, p. 208) is based on Moore's (1894) earlier work.

The most extended studies of the chemical composition of metal archaeological specimens by an American are those of William C. Root, a chemist at Bowdoin College, Maine. He began his research about 1930. Since 1937 he has published on the analyses of hundreds of specimens, and his reports continue to appear. Not only has Root made his specialized services available to archaeologists, but some of his writings also include descriptions of the artifacts and discussions of the archaeological problems. Most of Root's work has been on Mesoamerican and on Central and South American materials. A detailed discussion of the chemistry and metallography of archaeological specimens from this culturally complex area is beyond the scope of this paper. It should be noted, however, that the composition of many metal artifacts in this area is a result of alloying and mixing metals from different sources. In these cases, the trace elements in the metal can not be reduced to a constant that is independent of culture as can probably be done in northern and eastern North America where metals are not known to have been alloyed. The only known analyses of native copper deposits in the area are from northern Mexico (Lothrop, 1952, p. 22).

It appears that Root was the first to apply the spectrochemical method of trace element analysis to archaeological material. He briefly describes his technique in one of his earliest published reports (1937*a*, p. 307), and he states that he used the same method for the analyses in his 1943 and 1949 reports. By modern standards, Root's earlier technique was crude. It was useful only for metallic elements. He made his own standards, he constructed his own references to identify the spectral lines, and it was semiquantitative at best. He used "*ordinary* photographic film," and "*about* one milligram of metal." (Root, 1937*a*, p. 307 [Italics mine].) It may also be significant that Root did not do all the actual analyses himself (1937*a*, p. 307; 1949*b*, p. 10; and Haury, 1947, p. 81). Much of Root's work has been concerned with alloys, for which his techniques may be adequate, but they do not seem to be adequate for quantitative or qualitative trace element analysis. He has clearly stated that he considers spectrochemical analysis to be a qualitative, or at best a semiquantitative, technique (1951, p. 85; 1953, p. 266; 1957, p. 53) for the identification of trace elements; but quantitative spectrochemical analysis has been widely used in research and industry for over fifteen years. Root believes that other techniques must be used for quantitative analysis, but that qualitative spectrochemical analyeses are adequate for most archaeological problems (Root, 1957, p. 53).

Root's analyses of copper artifacts and native copper from northern Mexico and the American southwest show that, in contrast to the samples he has analyzed from areas farther to the south, silver is usually the only impurity found. Other trace elements occasionally occur in smaller amounts than does silver, but Root's analyses do not suggest that they have distributional significance (Root, in Lothrop, 1952, p. 21-22, tables 13-14). Other investigators of native copper samples from northern Mexico and the American southwest have tested for some of the same elements that Root did. They have always found at least some trace elements in addition to silver, and often in greater amounts than silver (Moore, 1894; Voce, 1948; Hurst and Larson, 1958). This can probably be attributed, at least in part, to the sensitivity of the methods used.

Root's statements about copper from the Lake Superior area are particularly interesting. In some published excerpts from an unpublished manuscript he says: "Two analyses of native copper from Lake Superior (Phillips, 1925*a*) show the presence of about .01 per cent of arsenic in the copper." (Root, 1937*b*, p. 276.)

The context in which this statement occurs is a characterization of the trace element content of copper from the Lake Superior area (arsenic), the American southwest (silver), and central Mexico (tin, lead, iron, arsenic, antimony, bismuth). Unfortunately, a more precise reference to the cited article by Phillips is not given. Phillips' known publications indicate that several trace elements, including arsenic, are found in Lake Superior copper, although he says that silver and iron are characteristic (Phillips, 1925*a*). More recently, Root has revised his opinion: "Analyses of native copper from Lake Superior show that it also is pure except for a little silver. . . .

"The metal in the copper objects from the Southwest is thus similar in composition to the native copper found both in the Southwest and in the Lake Superior region, and to the copper found in metal objects from both the west and east coasts." (Root, in Lothrop, 1952, pp. 20-21.)

Root cites that Phillips (1925*b*) as a basis for these statements on Lake Superior native copper, but in this particular article Phillips says nothing about trace elements in Lake Superior native copper, and in a previous article by Phillips (1925*a*) analyses are given which show that several trace elements are present in Lake Superior native copper. Recently Root analyzed a copper bead from northwestern United States, and found "a trace of silver and a (?) trace of lead" (Butler and Osborne, 1959, p. 220). Again he affirms that "The Lake Superior copper, which is the only copper of prehistoric origin from the northern part of the United States that I have analyzed, is also pure copper except for a little silver." (Root, in Butler and Osborne, 1959, p. 220.) A recent spectrochemical analysis of three specimens of Lake Superior native copper by Hurst (Hurst and Larson, 1958) shows the presence of 12 of 14 elements tested.

Archaeologists have published several general statements about trace elements in native copper. In his report on the Osceola Site, near Potosi, Grant County, Wisconsin, Robert Ritzenthaler (1946, p. 191) states: "Lake Superior copper is identifiable as more than 99% pure with only slight traces of iron, silver, cobalt, arsenic, and nickel." He does not cite a source for his statement. None of the published analyses of native copper from Lake Superior have identified cobalt.

P. Rivet and H. Arsandaux (1946) have published the most extensive work on prehistoric metallurgy in the New World. Although they did not analyze for trace elements, they thought that such analysis would be significant (p. 3). Their discussion of copper in North America is brief, and is mostly based on Moore's early work (1894).

Martin, Quimby, and Collier (1947, p. 45), in their chapter, "Objects of Copper," have cited Moore's data (1894), and they state: ". . . native copper from North America never shows a trace of lead and contains but minute traces of silver, arsenic, nickel, and cobalt." Modern analysies frequently show lead, but cobalt has been detected in only one specimen from the United States (Hurst and Larson, 1958, p. 179, Table 1).

Incomplete trace element analysis of a copper bell from Arizona was published by Haury (1947). The inclusions in the copper were independently identified as copper oxide by Colin E. Fink and as copper sulphide by B. H. McLeod. The archaeologist was forced to state that it "poses a metallurgical problem on which I can shed no light" (p. 81).

Spectrochemical analyses for sixteen trace elements in sixteen native copper samples from Europe, Asia, Australia, and North America by Eric Voce (1948) revealed variation between samples, but it also showed some rather striking inconsistencies in different analyses of the same sample. Nevertheless, he thought that "Certain indication of impurities characteristic of the different geographical localities can be discerned by a close examination of the table . . . it seems possible that a table such as this, but considerably extended, might serve as a guide to the locations of the source of artifacts fabricated from native copper without melting." (P. 21.)

Voce was the first to note that elements present in the gangue may become mixed with the copper. Moore was aware of this, but he disregarded it, and Phillips, and Root make no reference to it. Some of the elements commonly present in the gangue include lead, arsenic, iron, silicon, aluminum, and magnesium. Differences in analyses for the same element in different parts of the same sample may be partly due to gangue inclusions, so multiple analyses of each specimen are desirable.

Forbes (1950, p. 292), in his comprehensive survey of prehistoric metallurgy, mentions that silver, arsenic, and antimony are found in copper from modern mines in northern Michigan. He follows Phillips (1925*a*) in saying that iron and silver are found as trace elements in copper artifacts from central United States. Uncritical acceptance of the statements by Forbes and Phillips leads to the conclusion that the copper in the analyzed archaeological specimens from central United States did not come from the Lake Superior area.

The Wulfing plates, from near Malden, Dunklin County, Missouri, were studied by Lawrence Bonham and Allen K. Schleicher. Virginia D. Watson (1950) has briefly described their technique and reported the results of their analysis:

> Samples of the copper in each of the Wulfing plates, as well as those from three copper mines in Upper Michigan (Quincy, Calumet, and Hecla), were subjected to spectrographic qualitative analysis . . . The copper in the Wulfing plates is remarkably pure—much more so than that in the three mine samples—showing only faint traces (less than 0.01%) of other metals and completely lacking usual tracers for Michigan copper such as arsenic and cobalt. Thus, for identification of the mine(s) from which the copper used in the Wulfing plates came, it would be necessary to make a spectrographic quantitative analysis. This is impractical for two reasons: a) portions of the Wulfing plates themselves would have to be destroyed to obtain ample copper samples; and b) the analysis would probably occupy a technician for at least a month. For the present, then, we must content ourselves with the knowledge that the copper used in the manufacture of the Wulfing plates, because of its extreme purity, probably came from Upper Michigan. . . .(pp. 2-3).

Watson says that the Wulfing plates lack the "usual tracers for Michigan copper such as arsenic and cobalt." Arsenic has been found in most samples of Michigan native copper that have been analyzed, but cobalt can not be considered characteristic of

Michigan copper, as was pointed out before. Watson's comment about the high purity of the plates as compared to Michigan copper is particularly interesting, although she does not specifically state that the Michigan samples were *native* copper. Assuming that they are native copper, and since the Wulfing plates contain no arsenic, and are "much more" pure than the Michigan copper analyzed for her, there is a strong suggestion that the copper may not be Michigan native copper. The available studies are conflicting on the relative purity of native copper from different regions, but only highly refined copper is "much more" pure than native copper. Watson has, in addition, considerably exaggerated the sample size and time required for spectrochemical analysis.

Joseph E. Cox, Jr., spectrochemically analyzed the Mangum plate, from near Port Gibson, Mississippi (Cotter, 1952, p. 67), and native copper specimens from Michigan, Missouri, Cuba, Chihuahua (New Mexico), Arizona, and Colorado. Unfortunately, neither his techniques are described nor his data presented. Cotter states that "Results showed: (1) The three samples from the Mangum Plate fragments are of similar composition in major and minor trace elements; (2) in the analyses of native copper ores from 12 mining districts, samples from Keweenaw Point, Michigan, and Clifton, Arizona have compositions corresponding to that of the plate material." (P. 67.)

The best published description of the technique of spectrochemical analysis of specimens relative to North American archaeology is that by Hurst and Larson (1958). A copper celt from the Etowah site, near Cartersville, Georgia, and native copper specimens from North Carolina, Georgia, New Mexico, and Michigan were analyzed. The procedure of analysis is outlined, and a brief survey of relevant literature is given. Hurst describes his technique, but adds: "As the experimental conditions show, no attempt was made to achieve maximum detection of trace elements. Some care was given, however, to the shaping of the electrodes, preparation, sizing, packing of the samples, and excitation and plate development conditions to insure that the spectra are comparable." (Hurst and Larson, 1958, p. 178.) Hurst thought the analyses suggest that the Etowah celt was made of Georgia native copper. However, his presentation of the trace elements by relative abundance does not make his work quantitatively comparable to that of other analysts.

In each of the three samples of Southwestern native copper analyzed by Hurst (Hurst and Larson, 1958) and Voce (1947), several trace elements were detected, whereas Root's analysis of six native copper specimens from Arizona showed silver in four specimens, lead in one specimen, and no trace elements in two specimens (Root, in Lothrop, 1952, p. 21, Table 13). The consistency among Hurst's three Michigan samples is very good. On the other hand, one of the three Georgia samples was "uniquely different," but this unique sample is not described.

Hurst and Larson's opening statement deserves comment. They note that "For some time it has been almost tacitly accepted that most or all of the pre-Columbian copper artifacts found in the eastern United States were manufactured of native copper recovered from the *glacial drifts* of the western Great Lakes region" because of the abundance of copper artifacts in that area, the quantity and availability of the copper, the scarcity of other deposits, and that "*all* the copper artifacts so far analyzed show compositional similarities to the Great Lakes copper." (P. 177 [italics added].) Whether or not it is true that archaeologists have been laboring under these delusions, the evidence for extensive aboriginal *mining* of copper from open pits in the Lake Superior area has been known since Whittlesey's *Ancient Mining on the Shores of Lake Superior* appeared in 1863. This was preceded by several obscure, brief accounts. Documentary evidence for the mining of copper by Indians in eastern and southeastern United States was summarized by Rickard in 1934 (pp. 266-71). It has been common knowledge for some time that native copper occurs in many places as Hurst and Larson point out in the case of Georgia (also see T. Watson, 1923). Moore (1894, pp. 233-37, 241) thought that most of the copper in southeastern United States was derived from the Lake Superior area, and that the Southeast was an unlikely source for native copper; but he also thought, on the basis of trace element analyses, that some of the copper used in Florida came from Cuba, and possibly from Mexico and southwestern United States.

The most exhaustive analysis for trace elements in archaeological specimens from North America was reported by W. J. Kroll (1957) on copper beads from Oregon. Spectrochemical analysis by S. M. Shelton of thirty-six beads showed that twenty-five of the thirty-seven elements tested for were not present in any of the beads. Kroll indicates the amounts of trace elements in each bead by ranges, but in a gravimetric analysis of twelve of the thirty-six specimens he gives exact percentages. He found that the copper beads are not pure enough to be either electrolytic copper, or native copper from the Great Lakes, and he concluded that the specimens are probably early postcontact trade items.

In a two-volume history of metals by Leslie Aitchison (1960), reference is made to the work of Phillips (1925*a*) and Rickard (1930), but some of Aitchison's generalizations are untenable.

Outside of the archaeological literature, only a few references to the trace element content of North American native copper have been found. H. C. H. Carpenter (1914, p. 233) gives an analysis of Lake Superior native copper by Bardwell, in which antimony, arsenic, and silver were found. H. O. Hofman (1924, p. 66), citing Douglas (1895), says that "Native copper is very pure, containing 99.92 per cent Cu (copper) with small amounts of Ag (silver) and Fe (iron), perhaps some traces of Ni (nickel) and As (arsenic)." Kroll (1957, p. 228) refers to this source: "According to H. O. Hofman, a copper content of 99.92 per cent can be expected in native copper, the main impurities being nickel, bismuth, and arsenic."

J. W. Mellor (1928, p. 6) says that "Native copper is usually fairly pure, but it may contain small amounts of silver and bismuth."

Speaking of native copper in the Lake Superior district, Joseph Newton and Curtis Wilson (1942, p. 4) state that "The metal is very pure, containing 98 to 99.92 per cent copper with small amounts of silver which are mechanically enclosed and not alloyed. . . .Some iron, arsenic, nickel, bismuth, and mercury may also be present but strangely no gold."

In an effort to salvage something from the studies of trace elements in archaeological specimens, all the trace element analyses of North American native copper and archaeological copper specimens have been tabulated. A portion of this tabulation, showing the analyses of native copper, is reproduced in Tables XII-XVI. It is clear that there is more consistency between analyses by the same analyst of specimens from different areas than there is between specimens from the same area examined by different analysts. When all of the analyses are considered, no distinctive attributes can be discerned for any area. Selective use of the data does raise some interesting possibilities, but they can not be confirmed with the available data. For example, when only Moore's (1894) data for the Lake Superior area are considered, the sample from Isle Royale is distinguished from the Upper Michigan samples. The Isle Royale sample has more silver than iron, and nickel is present; all but one of the Upper Michigan samples have more iron than silver, and nickel was not detected in any of them. Arsenic, iron, and silver have been detected in native copper from all parts of North America.

TABLE XII
TRACE ELEMENTS IN LAKE SUPERIOR NATIVE COPPER
(In Per Cent)

Provenience	Kearsarge Mine	Tamarack Mine	Isle Royale	Phoenix Mine	Quincy Mine	Quincy Mine	Atlantic Mine	Central Mine	Osceola Mine	Franklin Mine	Glacial Drift, Illinois	Lake Superior	Lake Superior	Keweenaw Peninsula	Lake Superior	Lake Superior	Michigan	Ontonagon Co., Michigan	Michigan
Analyst.....	Harry F. Keller	Harry F. Keller	Harry F. Keller	Harry F. Keller	Harry F. Keller	A.R.Ledoux & Co.	A.R.Ledoux & Co.	A.R.Ledoux & Co.	A.R.Ledoux & Co.	A.R.Ledoux & Co.	A.R.Ledoux & Co.	Bardwell	U.S.Bureau of Standards*	Analyst?	E. Voce	Analyst?	Vernon J. Hurst §	Vernon J. Hurst	Vernon J. Hurst
Publication..	Moore, 1894	Moore, 1894	Moore, 1894	Moore, 1894	Moore, 1894	Moore, 1894 (2 analyses)	Moore, 1894	Moore, 1894	Moore, 1894	Moore, 1894	Moore, 1894	Carpenter, 1914	Phillips, 1925 a	Phillips, 1925 b	Voce, 1948	Forbes, 1950: 292	Hurst & Larson, 1958	Hurst & Larson, 1958	Hurst & Larson, 1958
Aluminum Al															tr		11	11	11
Antimony Sb			0			0	0	0	0	0	0	0.0022	tr 0.0000 †		0	0.002			
Arsenic As	tr		tr	tr	0	0.0010	0.0028	0.0016	tr	0	0	0.0019	0.0006- 0.0099		0	0.002	10	10	10
Bismuth Bi			0						0	0	0				0.0001				
Cadmium Cd																			
Chromium Cr																			
Cobalt Co			0			0			0	0					0		0	0	0
Germanium Ge																			
Gold Au			0												0				
Iron Fe	0.0223	0.0240	0.0068	pr	tr				0.0290	0.018	0.014		0.0014- 0.0063	0	0.0002 ‡ 0.005		12	12	12
Lead Pb			0						0	0	0		0- 0.0011		0 0.0003 ‡		6	0	6
Magnesium Mg																	12	11	13
Manganese Mn			0												0		8	8	11
Mercury Hg																			
Nickel Ni			0.0037	0	0	0			0	0			0.001- 0.0108		0		6	6	6
Oxygen O			0																
Phosphorus P															0		10	10	10
Platinum Pt																	0	0	0
Selenium Se																			
Silicon Si	0.0210	0.0193													<0.008		14	15	16
Silver Ag	0.0183	0.0151	0.0271	tr	pr	0.0253	0.0012	0.0145	0.0111	tr	0.007	0.229	0.057- 0.071	0	0	0.15	2	2	1
Sulphur S			0																
Tellurium Te															0				
Thallium Tl																			
Tin Sn			0												0				
Titanium Ti																	6	6	6
Vanadium V																			6
Zinc Zn									0	0	0				0				
Nickel & Cobalt Ni & Co											0.006								

NOTE.- 0 = not detected; tr = very small amount detected; pr = present, but amount not indicated; blank space = not tested for.
* Data based on range of numerous samples.
† This must be a misprint, but it appears in both the London and Menasha publications.
‡ Different parts of the same specimen.
§ Hurst's figures indicate relative abundance on a scale of 1 to 20.

TABLE XIII
TRACE ELEMENTS IN SOUTHEAST NATIVE COPPER
(In Per Cent)

Provenience		West Jefferson, Ashe County, No. Carolina	Oglethorpe County, Georgia	Fannin County, Georgia	Cobre Mountains, Cuba
Analyst		Vernon J. Hurst	Vernon J. Hurst	Vernon J. Hurst	A. R. Ledoux & Co.
Publication		Hurst & Larson, 1958	Hurst & Larson, 1958	Hurst & Larson, 1958	Moore, 1894
Aluminum	Al	12	10	9	
Antimony	Sb				tr
Arsenic	As	14	0	0	0.0087
Bismuth	Bi				0
Cadmium	Cd				
Chromium	Cr				
Cobalt	Co	0	0	0	0
Germanium	Ge				
Gold	Au				
Iron	Fe	14	6	10	0.019
Lead	Pb	4	8	9	0
Magnesium	Mg	13	10	5	
Manganese	Mn	12	0	0	
Mercury	Hg				
Nickel	Ni	8	0	0	0
Oxygen	O				pr
Phosphorus	P	10	0	0	
Platinum	Pt	2	0	0	
Selenium	Se				
Silicon	Si	20	15	6	
Silver	Ag	2	2	2	0.0056
Sulphur	S				
Tellurium	Te				
Thallium	Tl				
Tin	Sn				0
Titanium	Ti	11	6	6	
Vanadium	V	6	0	0	
Zinc	Zn				0
Nickel & Cobalt	Ni & Co				

NOTE. – 0 = not detected; tr = very small amount detected; pr = present, but amount not indicated; blank space = not tested for.

TABLE XIV
TRACE ELEMENTS IN SOUTHWEST NATIVE COPPER
(In Per Cent)

Provenience....	Chino, N. Mex.	Santa Rita, N. Mex.	Copper Queen Mine, Bisbee, Arizona		Fry Mine, Clifton, Ariz.	Arizona	Arizona	Arizona	Arizona	Arizona	Arizona
Analyst	E. Voce	Vernon J. Hurst	Harry F. Keller		A. R. Ledoux & Co.	W. C. Root	W. C. Root	W. C. Root	W. C. Root	W. C. Root	W. C. Root
Publication	Voce, 1948	Hurst & Larson, 1958	Moore, 1894 (2 runs on same spec.)		Moore, 1894	Lothrop, 1952	Lothrop, 1952	Lothrop, 1952	Lothrop, 1952	Lothrop, 1952	Lothrop, 1952
Aluminum Al	0	0									
Antimony Sb	0		0.002		0	0	0	0	0	0	0
Arsenic As	0.02	0	0	0	0	0	0	0	0	0	0
Bismuth Bi	0		0	0	0	0	0	0	0	0	0
Cadmium Cd						0	0	0	0	0	0
Chromium Cr						0	0	0	0	0	0
Cobalt Co	0	10	0	0	0	0	0	0	0	0	0
Germanium Ge						0	0	0	0	0	0
Gold Au	0		0	0		0	0	0	0	0	0
Iron Fe	0	14	0.0491	0.0503	0.045	0	0	0	0	0	0
Lead Pb	0	6	0	0	0	0.01	0	0	0	0	0
Magnesium Mg		5									
Manganese Mn	0	0									
Mercury Hg											
Nickel Ni	0	6	0	0	0	0	0	0	0	0	0
Oxygen O			0.1220	0.1094							
Phosphorus P	0	10									
Platinum Pt		0				0	0	0	0	0	0
Selenium Se			0	0							
Silicon Si	<0.008	15									
Silver Ag	0.005	2	0.0039	0.0037	0.003	2.0	2.0	2.0	2.0	0	0
Sulphur S			tr	0							
Tellurium Te	0		0	0							
Thallium Tl											
Tin Sn	0		0	0		0	0	0	0	0	0
Titanium Ti		10									
Vanadium V		0									
Zinc Zn	0					0	0	0	0	0	0
Nickel & Cobalt Ni & Co											

NOTE. – 0 = not detected; tr = very small amount detected; pr = present, but amount not indicated; blank space = not tested for.

TABLE XV
TRACE ELEMENTS IN NORTHERN MEXICO NATIVE COPPER
In Per Cent

Provenience ...		H. S. Graham's Mine, Coahuila	Cananea, Sonora	Cananea, Sonora	Descubridora, Durango	Concepcion del Oro, Zacatecas
Analyst........		Harry F. Keller	W. C. Root	W. C. Root	W. C. Root	W. C. Root
Publication		Moore, 1894	Lothrop, 1952	Lothrop, 1952	Lothrop, 1952	Lothrop, 1952
Aluminum	Al					
Antimony	Sb	0.0054	0	0	0	0
Arsenic	As	0.0149	0	0	0	0
Bismuth	Bi	?	0	0	0	0
Cadmium	Cd					
Chromium	Cr					
Cobalt	Co	0				
Germanium	Ge					
Gold	Au	0	0	0	0	0
Iron	Fe	0.0168				
Lead	Pb	0	0	0	0	0
Magnesium	Mg					
Manganese	Mn					
Mercury	Hg					
Nickel	Ni	0				
Oxygen	O					
Phosphorus	P					
Platinum	Pt					
Selenium	Se	0				
Silicon	Si					
Silver	Ag	tr	0	0	0	0
Sulphur	S					
Tellurium	Te	0				
Thallium	Tl					
Tin	Sn	0	0	0	0	0
Titanium	Ti					
Vanadium	V					
Zinc	Zn					
Nickel & Cobalt	Ni & Co					

NOTE. — 0= not detected; tr= very small amount detected; pr= present, but amount not indicated; blank space= not tested for.

TABLE XVI
TRACE ELEMENTS IN NATIVE COPPER HAVING NO SPECIFIC LOCATION DATA
(In Per Cent)

Kind of Copper		Native Copper	Lake Superior Native Copper	Lake Superior Native Copper	Lake Superior Copper
Opinion..........		H. O. Hofman	Joseph Newton & Curtis Wilson	W. C. Root	Robert Ritzenthaler
Publication.......		Hofman, 1924	Newton & Wilson 1942	Butler & Osborne, 1958	Ritzenthaler, 1946
Aluminum	Al				
Antimony	Sb				
Arsenic	As	?	pr		pr
Bismuth	Bi		pr		
Cadmium	Cd				
Chromium	Cr				
Cobalt	Co				pr
Germanium	Ge				
Gold	Au		0		
Iron	Fe	pr	pr		pr
Lead	Pb				
Magnesium	Mg				
Manganese	Mn				
Mercury	Hg		pr		
Nickel	Ni	?	pr		pr
Oxygen	O				
Phosphorus	P				
Platinum	Pt				
Selenium	Se				
Silicon	Si				
Silver	Ag	pr	pr	pr	pr
Sulphur	S				
Tellurium	Te				
Thallium	Tl				
Tin	Sn				
Titanium	Ti				
Vanadium	V				
Zinc	Zn				
Nickel & Cobalt	Ni & Co				

NOTE. — 0 = not detected; tr = very small amount detected; pr = present, but amount not indicated; blank space = not tested for.

The data were manipulated in several ways by visual inspection and by tabulation of the quantitative and qualitative data, but they are too few to allow statistical treatment, especially since the theoretical basis for the distribution of trace elements in different copper deposits is not understood. It is obvious that many specimens of native copper from each region must be carefully analyzed for a large number of trace elements before the usefulness of trace elements in archaeological research can be established.

POTENTIALITIES OF TRACE ELEMENT ANALYSIS IN ARCHAEOLOGY

Cursory examination of some of the technical literature on spectrochemical analysis and trace elements, and consultation with several specialists, has elicited the information presented in this section. These investigations indicate that it is theoretically possible to use trace elements to characterize copper from different regions. Even within one region, there may be characteristic differences, but these should not overshadow the regional characteristics. Although specific characteristics of different mines in one region may not always be discernible with present techniques, the characterization of different districts should pose no problem. The existence of regional and subregional characteristics of mill concentrates and smelted (nonelectrolytic) copper has been empirically demonstrated (for example, see Eichrodt and Schloen, 1955, pp. 214-19; and Broderick, 1929). It is unlikely that these characteristics are entirely due to different smelting processes.

Other methods of distinguishing native copper sources might be used, but they are also concerned with trace elements. The gravimetric method is usually less satisfactory for trace elements in amounts less than about .01 per cent, and it is very time consuming when many elements are being analyzed.

> X-ray fluorescence is fast, non-destructive, and requires only small samples. However, it is generally limited to elements above Titanium on the periodic table, and is generally not more sensitive than 0.1 per cent, although with special techniques, sensitivities on the order of 0.01 per cent are possible. (James A. Whelan, personal communication, 1961.)

These techniques can be called on for special problems, but from a practical standpoint the spectrochemical method is preferable since it efficiently identifies many elements, permits sensitive quantitative analysis to parts per million for some elements, and allows accurate analysis of samples smaller than 20 milligrams. An experienced technician can run about five samples per day, including duplicate runs and standards, with the spectrograph. When the impurities in a metal become larger than traces, other methods must be used for quantitative analysis. Some elements, such as oxygen and sulphur which are important in copper ores, and selenium cannot be detected spectrographically (Caley and Easby, 1959, p. 63; Voce, 1948, p. 19).

In reviewing the literature on trace element analysis of archaeological specimens from North America, two major problems were noted: The unacknowledged discrepancies in the work of different analysts, and the few cross references to the work of others, Hurst and Larson (1958) being an exception to the latter. It appears that some of those who are dealing with archaeological problems are rather naïve about the validity of trace element analysis, although specialists are well aware of the difficulties (for example, see Fairbairn, and others, 1951).

Spectrochemical methods have developed rapidly in recent years. Increased sensitivity of equipment has made the necessity of holding all variables constant more important than ever. Quantitative scales can now be accurately constructed from commercially available standards (samples with known amounts and kinds of trace elements), against which each unknown specimen should be run. Not only does this allow the work of one analyst to be more consistent, but it also improves the comparability of analyses carried out by different laboratories. The possibility of error is greatly increased when very small traces are being measured. During the uranium rush in western United States in the early 1950's, some assay laboratories installed spectrographs to identify trace elements useful in uranium prospecting. Their inexperience, and specimen contamination in the field and laboratory produced many anomalous results.

Far from being restricted to the metallic elements, as Root was, analysts now find it practical to make quantitative or semi-quantitative determinations on over forty elements. For sensitive quantitative work, standards for at least seventeen elements are available (Michaelis, 1956, p. 49). The implication of more rigid procedures also improves the usefulness of the method. Precision is increased by running standards numerous times to determine the mean and standard deviation of error for each element, and by running unknown specimens two or three times. In addition, the calculated sensitivity of the laboratory for each specimen can be compared to the many published tables which show the sensitivity attained by other laboratories. Further information can be found in any recent text on spectrochemical analysis.

B. H. McLeod (1945, p. 185), W. S. Root (1951, p. 91), and F. G. Hawley (1953, p. 101) have expressed doubt that the source of copper can be determined by trace element analysis. Hawley states:

> It is now realized that, although spectrographic analysis is accurate qualitatively, it is not always reliable in determining small differences in amounts of most elements. Most of the copper minerals found near the surface in both Arizona and Mexico, and hence usually oxidized, are comparatively pure and contain the same foreign elements in small but somewhat varying amounts. In areas both north and south of the international border, these impurities vary in different mines and even in different parts of the same mine, a condition which diminishes the reliability of spectrographic analysis in determining original provenience of the ore from which the metal was derived.

About fifteen years ago the British launched a study of trace elements in metal artifacts, and concerning native copper they said:

> The task is likely to be a big one. With elements reckoned in parts per million there is as yet no evidence to suggest that an estimation made on a small fragment of a single specimen is in any way representative of the mineralized area as a whole, or even for all parts of the specimen submitted. . . .The chance that sufficient analyses to be of value for our purpose will ever be made, or even that sufficient material for analyses will ever be available, seems remote. . . .For copper obtained by smelting ores, of which, in early times, the carbonates alone are of importance, the position is very different (Bromehead, 1948, pp. 6-7).

These statements seem overly pessimistic, but the dearth of adequate empirical data makes it impossible to evaluate them.

Very little of the literature on the analysis of Old World copper archaeological specimens has been examined, but those seen, with the exception of the one already cited (Voce, 1947), are concerned with alloys, or ores having large impurities. An excellent introduction to the problem of trace elements in copper ores, as opposed to native copper, is given by Biek (1957).

Just prior to final preparation of this discussion, H. H. Coghlan's recent paper (1960) was brought to my attention. Coghlan's excellent discussion (pp. 2-7) of the methods and limitations in trace element analysis of archaeological specimens is so similar to what I have already written that it seems more instructive to refer the interested reader to Coghlan's paper than to discuss it here. The independent development of these two similar viewpoints from dissimilar backgrounds is very interesting.

The discussions (pp. 24-33) following Coghlan's paper cannot be accepted without several reservations, however. For example, R. Pittioni states that "in natural raw copper the only impurity is silver." (P. 26.) Analyses on a world-wide scale by Voce (1948), and in North America by everyone except Root (in Butler and Osborne, 1958, p. 220), have always detected other trace elements in native copper. The basis of the statements by Pittioni and Root remains unclear.

METALLOGRAPHIC STUDIES

Examination of the physical structure in cross sections of copper archaeological specimens for information about the manufacturing processes used by the North American Indians has been applied less widely, and by fewer workers, than have studies of trace elements. The writer's interest in metallographic studies has been less intense than in trace element studies of archaeological material, so the following comments are relatively brief.

In metallographic analysis, the physical structure is observed with a microscope on polished and etched cross sections. The most prominent features seen in the cross section are the crystals, or grains, as metallographers call them. Dark lines mark the grain boundaries. The plane of the cross section should be cut parallel to the direction of hammering in hammered specimens so that the distortion of the grains can be observed with maximum clarity. The unit cells in each grain are all oriented in the same direction, but the grains are oriented in different directions; so in a cross section the intensity of the light reflected from all the unit cells in a grain is uniform, but the light intensity varies from grain to grain. The various shades of the grains are clearly visable in good photographs (Wilson and Sayre, 1935, Pl. 12; McLeod, 1937, Pl. ccxv, a).

In unworked native copper, the grains tend to be equidimensional (Frank, 1951, p. 58, Fig. 37, f). Wilson and Sayre (1935, p. 109), however, state that no grains are visable in unworked or in cold-worked native copper. It seems probable that the grains, in the specimens which Wilson and Sayre observed, were considerably larger than the field of their microscope, or that they were looking at the large surface of a distorted grain.

Cold-working sets up strains in the copper causing it to become more brittle, and increasing the hardness of native copper from 87 (78.1 according to Coghlan, 1951, p. 91) to 135 on the Brinell hardness scale (Forbes, 1950, p. 322).

> In most cases, it is found that the extent of cold deformation has a definite limit, as the metal will become more and more brittle and finally approach the point of failure by cracking. [Prior to cracking] it can be restored to a condition suitable for further cold working only by an annealing operation.

> During cold deformation, the individual grains of the metal become more elongated and increasingly distorted. (Toussaint, 1955, p. 654.)

In the case of extreme cold-working, the grains become very flat, and in a cross section the boundaries may be too close to allow resolution in the microscope.

Heating of cold-worked copper releases the strain, and reduces the brittleness and hardness. The grains tend to regain their equidimensional form, i.e., are recrystallized, as the heat is increased. Although both time and temperature factors are involved, the brittleness, hardness, and grain form are restored to the condition characteristic of unworked copper when native copper is heated to about 200° to 225° C. When the characteristics of cold-working have been eliminated, the copper is said to be recrystallized. When the recrystallization is brought about by intentional heating, it is called annealing. Impurities in the copper may raise the annealing temperature, but the annealing temperature of native copper can be easily attained in an open wood fire. Copper that is hot-worked at the annealing temperature will have the same grain form as copper that is cold-worked and then annealed (Voce, 1961, p. 69). Grain size is affected by both time and temperature factors.

Recrystallization may come about at ordinary temperatures through time alone (Thompson, 1958, p. 1), but whether this involves a few, or many, thousands of years is not known (Voce, 1961, p. 70). As long as this variable remains undefined, the significance of grain form in copper artifacts, especially in older specimens, is uncertain. In the copper artifacts from the western Great Lakes area analyzed by Wilson and Sayre (1935, Pl. 12) and by Frank (1951, p. 58, Fig. 37, a-d) the grains are not severely distorted. It seems possible that the specimens have not been annealed after the final cold-hammering, and that the grains have recrystallized with age.

In addition to distorting the grains, cold-working also causes twins and slip bands to form. Twins are closely parallel, dark, straight lines cutting across the grains (for example, see Wilson and Sayre, 1935, Pl. 12; Frank, 1951, p. 58, Fig. 37, a-d; and Thompson, 1958, Pl. B, a). Twinning is a reorientation of the unit cells, so that in addition to the different intensities of light reflected from different grains, the twins separate different intensities of light in each grain (for example, see Thompson, 1958, Pl. B, a). Slip bands are very closely parallel, light, slightly wavy lines cutting across the grains at about a 45° angle to the long axis of the copper grain (for example, see Thompson, 1958, Pl. B, d; and Wilson and Sayre, 1935, Pls. 12, 2). The slip bands may obscure the twins, and in a severely worked specimen neither the slip bands nor the twins may be distinguishable. Twins and slip bands form easily, and they have been noted in unworked native copper (Frank, 1951, p. 58, Fig. 37, f, slip bands near upper left corner). Thompson (1958, p. 2) suggests that slip bands will form by the stress caused during the removal of native copper from its matrix. When the copper is annealed, the slip bands disappear, but the twins remain.

If a copper archaeological specimen has distorted grains, present evidence suggest that there is no sure way to tell if the object has been annealed prior to hammering. If the specimen shows extensive twinning, it has probably been hammered, but "unhammered" specimens may show a few twins, as was pointed out above. Wilson and Sayre (1935, p. 111) erroneously say that "Twinning always shows that the copper has been mechanically worked and then annealed." Their own evidence does not appear to support this statement, as Shepard (1936, p. 139) has already pointed out.

When copper is melted (about 1100° C.) in an oxidizing atmosphere, spherical inclusions of copper sulphide, copper oxide, or other impurities may be introduced into the copper, and they arrange themselves along the grain boundaries. The presence of impurities may cause a decrease in the workability of the copper. When copper that has been melted is worked, the inclusions are deformed in the same direction as the crystals (for example, see McLeod, 1945, p. 227, Pl. 14). Remelting restores the inclusions and grains to their equidimensional shapes. Annealing of copper that has been melted usually restores only the grains to an equidimensional form, while the inclusions remain deformed. However, if the inclusions have a lower melting point than the copper, they may melt and spheroidize in the annealing process. In addition, prolonged annealing tends to spheroidize the inclusions and to grow large grains. McLeod (1957, p. 234) reports historic tubular beads from the state of Washington made from a sheet of copper having very even thickness, as if rolled, and showing spherical inclusions. The exterior of the sheet shows that it had been heated very hot, and that it is possible that the inclusions contained: "sufficient impurities to lower the melting point of the mixture and when the sheet was heated to a high temperature not only did the crystal structure reform, but the inclusions reached a very nearly spherical shape." (P. 234.) Apparently, McLeod means that the bead was heated enough to anneal the copper and to melt the inclusions, but not enough to melt the copper.

Some bells from Snaketown, Arizona, have inclusions which are arranged as if outlining nonexistent grains (McLeod, 1937). The inclusions are also present on the boundaries of the visable crystals. McLeod attributes this to prolonged heat treatment or to extremely slow cooling. In either case the rearrangement of the grains occurred after the original solidification of the metal. Prolonged heating could be due to an attempt to temper the copper (by age hardening?) or to remove gas inclusions, according to McLeod. Copper alloys are age hardened by heating to a high temperature, quenching, and then prolonged heating at a suitable lower temperature. Native copper can not be age hardened. Some metals, but not copper, can be hardened by heating and quenching. To relieve the strains of the hardening process, the metal is tempered by prolonged heating at a suitable lower temperature (Read, 1934, p. 386). The tempering of iron and the annealing of copper are similar processes, and they both relieve strain. Tempering is not a hardening process, and it does not involve any "tempering agent" as Martin, Quimby, and Collier (1947, p. 42) seem to imply.

In addition to information about the treatment of the copper, metallographic examination has been used to distinguish native copper from ore-derived copper.

> There does seem some possibility that native copper, so long as it has not been remelted, can be identified by the complete absence of oxide inclusions, but even here it would be nice to have further information regarding the possibility of the existence of other inclusions such as sulphides which, when small, are most difficult to distinguish from the oxide itself. The identification, then, of copper as being native is a matter of no small difficulty which can probably not always be done with complete certainty. . . .(Thompson, 1958, p. 1).

Thompson (*ibid.*) has emphasized that the structures and grain arrangements seen in copper are reflections of how it has been treated, and that they do not distinguish between native copper and ore-derived copper. Concerning the presence of inclusions, Voce (1961, p. 70) says that "The presence of cuprous oxide proves conclusively that the copper was melted without much protection from the air; it could not possibly have been wrought from a piece of unmelted native copper."

McLeod (1957, p. 233) makes a similar statement. A rather vague statement by Hawley (1953, p. 103) may also be relevant: "When copper is cast, small crystals of metallic copper, as well as small segregations of copper oxide and small spheres of copper sulfide form throughout the cooling metal. If this metal is polished and then etched and examined microscopically, the crystals may be seen to have approximately equal dimensions. The sulfide appears as small round inclusions. Native copper may have some of these characteristics."

The absence of oxide inclusions is not an entirely reliable guide in distinguishing native copper from ore-derived copper. If copper is annealed at a high temperature, the oxide inclusions may disappear (McLeod, 1945, p. 183), and they are absent from some refined coppers (Thompson, 1958, p. 1). However, if all the chemical, metallographical, and archaeological evidence is brought to bear on the problem, some fairly confident statements can probably be made about many specimens, but it may be an oversimplification to say that ". . . .the metallurgist can always differentiate between a metal which has been melted, and an unmelted native copper which has not been subjected to any form of heat treatment." (Coghlan, 1951, p. 92.)

Some of the uncertainties of metallographic studies are evident in an examination of Arlington H. Mallery's (1951, p. 231-38) evidence for prehistoric casting of copper in eastern United States. Inclusions in cast copper are typically arranged around the grain boundaries, as shown in Mallery's photographs of specimens from Mexico and Guatemala (also see McLeod, 1937, Pl. ccxiv, a, a, Pl. ccxv, a, b; 1945, p. 225, Pl. 13). None of Mallery's illustrated specimens from eastern United States show this typical structure. The inclusions can be clearly seen in only four of his seven photographs of eastern United States specimens, and in these four photographs the field is too small to determine how the inclusions are arranged. On the other hand, the presence of oxide inclusions in the specimens suggest that the artifacts were not made from unmelted native copper.[2] Since Mallery's evidence supports a viewpoint not generally accepted by American archaeologists, it is unfortunate that he has neither discussed the metallographic evidence of Wilson and Sayre (1935) and Frank (1951) supporting this traditional viewpoint, nor documented his own evidence more carefully.

CONCLUSIONS

The raw data of trace element and metallographic studies of copper archaeological specimens from North America have been reviewed in detail. The technique of acquiring and interpreting the data pivot on the data themselves. Where the data are conflicting or not comparable, the techniques of analysis need

2. Compare with Drier's findings on pp. 135-37.

revision, and the interpretations based on the analyses are probably not dependable. For these reasons many of the trace element data that have been presented in the analyses of archaeological problems are not very useful. It almost seems that archaeologists reporting trace element data have been reluctant to doubt the infallibility of the "exact sciences." Only one instance has been noted where conflicting information was mentioned (Haury, 1947, p. 81).

A much wider application of metallographic studies is necessary. For example, Hurst and Larson (1958, p. 178) have raised the possibility that copper was prehistorically smelted in Tennessee. As far as known, there are no metallographic analyses of copper archaeological specimens from southeastern United States. New potentialities of metallographic analysis in this and other areas need investigation.

A modern study of trace elements in copper may demonstrate that this type of investigation can be much more useful to archaeological research than the older studies suggest. Certainly, greater precision and sensitivity can be achieved. It remains to be demonstrated, however, whether or not the trace elements in different native copper deposits are distinctive enough to be useful in the determination of the origin of prehistoric copper artifacts. The available evidence does suggest that many specimens will have to be carefully analyzed before any conclusions about the usefulness of the technique can be made.

Addendum. Mildred M. Wedel's stimulating study (_Missouri Archaeologist_, Vol. 21, Nos. 2-4, 1959) of twenty-four trace elements in seven copper archeological specimens from the Midwest came to my attention too late for discussion. The technique is not described. Each element was run twice, but the basis of the single published figure for each element in each specimen is not given. The relatively high impurity in the float copper specimen may be due to the sampling technique. If clean specimens had been analyzed, purity alone might have indicated whether they were unmelted native copper or smelted copper. Wedel's statements about bismuth, antimony, and zinc should be compared with Table XII. Wedel's work called attention to three additional studies: Smith and Grange (_Bureau of American Ethnology_, _Bulletin 169_, 1958), Solecki (_Bureau of American Ethnology_, _Bulletin 151_, 1953), and Vickers and Bird (_American Antiquity_, Vol. 15, No. 2, 1949).

REFERENCES AND ADDITIONAL SOURCES

Adams, Charles C.
1906 An Ecological Survey in Northern Michigan. A report from the University Museum, University of Michigan. State Board of Geological Survey for 1905. Lansing.

Aitchison, Leslie
1960 A History of Metals. New York: Interscience Publishers, Inc.

Baerreis, David A., Hirshi Daifuku, and J. E. Lunstead
1954 The Burial Complex of the Reigh Site, Winnebago County, Wisconsin. The Wisconsin Archeologist, N. S., Vol. 35, No. 1, pp. 1-36. Milwaukee.

Bannister, C. O.
1925 (no title.) Institute of Metals, Journal, Vol. 34, p. 267. London.

Barrett, S. A.
1925 Aboriginal Copper Mines at McCargoe's Cove, Isle Royale. *In:* Yearbook of the Public Museum of the City of Milwaukee, 1924, Vol. 4, pp. 25-31.

Bell, Charles N.
1928 An Implement of Prehistoric Man. Thirty-sixth Annual Archaeological Report, 1928. Appendix to the Report of the Minister of Education, Ontario, pp. 51-54. Toronto.

Bemis, Samuel Flagg.
1935 The Diplomacy of the American Revolution. Washington, D. C.: The American Historical Association.

Bergsøe, Paul
1938 The Gilding Process and the Metallurgy of Copper and Lead Among the Pre-Columbian Indians. Ingeniørvidenshabelige Skrifter, Nr. A46. Copenhagen.

Biek, L.
1957 The Examination of Some Copper Ores. Man, Vol. 57, pp. 72-76. London.

Bigelow, Martha M.
1957 Isle Royale National Park Movement, A Study in Frustrations. Michigan History, Vol. 41, pp. 34-44. Lansing.

Biggar, H. P., (ed.)
1924 Publications of the Public Archives of Canada, No. 11. The Voyages of Jacques Cartier. Ottawa.
1925 The Publications of the Champlain Society, Vol. 2, The Works of Samuel De Champlain. Toronto.
1929 The Publications of the Champlain Society, Vol. 3, The Works of Samuel De Champlain. Toronto.

Binford, Lewis R.
n.d. A Proposed Attribute List for the Description and Classification of Projectile Points. Anthropological Papers, Museum of Anthropology, The University of Michigan. Ann Arbor.

Blue, A.
1894 Mine Report. Third Report of the Bureau of Mines, 1893. Toronto.

Broderick, T. M.
1929 Zoning in Michigan Copper Deposits and its Significance, Pt. I. Distribution of Arsenic in the Michigan Native Copper Deposits. Economic Geology, Vol. 24, No. 2, pp. 149-62. Lancaster, Pa.: Economic Geology Publishing Co.

Bromehead, C. E. N.
1948 The Geology of Copper from the Archaeological Point of View. Man, Vol. 48, Art. 3, pp. 5-7. London, England.

Brown, Charles E.
1904 The Native Copper Ornaments of Wisconsin. The Wisconsin Archaeologist, Vol. 3, pp. 101-21. Milwaukee.

Brown, Clair A.
1933 Ferns and Flowering Plants of Isle Royale, Michigan. U.S. Department of Interior. National Park Service, Emergency Conservation Work. Washington, D. C.

Butler, B. Robert, and Douglas Osborne
1959 Archaeological Evidence for the use of Atlatl Weights in the Northwest. American Antiquity, Vol. 25, No. 2, pp. 215-24. Salt Lake City: University of Utah.

Caley, Earle R., and Dudley T. Easby
1959 The Smelting of Sulphide Ores of Copper in Preconquest Peru. American Antiquity, Vol. 25, No. 1, pp. 59-65. Salt Lake City: University of Utah.

Carpenter, H. C. H.
1914 The Extraction of Native Copper at Calumet, Lake Superior, U.S.A. Institute of Metals, Journal, Vol. 12, pp. 230-33. London.

Carver, Jonathan
1796 Three Years Travels Through the Interior Parts of North America. Philadelphia: Joseph Crukshank.

Coghlan, H. H.
1951 Native Copper in Relation to Prehistory. Man, Vol. 51, Art. 156, pp. 90-93. London.
1960 Metallurgical Analysis of Archaeological Materials: I. Viking Fund Publications in Anthropology, No. 28, pp. 1-20. Chicago: Quadrangle Books, Inc.

Cole, Fay-Cooper, and Thorne Deuel
1937 Rediscovering Illinois. Chicago: The University of Chicago Press.

Cooper, Dennis Glenn

1949 Geographic Influences on the History and Development of Isle Royale, Michigan. Papers of the Michigan Academy of Science Arts, and Letters, Vol. 24, Pt. 3, pp. 1-8. Ann Arbor: The University of Michigan Press.

Cotter, John L.

1952 The Mangum Plate. American Antiquity, Vol. 18, No. 1, pp. 65-68. Salt Lake City: University of Utah.

Croft, Henry

1856 Report on Copper Implements Found Near Brockville. The Canadian Journal, N. S., Vol. 1, No. 4, pp. 334-36. Toronto.

Davis, A. C.

1875 Antiquities of Isle Royale, Lake Superior. Annual Report of the Board of Regents of the Smithsonian Institution for 1874, pp. 369-70. Washington, D. C.

Dawson, J. W.

1857 On the Geological Structure and Mineral Deposits of the Promontory of Mamainse, Lake Superior. The Canadian Naturalist and Geologist, Vol. 2, pp. 1-12, Montreal.

Douglas, James

1895 Aboriginal Metallurgists. The Mineral Industry in 1894, Vol. 3, pp. 243-48. New York and London: The Scientific Publishing Company.

Drier, Roy W.

1939 A New Method of Sherd Classification. American Antiquity, Vol. 5, No. 1, pp. 31-35. Menasha, Wis.

Dustin, Fred

1932 A Summary of the Archaeology of Isle Royale, Michigan. Papers of the Michigan Academy of Science, Arts, and Letters, Vol. 16, pp. 1-16. Ann Arbor: The University of Michigan Press.

1957 An Archaeological Reconnaissance of Isle Royale. Michigan History, Vol. 41, pp. 1-34. Lansing.

Eichrodt, C. W., and J. H. Schloen

1955 Electrolytic Copper Refining. *In:* Allison Butts, Copper, The Science and Technology of the Metal, Its Alloys and Compounds. American Chemical Society Monograph Series, No. 122, pp. 165-222. New York: Reinhold Publishing Co.

Elson, John A.

1957 Lake Agassiz and the Mankato-Valders Problem. Science, Vol. 126, No. 3281, pp. 999-1002. Washington, D. C.

Fairbairn, H. W., and others

1951 A Cooperative Investigation of Precision and Accuracy in Chemical, Spectrochemical and Modal Analysis of Silicate Rocks. United States Geological Survey, Bulletin, No. 980. Washington, D. C.

Farrand, William R.
1960 Former Shorelines in Western and Northern Lake Superior Basin. Doctoral thesis, University of Michigan Library. Ann Arbor.

Fenton, William E.
1940 Problems Arising From the Historic Northeastern Position of the Iroquois. *In:* Essays in Historical Anthropology of North America. Smithsonian Miscellaneous Collections, Vol. 100, pp. 159-251. Washington, D. C.

Ferguson, William P. F.
1923 Michigan's Most Ancient Industry: The Prehistoric Mines and Miners of Isle Royale. Michigan History Magazine, Vol. 7, pp. 155-62. Lansing.
1924 The Franklin Isle Royale Expedition. *Ibid.*, Vol. 8, pp. 450-68.

Flaskerd, George
1940 A Schedule of Classification, Comparison and Nomenclature for Copper Artifacts in Minnesota, The Minnesota Archaelogist, Vol. 6, No. 2, pp. 34-50. Minneapolis.

Forbes, R. J.
1950 Metallurgy in Antiquity; A Notebook for Archaeologists and Technologists. Leiden: E. J. Brill.

Foster, J. W., and J. D. Whitney
1850 Report on the Geology and Topography of a Portion of the Lake Superior Land District in the State of Michigan. Copper Lands. House Executive Documents, No. 69, Pt. 1, Washington, D. C.

Foster, William
1934 Grecian and Roman Stucco, Mortar and Glass. Journal of Chemical Education, Vol. 2, pp. 223-25. Easton, Pa.

Fox, George R.
1911 The Ancient Copper Workings on Isle Royale. The Wisconsin Archeologist, Vol. 10, pp. 73-100. Milwaukee.

Frank, Leonard
1951 A Metallographic Study of Certain Pre-Columbian American Implements. American Antiquity, Vol. 17, No. 1, pp. 57-59. Salt Lake City: University of Utah.

Fryklund, P. O.
1941 A Catalog of Copper. The Minnesota Archaeologist, Vol. 7, No. 3, pp. 5-15. Minneapolis.

Gaul, James H.
1943 Observations on the Bronze Age in the Yenisei Valley, Siberia. In: Studies in the Anthropology of Oceania and Asia. Papers of the Peabody Museum of American Archaeology and Ethnology, Harvard University, Vol. 20, pp. 149-86. Cambridge: Harvard University Press.

Gillman, Henry
1873 Ancient Works at Isle Royale, Michigan. Appletons' Journal of Literature, Science, and Art, Vol. 10, pp. 173-75. New York.
1874 The Mound-Builders and Platycnemism in Michigan. Annual Report of the Board of Regents of the Smithsonian Institution for 1873, pp. 364-90. Washington, D. C.
1876 The Ancient Men of the Great Lakes. Proceedings of the American Association for the Advancement of Science, Vol. 24. Washington, D. C.

Gimbutas, Marija
1957 Borodino, Seima and their Contemporaries. Proceedings of the Prehistoric Society for 1956. New Series, Vol. 22, pp. 143-72. Cambridge, England.

Harvey, Frederick L.
1903 History of the Washington National Monument and the Washington National Monument Society. Senate Document No. 224, 57th Congress, 2d Sess. Washington, D. C.

Haury, Emil W.
1947 A Large Pre-Columbian Copper Bell from the Southwest. American Antiquity, Vol. 13, No. 1, pp. 80-82. Menasha, Wis.

Hawley, F. G.
1953 The Manufacture of Copper Bells found in Southwestern Sites. Southwestern Journal of Anthropology, Vol. 9, No. 1, pp. 99-111. Albuquerque: University of New Mexico Press.

Henry, Alexander
1901 Travels and Adventures in Canada and the Indian Territories Between the Years 1760 and 1776. Edited by James Bain, 1901. Toronto.

Hinsdale, Wilbert B.
1931 Archaeological Atlas of Michigan. Michigan Handbook Series No. 4. University Museums, University of Michigan. Ann Arbor.

Hodge, F. W. (ed.)
1912 Handbook of American Indians North of Mexico. Bureau of American Ethnology Bulletin No. 30. Smithsonian Institution. Washington, D. C.

Hofman, H. O.
1924 Metallurgy of Copper. 2d ed., rev. Carle R. Hayward, New York: McGraw-Hill Book Co.

Holmes, William H.
1901 Aboriginal Copper Mines of Isle Royale, Lake Superior. American Anthropologist, Vol. 3, pp. 684-96. Lancaster, Pa.

Hough, Jack L.
1958 Geology of the Great Lakes. Urbana: University of Illinois Press.

Houghton, J. J.
1879 Ancient Copper Mines of Lake Superior. Wisconsin Historical Collections, Vol. 8, pp. 140-51. Madison.

Hubbard, Lucius L.
1898 Keweenaw Point, with Particular Reference to the Felsites and their Associated Rocks. Geological Survey of Michigan, Vol. 6, Pt. 2. Lansing.

Hubbs, Carl L., and Karl F. Lagler
1949 Fishes of Isle Royale, Lake Superior, Michigan. Papers of the Michigan Academy of Science, Arts, and Letters. Ann Arbor: The University of Michigan.

Hurst, Vernon J., and Lewis H. Larson, Jr.
1958 On the Source of Copper at the Etowah Site, Georgia. American Antiquity, Vol. 24, No. 2, pp. 177-81. Salt Lake City: University of Utah.

Hyypio, Peter, and W. R. Farrand
N.D. Studies of Pollen from Portage Lake, Houghton County, Michigan. Umpublished manuscript to be submitted to Science magazine.

Jenks, Albert E.
1937 Minnesota's Browns Valley Man and Associated Burial Artifacts. Memoirs of the American Anthropological Association, No. 49. Menasha.

Kellogg, Louise Phelps
1925 The French Régime in Wisconsin and the Northwest. State Historical Society of Wisconsin. Madison.

Kinietz, W. V.
1940 The Indians of the Western Great Lakes, 1615-1760. Occasional Contributions from the Museum of Anthropology of the University of Michigan, No. 10. Ann Arbor: The University of Michigan.

Kroll, W. J.
1957 Report on the Composition of Indian Copper Beads Found at the McNary Dam, Oregon. Bureau of American Ethnology, Bull. No. 166, pp. 227-31. Washington, D. C.

Lane, Arthur C.
1898 Geological Report on Isle Royale, Michigan. Geological Survey of Michigan, Vol. 6, Pt. 1. Lansing.

Lawson, Andrew C.
1893 Sketch of the Coastal Topography of the North Side of Lake Superior with Special Reference to the Abandoned Strands of Lake Warren. Twentieth Annual Report, for the Year 1891. The Geological and Natural History Survey of Minnesota, pp. 182-289. Minneapolis.

Lee, Hulbert A.
1959 Surficial Geology of Southern District of Keewatin and the Keewatin Ice Divide, Northwest Territories. Geological Survey of Canada, Bull. 51. Ottawa.
1960 Late Glacial and Postglacial Hudson Bay Sea Episode. Science, Vol. 131, No. 3413, pp. 1609-11.

Leverett, Frank, and F. B. Taylor
1915 The Pleistocene of Indiana and Michigan and the History of the Great Lakes. United States Geological Survey, Monograph, Vol.. 53. Washington, D. C.

Lilly, Eli
1937 Prehistoric Antiquities of Indiana. Indianapolis: Indiana Historical Society.

Loehr, Max
1956 Chinese Bronze Age Weapons. Ann Arbor: The University of Michigan Press.

Logan, Wm. E.
1863 Geology of Canada. Geological Survey of Canada; Report of Progress from its Commencement to 1863. Montreal: Dawson Brothers.

Long, John
1791 Voyages and Travels of an Indian Interpreter and Trader, etc. London, England.

Lothrop, Samuel Kirkland
1952 Metals from the Cenote of Sacrifice, Chichen Itza, Yucatan. Peabody Museum of Archaeology and Ethnology, Memoirs, Vol. 10, No. 2. Cambridge, Mass.

MacNeish, Richard S.
1952 A Possible Early Site in the Thunder Bay District, Ontario. Report of the National Museum of Canada 1950-51, Bull. 126, pp. 23-47. Ottawa.
1958 An Introduction to the Archaeology of Southeast Manitoba. National Museum of Canada, Bull. No. 157. Ottawa.

Mallery, Arlington H.
1951 Lost America: The Story of Iron-Age Civilization Prior to Columbus. Columbus and Washington: The Overlook Company.

Manuel, W. A.
1935 How to Study Chemistry. Journal of Chemical Education, Vol. 12, pp. 579-80. Easton, Pa.

Martin, Paul S., George I. Quimby, and Donald Collier
1947 Indians Before Columbus. Chicago: University of Chicago Press.

McKern, W. C.
1942 The First Settlers of Wisconsin. Wisconsin Magazine of History, Vol. 25, pp. 153-69. Madison.

McLeod, B. H.
1937 An Examination of the Structure of Copper Bells. *In:* Harold Gladwin and others, Excavations at Snaketown, Material Culture. Medallion Papers, No. 25, pp. 278-81. Globe, Ariz., Gila Pueblo.
1945 Examination of Artifacts from Culiacán. App. II. *In:* Excavations at Culiacán, Sinaloa, by Isabel Kelly. Pp. 180-86. Ibero-Americana: 25. Los Angeles: University of California Press.
1957 Examination of Copper Artifacts from the McNary Site, Oregon. Bureau of American Ethnology, Bull. No. 166, pp. 232-34. Washington, D. C.

Meggers, William F., and Bourdon F. Scribner
1941 Index to the Literature of Spectrochemical Analysis, 1920-39. 2d ed. Philadelphia: American Society for Testing Materials.

Mellor, J. W.
1928 A Comprehensive Treatise on Inorganic and Theoretical Chemistry, Vol. 3. London: Longmans, Green and Co., Ltd.

Michaelis, Robert E.
1956 Report on Standard Samples and Related Materials for Spectrochemical Analysis, 1955. American Society for Testing Materials, Special Technical Publication No. 58-C. Philadelphia.

Miles, S. W.
1951 A Revaluation of the Old Copper Industry. American Antiquity, Vol. 16, No. 3, pp. 240-47. Salt Lake City: University of Utah.

Moore, Charles
1897 The Ontonagon Copper Boulder in the U.S. National Museum, Smithsonian Institution. Report of the U.S.N.M. for 1895, pp. 1021-30. Washington, D. C.

Moore, Clarence B.
1894 Certain Sand Mounds of the St. John's River, Florida. Journal of the Academy of Natural Sciences of Philadelphia, 2d Ser., Vol. 10, Pt. 2, pp. 129-246. Philadelphia.
1900 Certain Aboriginal Remains of the Alabama River. *Ibid.*, 2d ser., Vol. 11, Pt. 3, pp. 289-348. Philadelphia.
1903 Certain Aboriginal Mounds of the Central Florida West-Coast. *Ibid.*, Vol. 12, Pt. 3, pp. 359-494. Philadelphia.
1910 Antiquities of St. Francis, White, and Black Rivers, Arkansas. *Ibid.*, Vol. 14, Pt. 3, pp. 253-364.

Moore, Clarence B., and others.
1903 Sheet-Copper from the Mounds is not Necessarily of European Origin. American Anthropologist, N. S., Vol. 5, No. 1, pp. 27-49. Lancaster, Pa.

Newton, Joseph, and Curtis S. Wilson
1942 Metallurgy of Copper. New York: John Wiley & Sons, Inc.

Nute, Grace Lee
1943 Caesars of the Wilderness. New York: D. Appleton-Century Company.

O'Callaghan, E. B. (ed.)
1855 Documents Relating to the Colonial History of the State of New York, Vol. 9, Paris Documents, I-VIII, 1631-1744. Albany.

Olson, R.
1957 Was Our Biggest Historical Find our Biggest Hoax? Macleans Magazine, Vol. 70, pp. 30-31; 80-84. Toronto.

Packard, R. L.
1893 Pre-Columbian Copper-Mining in North America. Annual Report of the Board of Regents of the Smithsonian Institution for 1892, pp. 175-98. Washington, D. C.

Phillips, George Brinton
1922 The Composition of Some Ancient Bronze in the Dawn of the Art of Metallurgy. American Anthropologist, n.s., Vol. 24, No. 2, pp. 129-43. Menasha, Wis.
1925*a* The Primitive Copper Industry of America. American Anthropologist, N. S., Vol. 27, No. 2, pp. 284-89. Menasha, Wis. Also published, with appended discussions, *in*: Institute of Metals, Journal, Vol. 34, pp. 261-70. London.
1925*b* The Metal Industry of the Aztecs. American Anthropologist, Vol. 27, No. 4, pp. 550-57. Menasha, Wis.
1926 The Primitive Copper Industry of America. Pt. II. Institute of Metals, Journal, Vol. 36, pp. 99-106. London.
1928 The Earliest Ornamental Metal Work. America Anthropologist, N. S., Vol. 30, No. 3, pp. 465-69. Menasha.

Popham, Robert E., and J. N. Emerson
1954 Manifestations of the Old Copper Industry in Ontario. Pennsylvania Archaeologist, Vol. XXIV, pp. 1-19. Milton.

Potzger, J. E.
1942 Pollen Spectra from Four Bogs on the Gillen Nature Reserve, along the Michigan-Wisconsin State Line. The American Midland Naturalist, Vol. 25, No. 2, pp. 501-11. South Bend, Ind: University of Notre Dame Press.
1954 Post-Algonquin and Post-Nipissing Forest History of Isle Royale, Michigan. Butler University Botanical Studies, Vol. 11, pp. 199-208. Indianapolis.

Quimby, George I.
1937 Notes on Indian Trade Silver Ornaments in Michigan. Papers of the Michigan Academy of Science, Arts, and Letters, Vol. 22, pp. 15-24. Ann Arbor: The University of Michigan Press.
1938 Dated Indian Burials in Michigan. *Ibid.*, Vol. 23, pp. 63-72.
1939*a* Aboriginal Camp Sites on Isle Royale, Michigan. American Antiquity, Vol. 4, No. 3, pp. 215-23. Menasha, Wis.
1939*b* European Trade Articles as Chronological Indicators for the Archaeology of the Historic Period in Michigan. Papers of the Michigan Academy of Science, Arts, and Letters, Vol. XXIV, pt. IV, pp. 25-33. Ann Arbor: The University of Michigan.
1954. The Old Copper Assemblage and Extinct Animals. American Antiquity, Vol. 20, No. 2, pp. 169-70. Salt Lake City: University of Utah.

Quimby, George I., (Cont.)
1957 An Old Coper Site at Menominee, Michigan. The Wisconsin Archeologist, Vol. 38, No. 2, pp. 37-41. Milwaukee.
1958 New Evidence Links Chippewa to Prehistoric Culture. Chicago Natural History Museum Bulletin, Vol. 29, No. 1, pp. 7-8. Chicago.
1959 Review of Ronald J. Mason, Late Pleistocene Geochronology and the Paleo-Indian Penetration into the Lower Michigan Peninsula. American Antiquity, Vol. 24, No. 3, p. 327. Salt Lake City: University of Utah.
1960 Indian Life in the Upper Great Lakes 11,000 B.C. to A.D. 1800. Chicago.

Quimby, George I., and Albert C. Spaulding
1957 The Old Copper Culture and the Keweenaw Waterway. Fieldiana: Anthropology, Vol. 36, No. 8, pp. 189-201. Chicago.

Rainey, Froelich G.
1939 Archaeology in Central Alaska. Anthropological Papers of the American Museum of Natural History, Vol. 36, Pt. 4, pp. 351-405. New York.

Read, Thomas F.
1934 Metallurgical Fallacies in Archaeological Literature. American Journal of Archaeology, Vol. 38, No. 3, pp. 382-89. Archaeological Institute of America.

Reeder, John T.
1906 Evidences of Prehistoric Man on Lake Superior. Historical Collections: Collections and Researches Made by the Michigan Pioneer and Historical Society, Vol. 30, pp. 110-18. Lansing.

Reynolds, Thomas
1856 Discovery of Copper and Other Indian Relics, Near Brockyille. The Canadian Journal, N. S., Vol. 1, No. 4, pp. 329-34. Toronto.

Rickard, T. A.
1930 The Early Use of Metals. Institute of Metals, Journal, Vol. 43, pp. 297-365. London.
1934 The Use of Native Copper by the Indigenes of North America. Royal Anthropological Institute, Journal, Vol. 64, pp. 265-87. London.

Ridley, Frank
1957 Cultural Contacts of Iroquoian and Plains. The Pennsylvania Archaeologist, Vol. 27, No. 1, pp. 33-38. Milton.

Ritchie, William A., and Don W. Dragoo
1960 The Eastern Dispersal of Adena. New York State Museum and Science Service Bulletin, No. 379. Albany.

Ritchie, William A.,
1961 A Typology and Nomenclature of New York Projectile Points. New York State Museum and Science Service Bulletin Number 384. Albany.

Ritzenthaler, Robert E.
1946 The Osceola Site, an "Old Copper" Site near Potosi, Wisconsin. The Wisconsin Archeologist, Vol. 27, No. 3, pp. 53-70. Milwaukee.
1960 An "Old Copper" Crescent from Alberta, Canada. *Ibid.*, Vol. 41, No. 2, p. 134.

Ritzenthaler, Robert E., and others
1957 Reigh Site Report—Number 3. The Wisconsin Archeologist, Vol. 38, No. 4, pp. 278-310. Milwaukee.

Ritzenthaler, Robert E., and Warren L. Wittry
1952 The Oconto Site—An Old Copper Manifestation. *Ibid.*, Vol. 33, No. 4, pp. 199-223.

Rivet, Paul, and Henri Arsandaux
1946 La Metallurgie en Amérique Pré-Colombiene. Paris: Institut L'Ethnologie.

Root, William C.
1937*a* Analyses of Metal Artifacts from Coclé and Adjacent Regions. *In*: Samuel K. Lothrop, Coclé, an Archaeological Study of Central Panama, Pt. 1. Peabody Museum of Archaeology and Ethnology, Memoirs, No. 7, pp. 307-9. Cambridge.
1937*b* The Metallurgy of Arizona and New Mexico. *In:* Harold Gladwin, and others, Excavations at Snaketown, Material Culture. Medallion Papers, No. 25, pp. 276-77. Globe, Arizona, Gila Pueblo.
1942 Studies in the Use of Metals in Pre-Columbian America. American Philosophical Society, Yearbook, 1941, pp. 232-34. Philadelphia.
1943 A Study of Some Copper Objects from Guatemala. *In:* Bertha P. Dutton and H. R. Hobbs. Excavations at Tajumulco, Guatemala. School of American Research, Monograph, No. 9, pp. 115-16. Santa Fe, N. M.
1949*a* Metallurgy. *In:* Handbook of South American Indians. Vol. 5 of Bulletin 143 of the Bureau of American Ethnology. Smithsonian Institution, pp. 205-25. Washington, D. C.
1949*b* The Metallurgy of the Southern Coast of Peru. American Antiquity, Vol. 15, No. 1, pp. 10-37. Menasha.
1951 Metallurgical Analyses and Their Aid to Archaeology. *In*: Essays on Archaeological Methods. Anthropological Papers Museum of Anthropology, University of Michigan, No. 8, pp. 85-93. Ann Arbor.
1953 Report on Some Metal Objects from Zaculeu. *In*: Richard B. Woodbury and Aubrey S. Trick, The Ruins of Zaculeu, Guatamala, pp. 266-68, The William Byrd Press, Richmond, Virginia.
1957 Metallurgy. *In*: The Identification of Non-artifactual Archaeological Materials. Walter W. Taylor, ed. National Academy of Sciences—National Research Council Publication 565, pp. 52-54. Washington, D. C.

Rueping, H. J.
1944 A Fond du Lac Gravel Pit Burial. The Wisconsin Archeologist, n.s., Vol. 33, No. 44, pp. 199-223. Milwaukee.

Sharp, Robert P.
1953 Shorelines of the Glacial Great Lakes in Cook County, Minnesota. American Journal of Science, Vol. 251, February, 1953, pp. 109-39. New Haven.

Shepard, Anna O.
1936 Metallographic Study of Copper Artifacts. American Antiquity, Vol. 2, No. 2, pp. 139-40. Menasha.

Slafter, E. F.
1879 Prehistoric Copper Implements. Wisconsin Historical Collections, Vol. VIII, pp. 152-64. Madison.

Squier, E. G., and E. H. Davis
1848 Ancient Monuments of the Mississippi Valley. In: Smithsonian Contributions to Knowledge. Vol. 1, Washington, D. C.

Stanley, George M.
1932 Abandoned Strands of Isle Royale and Northeastern Lake Superior. Unpublished Doctoral thesis, University of Michigan Library, pp. 1-158.
1941 Minong Beaches and Water Plane in Lake Superior Basin. Geological Society of America Bulletin, Vol. 52, p. 1935. New York.

Swineford, A. P.
1884 Annual Report of the Commissioner of Mineral Statistics of the State of Michigan for 1883. Marquette.

Tanton, T. L.
1931 Fort William and Port Arthur, and Thunder Cape Map-areas, Thunder Bay District, Ontario. Geological Survey of Canada, Memoir 167, pp. 1-222. Ottawa.

Thayer, Burt
1940 Narrative of George Hodge. The Minnesota Archaeologist, Vol VI, No. 1, pp. 3-11. Crystal Bay, Lake Minnetonka: Lake Pokegama, Pine Co.

Thompson, F. C.
1958 The Early Metallurgy of Copper and Bronze. Man, Vol. 58, Art. 1, pp. 1-7. London.

Thompson, James E.
1954 Geology of the Mamainse Point Copper Area. Sixty-Second Annual Report of the Ontario Department of Mines, Pt. 4, Toronto.

Thwaites, Reuben G.
1899 The Jesuit Relations and Allied Documents. Vol. XXXVIII. Cleveland: Burrows Brothers.
1902 The French Regime in Wisconsin-I, 1634-1727. Wisconsin Historical Collection, Vol. XVI. Madison.
1906 The French Regime in Wisconsin-II, 1727-1748. *Ibid.*, Vol. 17. Also in: Allisson Butts, ed., Copper, The Science and Technology of the Metal, Its Alloys and Compounds.

Toussaint, W. F.
1955 Cold Working of Copper and Copper Alloys. American Chemical Society Monograph Series, No. 122, pp. 654-72. New York: Reinhold Publishing Corp.

Tucker, Sara Jones (ed.)
1942 Indian Villages of the Illinois Country: Atlas. Scientific Papers, Vol. 2, Pt. 1. Springfield: Illinois State Museum.

Upham, Warren
1905 Groseillers and Radisson, the First White Men in Minnesota, 1655-56, and 1659-60, and Their Discovery of the Upper Mississippi River. Collections of the Minnesota Historical Society, Vol. 10, Pt. II, pp. 449-594. St. Paul.

Verrill, A. Hyatt, and Ruth Verrill
1953 America's Ancient Civilizations. New York: G. P. Putnam's Sons.

Voce, Eric
1948 Notes on Some Analyses of Native Copper and Ancient Artifacts. Man, Vol. 48, Art. 17, pp. 19-21. London.
1961 Scientific Evidence Concerning Metal-Working Techniques. *Ibid.*, Vol. 61, pp. 68-71. London.

Wahlgren, Erik
1958 The Kensington Stone, A Mystery Solved. Madison: The University of Wisconsin Press.

Watson, Thomas L.
1923 Native Copper Deposits of the South Atlantic States Compared with those of Michigan. Economic Geology, Vol. 18, pp. 732-52. Lancaster, Pa.: Economic Geology Publishing Co.

Watson, Virginia Drew
1950 The Wulfing Plates, Products of Prehistoric Americans. Washington University Studies, N. S., Social and Philosophical Sciences, No. 8. St. Louis.

West, George A.
1929 Copper: Its Mining and Use by the Aborigines of the Lake Superior Region. Report of the McDonald—Massee Isle Royale Expedition, 1928. Bulletin of the Public Museum of the City of Milwaukee, Vol. 10, No. 1, pp. 1-184.

Whittlesey, Charles
1863 Ancient Mining on the Shores of Lake Superior. Smithsonian Contributions to Knowledge. Vol. 13, Contrib. No. 155, pp. 1-29. Washington, D. C.
1867 On the Weapons and Military Character of the Race of the Mounds. Memoirs Boston Society of Natural History, Vol. I, Pt. 4, pp. 475-81.
1872 Notice of Some Rare Polished Stone Ornaments. Western Reserve and Northern Ohio Historical Society Historical and Archaeological Tract No. 11. Cleveland.

Wilford, Lloyd A.
1941 A Tentative Classification of the Prehistoric Cultures of Minnesota. American Antiquity, Vol. 6, pp. 231-49. Salt Lake City: University of Utah.
1945 The Prehistoric Indians of Minnesota: The Headwaters Lakes Aspect. Minnesota History, Vol. 26, pp. 312-29. St. Paul.
1955 A Revised Classification of the Prehistoric Cultures of Minnesota. American Antiquity, Vol. 21, pp. 130-42. Salt Lake City: University of Utah.

Wilson, Curtis L., and Melville Sayre
1935 A Brief Metallographic Study of Primitive Copper Work. American Antiquity, Vol. 1, No. 2, pp. 109-12. Menasha, Wis.

Wilson, Daniel
1856 The Ancient Miners of Lake Superior. The Canadian Journal, N. S., Vol. 1, No. 3, pp. 227-37, Toronto.
1865 Prehistoric Man. 2d. Ed.; London: The MacMillan Co.

Wilson, L. R.
1935 The Nipissing Flora of the Apostle Islands Region. Bulletin of the Torrey Botanical Club, Vol. 62, pp. 533-35. Lancaster, Pa.: Business Press.

Winchell, N. H.
1881 Ancient Copper Mines of Isle Royale. Popular Science Monthly, Vol. 19, pp. 601-20. New York.
1882 Preliminary List of Rocks Collected by N. H. Winchell in 1879. *In:* The Geological and Natural History Survey of Minnesota, The Tenth Annual Report for the Year 1881, pp. 9-122. St. Paul.

Winchell, N. H. (ed.)
1911 The Aborigines of Minnesota. Minnesota Historical Society, St. Paul.

Winsor, Justin, (ed.)
1888 Narrative and Critical History of America, Vol. VII, Part 1. The United States of North America, Pt. II. Boston and New York.

Wittry, Warren L.
1951 A Preliminary Study of the Old Copper Complex. The Wisconsin Archeologist, N. S., Vol. 32, No. 1, pp. 1-18. Milwaukee.
1957 The Old Copper Complex: An Archaic Manifestation in Wisconsin. *Ibid.*, Vol. 38, No. 4, pp. 311-29.

Wrong, G. M. (ed.)
1939 The Long Journey to the Country of the Hurons, by Father Gabriel Sagard. Publications of the Champlain Society, Vol. 25. Toronto.

PLATES

PLATE I

Fig. 1. Pit 25 on Isle Royale before excavation in June, 1953. Henry Cornwall and R. W. Drier inspecting hammerstones. National Park Service Negative 14410.

Fig. 2. Hammerstones recovered from Pit 25. N.P.S. Neg. 14412.

PLATE II

Fig. 1. Pit 25 with excavation at about the 6-foot level. University of Michigan Museum of Anthropology Neg. 13856.

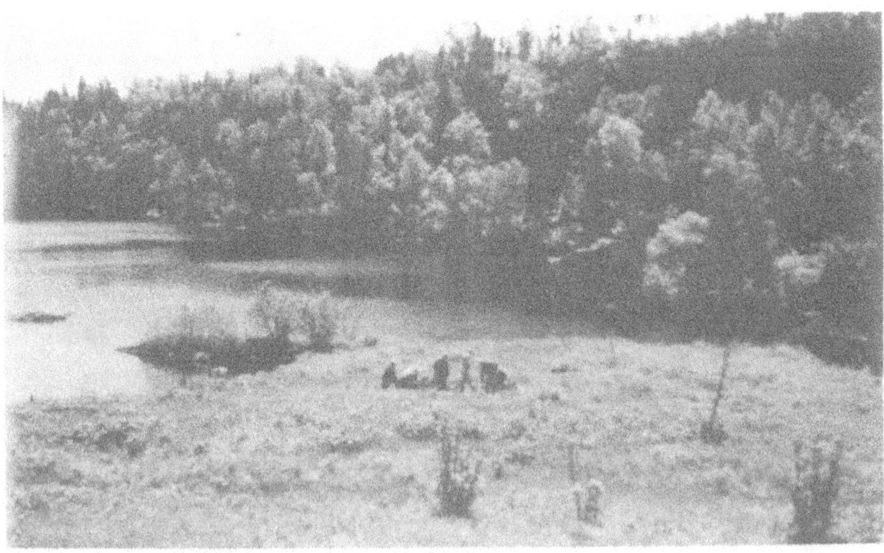

Fig. 2. Excavation party at work on test trench at Chippewa Harbor village site in June, 1953. U.M.M.A. Neg. 13857.

PLATE III

Fig. 1. Rim and decorated sherds from Chippewa Harbor test trench. N.P.S. Neg. 14422.

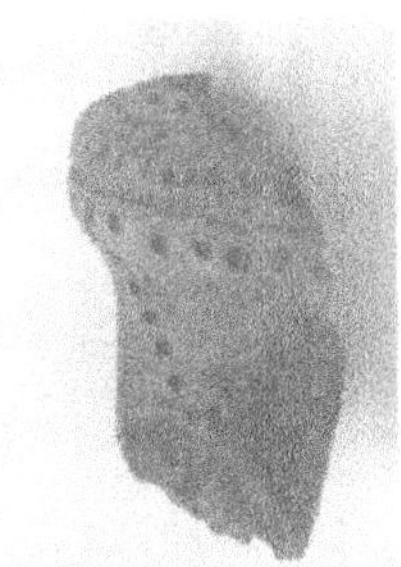

Fig. 2. Portion of clay pipe bowl from Chippewa Harbor site. N.P.S. Neg. 14424.

Fig. 3. Rim and body sherds from Chippewa Harbor. N.P.S. Neg. 14423.

PLATE IV

Fig. 1. Location of Indian Point Village site at east end of McCargoe Cove. N.P.S. Neg. 14418.

Fig. 2. Upper left group are from a small Blackduck-style vessel of Late Woodland time, and associated sherds. N.P.S. Neg. 14419.

Fig. 3. Late Woodland body sherds from a different area of Indian Point Village. N.P.S. Neg. 14417.

PLATE V

Copper nugget weighing 5,720 pounds found at a depth of 16 1/2 feet in the Minong Mine, Isle Royale, in 1874. The photograph is from a glass negative in the Burton Collection of the Detroit Public Library. The nugget is shown on a dock in Detroit. Note the uneven surface resulting from prehistoric attempts to remove sections for implements.

PLATE VI

Another view of the Minong copper nugget on a dock in Detroit in 1874. After being exhibited in Detroit it was shown at the Philadelphia Centennial Exposition in 1876. It was then smelted.

PLATE VII

View to the north of the Minong Mine area, Isle Royale, taken in 1892 by W. H. Holmes. The mining dumps of 1874-1883 are clearly shown and also the disastrous effect of forest fires on the vegetation. This photograph is from the files of the Smithsonian Institution Bureau of American Ethnology. B.A.E. Neg. 2285.

PLATE VIII

Tunnel of the Minong Mine in area of many prehistoric pits. Photograph by W. H. Holmes in 1892. B.A.E. Neg. 2272.

PLATE IX

Rubble fill of ancient copper pit near the Minong Mine, Isle Royale. This excavation was by W. H. Holmes, who is on the right, to obtain data for an exhibit at the Worlds Columbian Exposition in Chicago. B.A.E. Neg. 2273.

PLATE X

Hammerstones from ancient pit excavated by W. H. Holmes near the Minong Mine, Isle Royale. The size of the hammerstones may be judged by comparing them with the hand-pick, and with the silver dollar at left center. B.A.E. Neg. 2294.

PLATE XI

Fig. 1. Area of prehistoric copper pits near Minong Mine, Isle Royale, before excavation in 1924 by S. A. Barrett for the Milwaukee Public Museum. M.P.M. Neg. 113940.

Fig. 2. Lower and upper prehistoric pits after excavation by S. A. Barrett. M.P.M. Neg. 113945.

PLATE XII

Fig. 1. Larger hammerstones from pits excavated by S. A. Barrett near Minong Mine, Isle Royale. M.P.M. Neg. 7505.

Fig. 2. Hammerstones and fragments from pits excavated by S. A. Barrett near Minong Mine, Isle Royale. M.P.M. Neg. 7506.

PLATE XIII

An eighteen-ton mass of native copper uncovered in 1862 at the Mesnard Mine in Keweenaw County, Michigan. This block had been worked by Indians in order to detach sections of it to be made into implements. (From a print in the Burton Collection of the Detroit Public Library.)

PLATE XIV

Fig. 1. Copper Pit No. 1, near Point Mamainse, Ontario. J.B. Griffin standing in eastern side of pit.

Fig. 2. Copper Pit No. 1, near Point Mamainse, Ontario. J. B. Griffin sitting on western edge of pit.

PLATE XV

Fig. 1. Copper Pit No. 2 near Point Mamainse, Ontario.

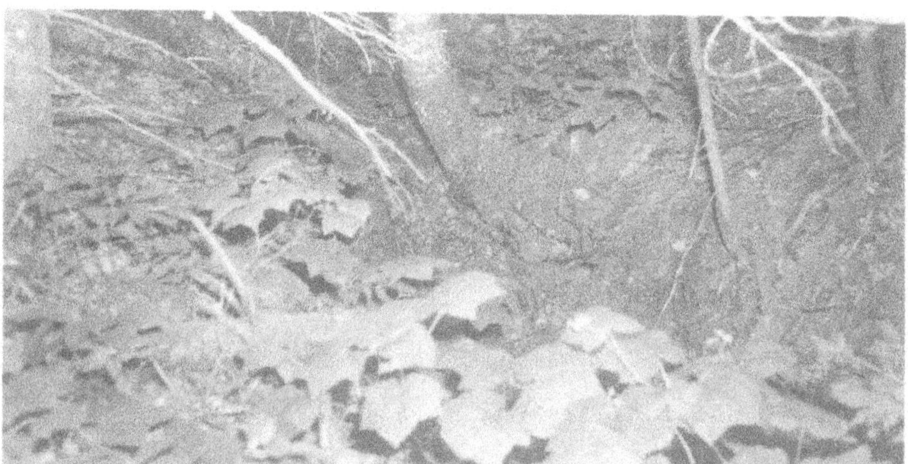

Fig. 2. Copper Pit No. 3 near Point Mamainse, Ontario.

PLATE XVI

Fig. 1. Southern section of Pic River site. View to the east from the beach with the Pic River on the right.

Fig. 2. View to the east of north and south exposures of occupied zone.

PLATE XVII

Fig. 1. G.I. Quimby at work clearing sand from occupied zone of Pic River site.

Fig. 2. Artifacts from the Pic River occupation zone. Two cord-marked sherds, a flint scraper, European glass beads, and a rim section of a brass or copper pot. Chicago Natural History Museum photograph.

PLATE XVIII

Fig. 1. The McCollum site from the railroad trestle over the southeast arm of Lake Nipigon, Ontario.

Fig. 2. The McCollum site in the foreground with the railroad tracks and Ontario Highway No. 11 in the background.

PLATE XIX

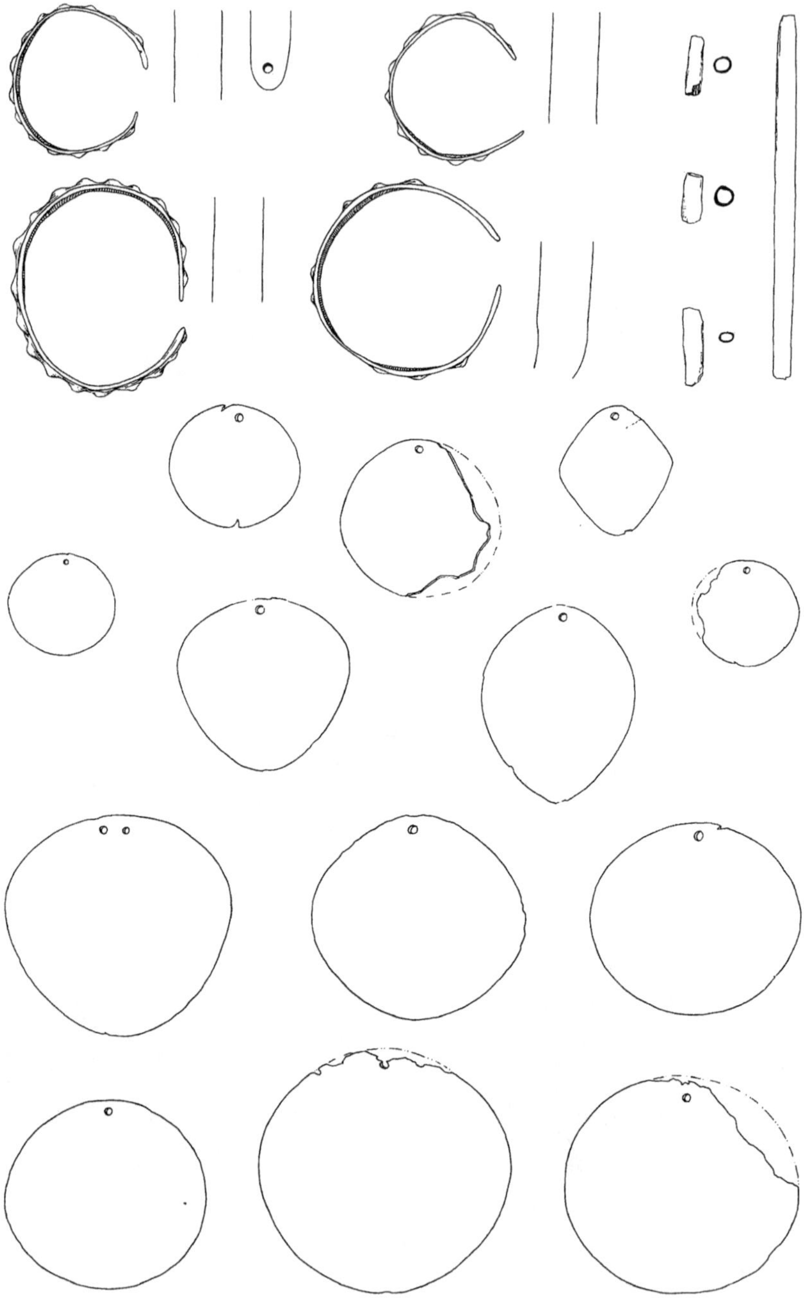

Copper discs, bracelets, and beads from the McCollum site, Nipigon District, Ontario.

PLATE XX

Socketed narrow points, broad-bladed beveled points, and socketed beveled knives from the McCollum site, Nipigon District, Ontario.

PLATE XXI

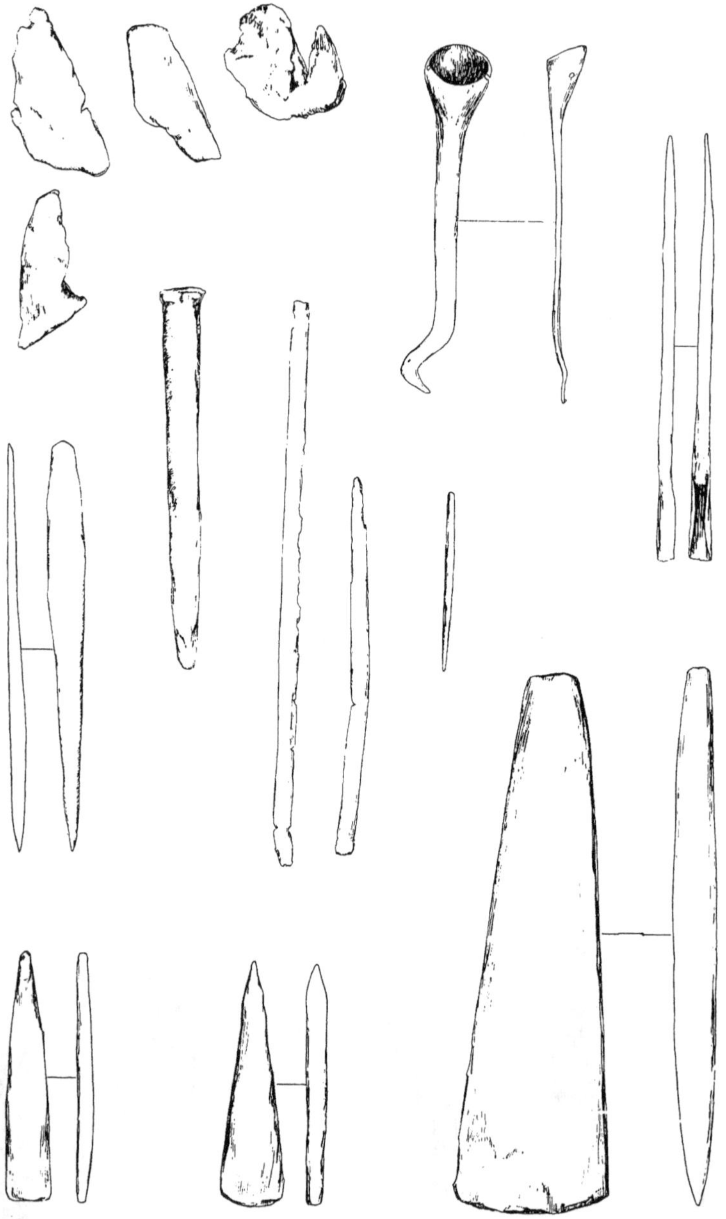

McCollum site–unworked copper fragments, awls, cylinders, adze, and narrow socketed point. An unidentified copper object is shown in vertical and lateral view in the upper right center.

PLATE XXII

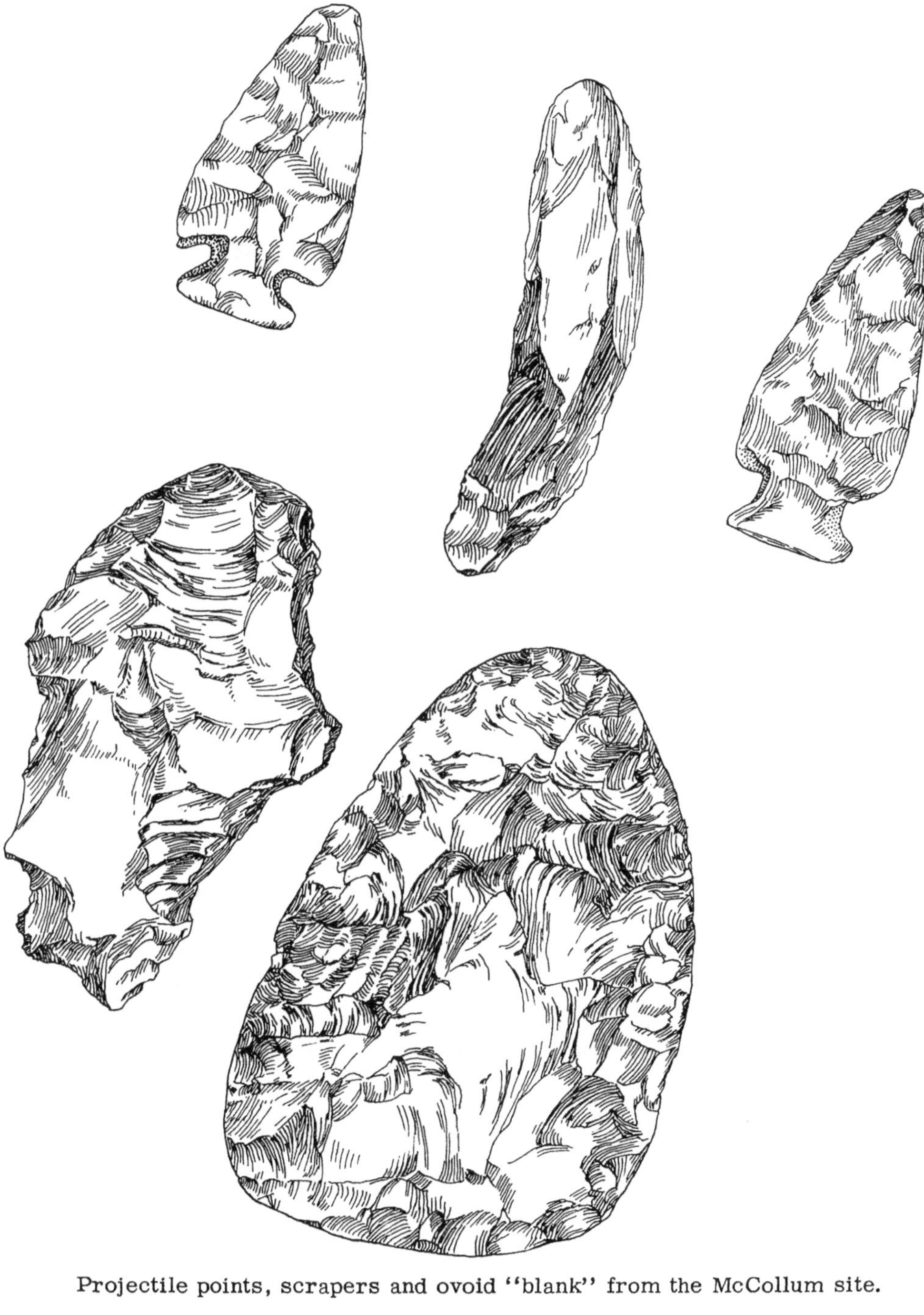

Projectile points, scrapers and ovoid "blank" from the McCollum site.

PLATE XXIII

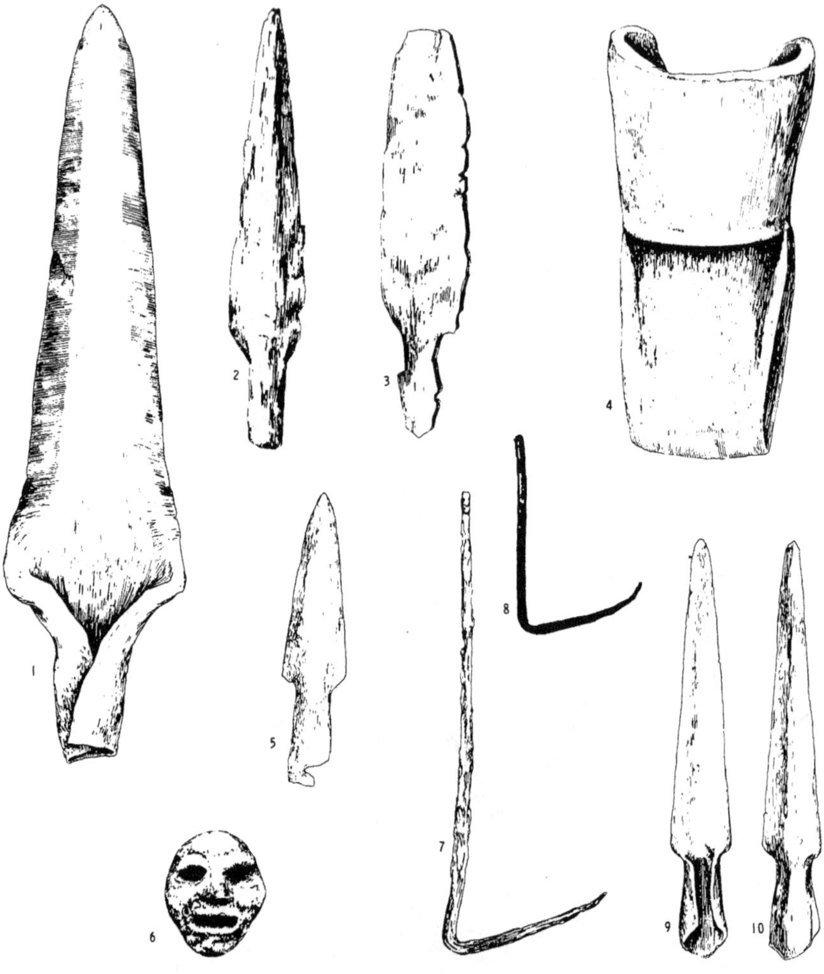

Artifacts from near Brockville, Ontario, and Ontonagan, Michigan.

1. Unusually long crudely socketed spear from Brockville. Length 30.5 cm.
2. Stemmed point from Brockville. Length 17.8 cm.
3. Stemmed point from Brockville with broken tip and eroded stem. Length at time of find was 14.5 cm.
4. Copper spud from Brockville. Length 15.3 cm.
5. Stemmed spear from Brockville with unusual hook in base. Length 12.7 cm.
6. Small mask of clay (?) from Brockville. Length 5 cm.
7. Copper hook or gaff from Pie Island, near Fort William, Ontario. Length 18.7 cm.
8. Copper hook or gaff from Pic River, one mile east of Heron Bay, Ontario. Length 33 cm.

9-10. Two views of socketed copper point with beveled edges from Ontonagan, Michigan area. Length about 30 cm.

PLATE XXIV

Three copper gaffs in the Lakehead College collection, Fort William, Ontario, Canada. The gaff on the left was brought up by a net from Black Bay, Lake Superior. The two on the right are from the north shore of Lac Seuel. (Information and print are from J. V. Wright, National Museum of Canada.)

PLATE XXV

Copper specimens from the Fort William, Ontario area in the Thunder Bay Historical Museum. (The photograph is through the courtesy of J. V. Wright, National Museum of Canada.)

PLATE XXVI

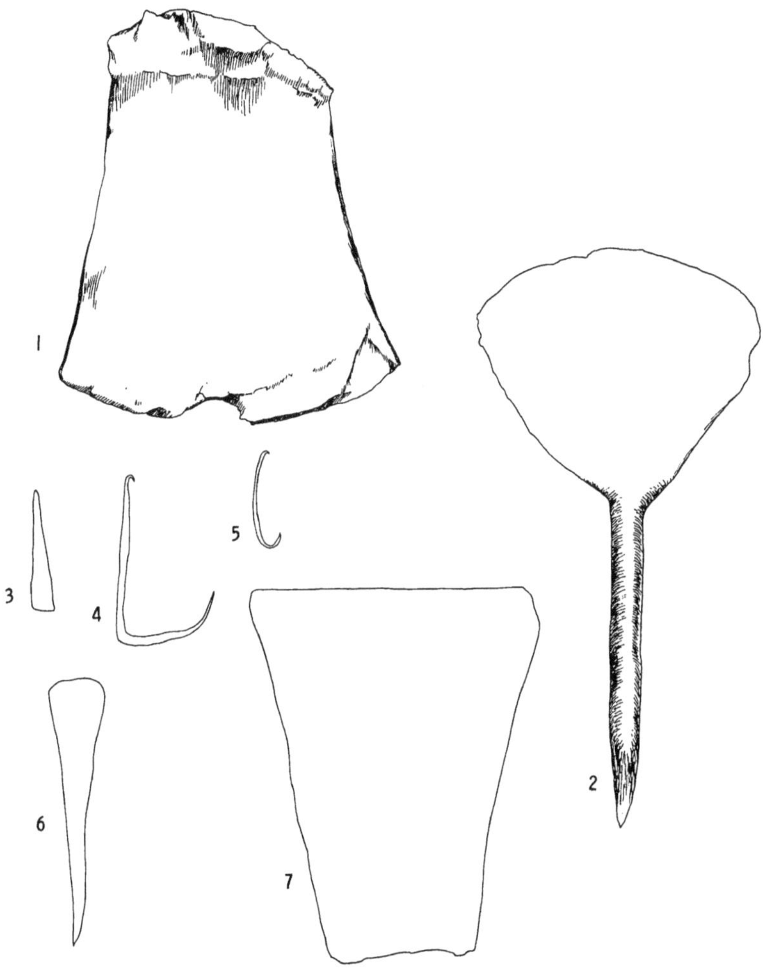

Miscellaneous Copper finds from Ontario and Manitoba.

1. Copper axe with battered butt from near Riding Mountain, Manitoba. Length 11.3 cm; width at bit, 9 cm; thickness 1/8" at cutting edge and 3/16" at the butt end.
2. Copper scraper (?) from a gravel pit near the town of Nipigon, Ontario. Cat. No. 28.298 of the Royal Ontario Museum, Toronto. Length 16 cm.
3. Small copper awl or point from the east shore of Lake Nipigon, Ontario. Nat. Mus. of Canada Cat. No. VIII-F-15235. Length 6 cm.
4. Fishhook from Fort William, Ontario. N.M.C. Cat. No. VIII-F-15672.
5. Fishhook from bed of Rainy River, Fort Frances, Rainy River District, Ontario. N.M.C. Cat. No. VIII-F-17471.
6. Copper awl or point from Fort William, Ontario. N.M.C. Cat. No. VIII-F-15674.
7. Spud from Fort William, Thunder Bay District, Ontario. N.M.C. Cat. No. VIII-F-15670.

Fig. 1. Bone spear point, projectile points, and copper knife from high dune area west of Grand Marais, Alger County, Michigan. U.M.M.A. Neg. 14220.

Fig. 2. Five Copper Specimens studied by Dr. W. C. Root from the Lower Peninsula of Michigan. U.M.M.A. Neg. 14218.

No. 1. An open-flanged copper point from Scott Lake near Rosebush, Isabella County, Michigan. Received by the Museum of Anthropology in March, 1952 as a part of the Dr. R. M. Kempton Collection. University of Michigan Museum of Anthropology Catalog Number 39001.

No. 2. A flanged copper point from near Eaton Rapids, Eaton County, Michigan. It was received by the Museum in March, 1952 from Mrs. Mary E. Goheen. U.M.M.A. 30464.

No. 3. One of two copper spear points probably from Montcalm County which were collected by Dr. G. E. Dakin. These were received by the Museum in May, 1939 from Mr. and Mrs. F. Earle Lyman. U.M.M.A. 22191.

No. 4. Small copper celt from the Converse Mound Group, Kent County, Michigan. Received by exchange in 1943. U.M.M.A. 27231.

No. 5. One of two copper celts from Denver twp., of Isabella County, Michigan which had been in the Collection of Dr. W. B. Hinsdale since before 1928. They were accessioned as part of the Museum collection in October, 1944. U.M.M.A. 27651.

PLATE XXVII

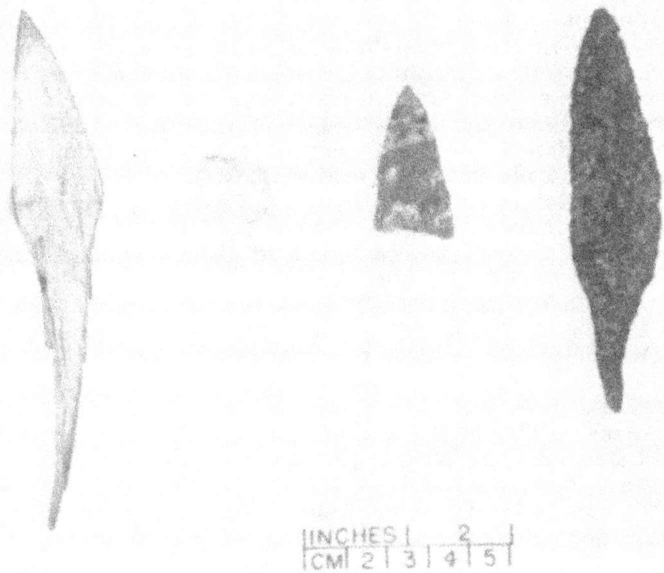

Copper Artifacts from Manitoba and Western Ontario.

1. Socketed point from the vicinity of Koostatak, around Fisher Bay, western Lake Winnipeg, Manitoba. Blade thickness 1/4". Clifford Martin Collection.
2. Folded socket point from near Rathwell, south-central Manitoba. Blade thickness 3/16". Manitoba Museum Collection Item 1071E.
3. Folded socket point from near Arborg, west of southern Lake Winnipeg, Manitoba. Blade thickness 1/4". M.M.C. Item L36E.
4. Folded socket point of uncertain origin but possibly from near Arden, west of southern Lake Manitoba. M.M.C.
5. Folded socket point of uncertain origin but possibly from near Arden, west of southern Lake Manitoba. M.M.C.
6. Folded socket point from Vivian, south of Lake Manitoba. Blade thickness 1/4". M.M.C. Item 619A.
7. Beveled knife blade with flat tang which has been bent, from Wampum, southeast Manitoba. Blade thickness 1/8". M.M.C. Item 1136E.
8. Slightly notched ovoid flat point from Balmoral, north of Winnipeg. M.M.C. Item 701.
9. Notched and stemmed flat point from Hartney, southwest Manitoba. Blade thickness 1/8". M.M.C. Item L64.
10. Folded socket point from Niverville, south of Winnipeg. D. H. Doerksen collection.
11. Flat, slightly notched point from Rainy Lake Falls, southwest Ontario. M.M.C. Item 563.

PLATE XXVIII

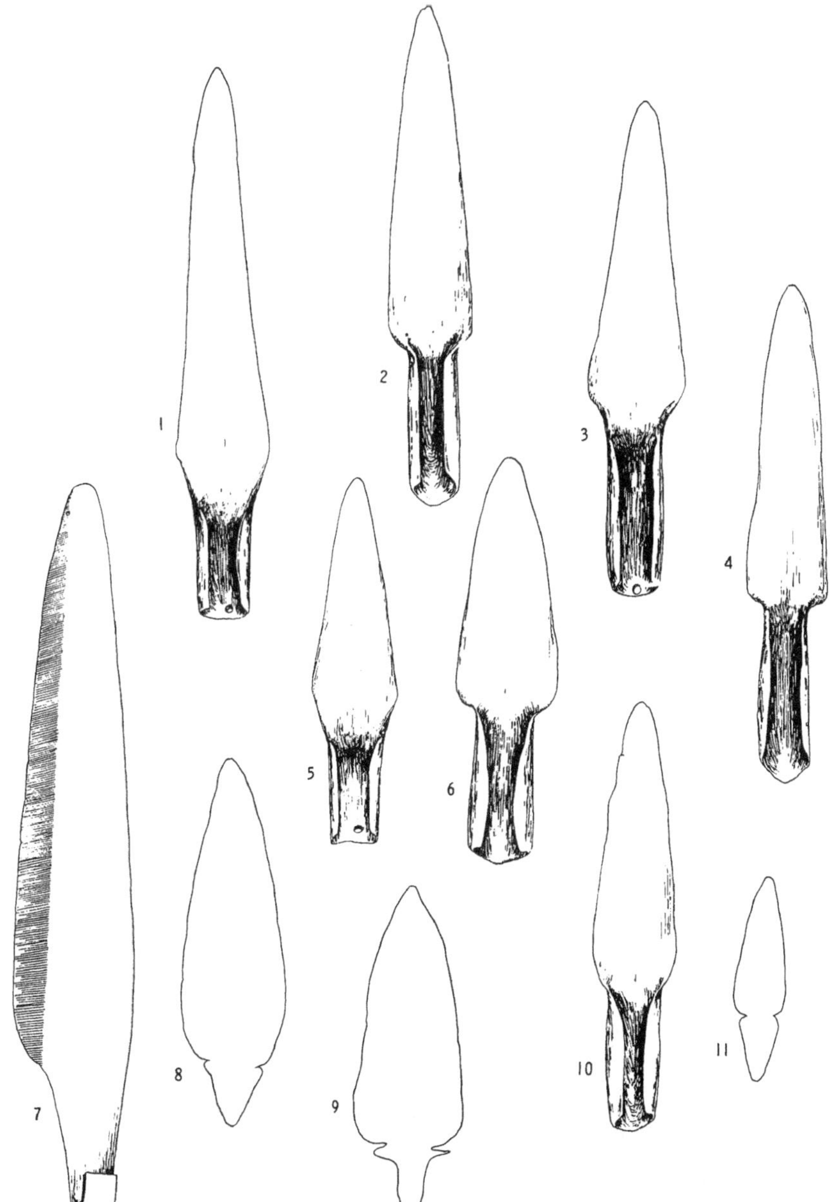

PLATE XXIX

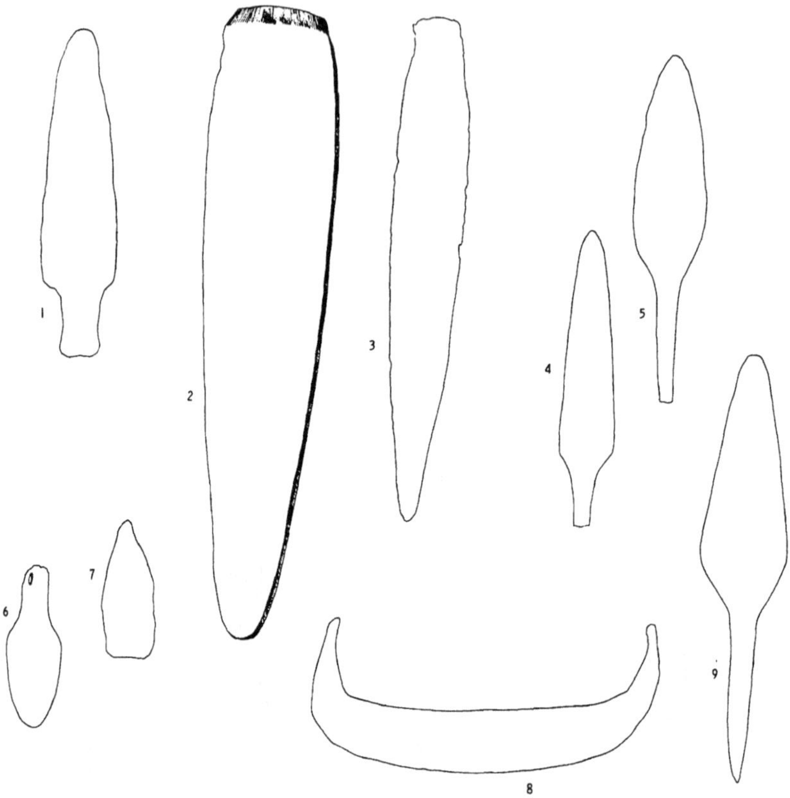

Copper Artifacts from Southern Manitoba and Western Ontario.

1. Stemmed point from Miami, south central Manitoba. Blade thickness, 3/16". M.M.C. Item L35E.
2. Long chisel with beveled bit. Thickness 1/2", weight 1 lb. 13 oz., from Piney, southeast Manitoba. M.M.C. Item E1171.
3. Long slender point from Nipigon, Ontario, 1/16" thick. M.M.C. Item 31.
4. Stemmed point 1/8" thick from Pointe du Bois, on Winnipeg River, eastern Manitoba. Clifford Martin Collection.
5. Stemmed point from Niverville, south of Winnipeg. Dyck collection.
6. Small stemmed point from McTavish, south of Winnipeg. M.M.C. Item 377.
7. Small triangular form from McTavish. Tickness 1/8". M.M.C. Item L33E.
8. Copper scraper or "woman's knife" from near Miami, south central Manitoba. Drawn from memory by R. W. Sutton. H. M. Dundas Collection.
9. Long stemmed point from Gladstone, west of southern end of Lake Manitoba. M.M.C. Item 489E.

PLATE XXX

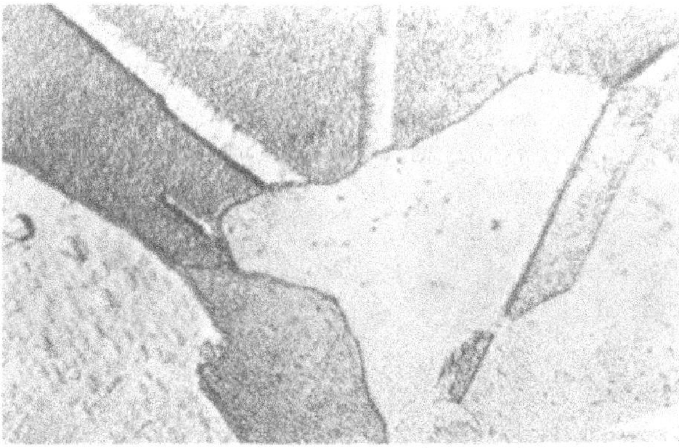

Fig. 1. Native copper. No eutectic. 1000 X.

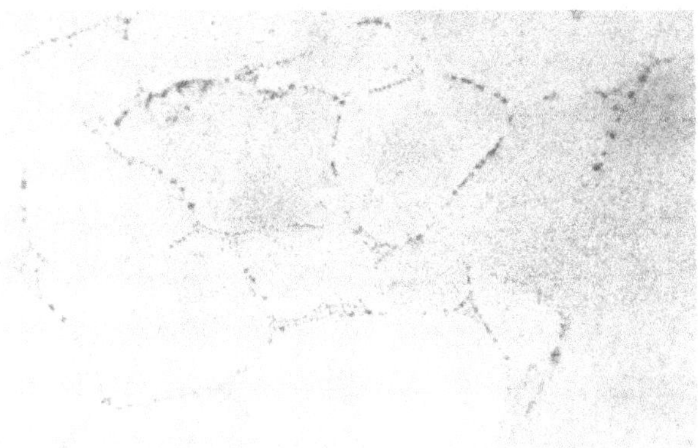

Fig. 2. Forged native copper, 500 X. Eutectic (dark spots) in grain boundaries.

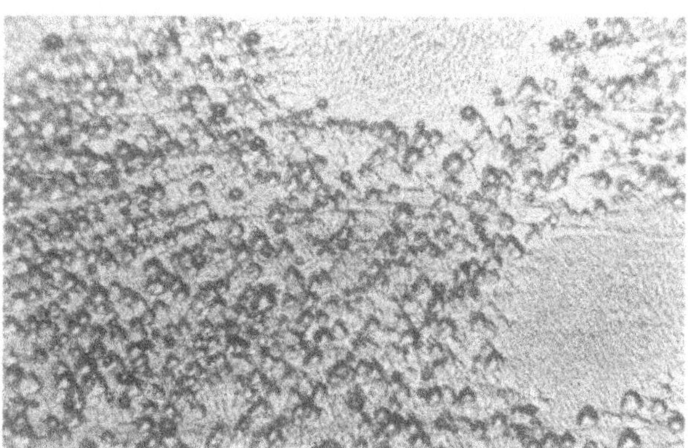

Fig. 3. Cast copper. Much eutectic throughout some grains. 500 X.

Microphotograph of native copper, forged native copper, and cast copper to show the presence and absence of copper—cuprous oxide eutectic.

PLATE XXXI

Copper artifacts analyzed by R. W. Drier. See List on pages 140-42.

Fig. 1. Awl from Isle Royale.
Fig. 2. Earspool fragment of Hopewellian type from Tennessee.
Fig. 3. Chisel with mushroom shape butt end from Houghton, Michigan.
Fig. 4. Projectile or spear point.
Fig. 5. Projectile point of simple conical form.
Fig. 6. Copper knife.
Fig. 7. Celt with hammered butt end from Houghton.
Fig. 8. Projectile or spear point.
Fig. 9. Knife with badly eroded socket edges.

PLATE XXXII

Copper artifacts analyzed R. W. Drier. See List, pp. 140-42 for further identification and size.

Fig. 1. Socketed knife handle.
Fig. 2. Unsocketed knife.
Fig. 3. Socketed projectile or spear point.
Fig. 4. Socketed projectile or spear point.
Fig. 5. Spud-cut lengthwise to measure hardness. The small holes along the cut edge of the right hand section are the result of the hardness test.
Fig. 6. Spud with overlapping edge due to forming in the solid state.
Fig. 7. Earspool fragment from Louisiana.
Fig. 8. Bipointed copper awl.
Fig. 9. Socketed spear point from Dane County, Wisconsin.
Fig. 10. Stemmed projectile point from Shawano County, Wisconsin.
Fig. 11. Socketed projectile or spear point from Manitowac County, Wisconsin.
Fig. 12. Socketed projectile or spear point from Dane County, Wisconsin.

PLATE XXXIII

Copper artifacts analyzed by R. W. Drier. See List, pp. 141-42 for further identification and size.

Fig. 1. Socketed projectile point from Portage County, Wisconsin.
Fig. 2. Stemmed point from Dane County, Wisconsin.
Fig. 3. Stemmed point from Ottawa County, Michigan.
Fig. 4. Stemmed point from Marquette County, Michigan.
Fig. 5. Rat-tail spear from Jefferson County, Wisconsin.
Fig. 6. Socketed point from Dane County, Wisconsin.
Fig. 7. Celt from Dodge County, Wisconsin.
Fig. 8. Socketed projectile point or spear from Dane County, Wisconsin.
Fig. 9. Long socketed spud from Dane County, Wisconsin.
Fig. 10. Stemmed point from Waushara County, Wisconsin.
Fig. 11. Long narrow celt from Dane County, Wisconsin.
Fig. 12. Large celt with recurved butt from Baraga County, Michigan.
Fig. 13. Long socketed point from Baraga County, Michigan.

www.ingramcontent.com/pod-product-compliance
Lightning Source LLC
LaVergne TN
LVHW050020250826
846302LV00008B/40